The Touch Taboo in Psychotherapy and Life

Touch has been a taboo in mainstream Western talking therapies since their inception. This book examines the effects on us of touch, and of touch deprivation — what we feel when we are touched, what it means to us, and the fact that some individuals and cultures are more tactile than others.

The author traces the development and perpetuation of the touch taboo, puts forward counterarguments to it, outlines criteria for the safe and effective use of touch in therapy, and suggests ways of dismantling the touch taboo should we wish to do so. Through moving interviews with clients who have experienced life-changing benefits of physical contact at the hands of their therapists, the place of touch in therapy practice is re-evaluated and the therapy profession urged to re-examine its attitudes towards this important therapeutic tool.

This book will be essential reading for therapists, counsellors, social workers, educators, health professionals and for any general reader interested in the crucial issue of touch in everyday life.

Tamar Swade has sustained several parallel careers, as psychotherapist, teacher, musician, entertainer, and creator of 'Theatre in Education' plays. She loves dancing, singing, being and running in nature, singing songs with small children, and often protests against injustices.

"This is a highly readable and fascinating book and long overdue. It makes a vitally important contribution important for both lay persons and professionals. All of us, but in particular psychotherapists, need to examine closely the critical role of touch in our own lives. And this book provides both understanding and tools to do precisely this. Its power derives from its amalgamation of both scientific evidence and personal experience both of clients and others. The author brings her own insights to bear based on her original research. She explores the origin of why touch has been so proscribed for psychotherapists and how negative this can be for the client. She provides sensitive guidance for the therapist who wants to incorporate touch more effectively in their practice."

— *Dr Richard Stevens, former Head of Psychology at the Open University and Chair of the Association for Humanistic Psychology, author of several books on psychology and occasional broadcaster on psychological topics.*

The Touch Taboo in Psychotherapy and Everyday Life

Tamar Swade

Routledge
Taylor & Francis Group
LONDON AND NEW YORK

First published 2020
by Routledge
2 Park Square, Milton Park, Abingdon, Oxon OX14 4RN

and by Routledge
52 Vanderbilt Avenue, New York, NY 10017

Routledge is an imprint of the Taylor & Francis Group, an informa business

© 2020 Tamar Swade

The right of Tamar Swade to be identified as author of this work has been asserted by her in accordance with sections 77 and 78 of the Copyright, Designs and Patents Act 1988.

All rights reserved. No part of this book may be reprinted or reproduced or utilised in any form or by any electronic, mechanical, or other means, now known or hereafter invented, including photocopying and recording, or in any information storage or retrieval system, without permission in writing from the publishers.

Trademark notice: Product or corporate names may be trademarks or registered trademarks, and are used only for identification and explanation without intent to infringe.

British Library Cataloguing-in-Publication Data
A catalogue record for this book is available from the British Library

Library of Congress Cataloging-in-Publication Data
A catalog record has been requested for this book

ISBN: 978-0-367-23402-7 (hbk)
ISBN: 978-0-367-23405-8 (pbk)
ISBN: 978-0-429-27969-0 (ebk)

Typeset in Times New Roman
by codeMantra

In memory of Ruth Swade, a remarkable human.

Contents

Acknowledgements ix

Introduction 1

SECTION I
Touch in everyday life 5

1 Animal touch research 7
2 Human touch research 20
3 Negative touch 53
4 The tactility scale 67
5 The origins of attitudes to touch; how tactile habits are formed 92
6 Touch in everyday life; what 'ordinary people' (non-clients) said about touch 104

SECTION II
Touch in psychotherapy 117

7 Can touch help or hinder therapy? clients' experience 119
8 Wisdom from the literature 151

9 Origins of the touch taboo in psychotherapy 160
10 Counterarguments to the touch taboo 170
11 Criteria for the successful use of touch in therapy 181
12 Dismantling the touch taboo 198
13 Overall summary, conclusions and final thoughts 217

Bibliography 221
Index 281

Acknowledgements

Thank you, first, to the participants in this research whose remarkable wisdom, insight and articulacy were the major spur to my writing this book. Thank you to my superbly gifted readers who commented on some or all of the various drafts of the manuscript: Dario Swade, whose zoom-lens brain enables him to leap about in the ideological forest canopy like a monkey-acrobat — seeing the overview, holding long theme-trails in mind — and at the same time, eagle-eyed, notice details and dive down to the forest floor to retrieve a missing comma or colon; Danny Gluckstein who read some of the original book, immediately got the gist, and said astutely, 'This is two books'; Ruth Thackeray, professional copy-editor whom nothing escapes, and who alerted me to an article by John Walsh (2000) according to which three kinds of people are close to extinction: the rag-and-bone man, the spinster, and the copy-editor; Ruth is living proof that at least one example of the latter species survives; Ann Harries, my novelist 'besty', whose appreciation of prose style (especially mine) is a delight; David Drake, another with awesome awareness of fine detail; supermind Richard Stevens whose enthusiasm for the book was so heartening; Elana Dallas and Sophie Khan, who struggled loyally through some of the very first draft; Angela Hobsbaum who applied her unerring acumen and expertise to proofreading the final draft; and Ian Horton who applauded the original dissertation on which this book is based. Any errors in the text are entirely mine and nothing to do with them.

Huge thanks to Doron Swade, effortlessly brilliant and articulate, for invaluable help and advice, particularly when the going was tough, and to other long-suffering friends and family for crucial help, encouragement and support — Joanne Zimmerman, Ruth

Swade, Sarah Sceats, Ilan Lazarus, Shelley Swade, Sally Donati, Jill Norman, Sheena Roberts, Tim Megarry, Anousheh Bromfield, Lynn Kramer, Hilary Henderson, Janet Riddett, Jenny West, Sue Ellman and Sarah Harrison, to mention but a few.

Thanks to the 70 friends and associates who participated so consummately in research on the title of this book; to Tessa, Wilf and Alice Hatchett and their lovely Mum Vicky for essential entertainment and light relief; to extraordinary therapist Chris Nikoloff from whom I learned so much about therapy and who first introduced me to Ashley Montagu's glorious book about touch; to my editor, Alec Selwyn, ever kind, friendly and unflappable; and to the virtuoso internet sleuths of the British Library — Paul Allchin, Vera Eterovic, Lorena Garcia Moreno and Lesley Haji-Gholam — who did *not* try to teach me how to work the library computers but instead understood at once that I was technologically a lost cause and traced obscure books and articles for me.

And thanks as big as the universe to wondrous Peter Kent for decades of unfailing support, computer repair and maintenance, ideas, jokes, printing, photocopying, hugs, hot-water-bottle-making and a million other feats of ballastry.

Love, and hugs if you like them.

Tamar Swade

Introduction

It was puzzlement that first led me to explore the issue of touch. As an undergraduate psychotherapist, certain aspects of traditional psychotherapy struck me as distinctly odd. One of these oddities, it seemed to me, was the blanket taboo against physical contact between therapist and client.

When I engage in non-erotic touch (a hug, for example) with someone I like and trust, I feel happy, healthy, alive, and my world is rich and colourful. If I am worried, sad or irritable, touch can allay these feelings and restore my sense of well-being. Since these kinds of positive feeling are major goals of any therapy, I was curious as to whether my own experience of affectionate physical contact was unusual or was more generally shared. If the latter, then therapy clients (and anyone else) might increase their well-being through experiencing touch; and if this were the case then withholding touch when it could help would be neglectful of clients' needs and might diminish my effectiveness as a therapist.

I am positing in the above that clients do not transform into some alien species on entering the therapist's room, that they instead take their human needs and personalities with them into therapy. Therefore, if ordinary people like me and others of my acquaintance benefit from physical contact in everyday life, it seemed probable that some clients would find it helpful in therapy. In order to explore this hypothesis I divided my material into two sections. The first (Chapters 1–6) investigates responses to touch in everyday life; the second (Chapters 7–12) examines whether or how much these responses transfer to therapy.

In more detail, for readers who like to be forewarned:

The first three chapters present an overview of research into touch spanning the 20th century and the early 21st.

Chapter 1 looks at research conducted with animal subjects. Readers concerned about animal welfare will be horrified by the cruelty of some of the experiments described. However, the cruelty has irrevocably occurred and in my view it would add insult to injury to disregard the results of this research; at least the animals in question will not have suffered and died to completely no avail if the findings to which they have so signally contributed are used to advance understanding. And early animal investigations into touch are not only important historically but offer striking insights into human as well as animal tactile needs.

Chapter 2 moves the focus from animals to humans and explores the potent effects on us of both touch and touch deprivation.

Chapter 3 deals with the devastating, often lifelong, impacts of negative physical contact, in particular physical and sexual abuse — for although this book is about humane touch, the picture of human tactility would be incomplete without mention of the malign touch perpetrated by psychologically ill or underdeveloped persons.

The next four chapters draw on my own research in the form of interviews with people from varied backgrounds, henceforth called 'participants' or 'interviewees':

Chapter 4 begins to explore the range of human touch habits — the varied amounts and types of touch we experience in childhood and later. These are placed on a *tactility scale* ranging from 'non-tactile' at one end to 'fully tactile' at the other.

Chapter 5 asks whether the societies in which we live influence our tactile attitudes and behaviours. For example, are Britons indeed less tactile than French or South American peoples, as popular belief has it — and might such cultural differences have bearing on the touch taboo in psychotherapy?

Chapter 6 presents participants' experience of touch in everyday life, their sensations, feelings and thoughts in response to physical contact. Social workers, educators, medical professionals... — anyone in a caring role — may find this chapter particularly relevant.

In Section 2, Chapter 7 again presents my own research in the form of excerpts from interviews, in this case with clients who had experienced touch in psychotherapy. For therapists and counsellors this chapter is probably the nub of the book, so these readers may wish to start with it.

Chapter 8 outlines the rich and detailed literature on therapeutic touch that exists to date.

Chapter 9 traces the origins of the touch taboo in psychotherapy — if the benefits of physical contact are as marked as the research suggests, how is it that the taboo exists at all? Chapter 10 proposes counterarguments to the touch taboo. Chapter 11 examines criteria for the safe and effective use of touch in therapy. Chapter 12 suggests ways of dismantling the touch taboo in everyday life and in therapy for those who wish to do so; and Chapter 13 presents brief overall conclusions and final thoughts.

Dramatis personae

Most of the persons mentioned in this book were research participants; a comparatively small number were therapy clients or case studies; and a handful are people I have known and observed in my non-work life.

I was enormously lucky in the individuals who volunteered as participants in this research. Their words were so wise and inspiring, and so valuable a contribution to current psychology, that I thought it a loss to the world not to make them more widely known. Hence this book.

I have changed participants' names in all but a few instances when they preferred to be quoted under their own name. I have also sometimes changed identifying details in their narratives in order to ensure their anonymity.

Verbatim reporting; use of italics

Besides the normal uses of italics, all words quoted verbatim from participants' interviews are in *'italics and inverted commas'*. The only exception to strict verbatim reporting of interviews is the omission of an occasional 'um' or 'er' for the sake of continuity.

Gender pronouns

I have not changed the gender of the actual research participants interviewed. However, when describing hypothetical persons I have alternated the use of 'he/him' and 'she/her'. As far as possible, I have attempted to divide the two descriptions evenly.

IMPORTANT NOTE ABOUT TOUCH

Unless otherwise stated the 'touch' referred to in this book is **non-sexual/non-erotic**. It includes any form of physical contact by means of which humans express warmth and caring — 'conversational' touch (the brief touches, for example on arm or shoulder, that sometimes occur during conversation); more prolonged contact with a body-part, such as hand-holding, a hand resting on someone's arm, or an arm round shoulders; and more or less full body contact, as in hugging, holding, rocking, cradling ... (Hunter & Struve, 1998:169–74; Smith, 1998b).

Section 1

Touch in everyday life

Chapter 1
Animal touch research

Well into the last century touch was not considered a proper subject for scientific investigation, and the 20th-century anatomist Frederick Hammett had no intention of straying into this uncharted field. His interest lay rather in the effects of thyroid secretion on animal growth. Nevertheless, quite by chance, Hammett arrived at one of the earliest touch-related findings, one with profound implications.

In order to discover how animals would fare without their thyroid and parathyroid glands, Hammett (1921,1922) removed these glands from 304 albino rats. The general consensus among investigators of the time was that such an operation was sure to be fatal. To their surprise, however, not all the rats died. Curious about this outcome, Hammett inquired into the rats' provenance and discovered that they had been drawn from two separate groups. Members of the one group had never experienced caring touch; they had instead received only the brief, perfunctory physical contact that occurred during feeding and cage-cleaning. They were fearful, highly-strung, aggressive, and when handled by experimenters were tense and resistant. The majority of deaths — 79% — occurred in this group within 48 hours of the operation.

The second group of rats had been frequently 'gentled' (gently stroked, caressed, petted, handled). Their personalities contrasted markedly with those of the non-gentled group; they were placid, fearless, friendly and, when handled, were 'relaxed and yielding' (Montagu, 1986:20). Only 13% of this group died after the operation. Hammett concluded that the gentling of the rats had produced a stability in their nervous systems which had enabled them to resist the loss of thyroid and parathyroid secretion. For most of the rats in this group, therefore, being gently petted had made 'all the difference between life and death' (Montagu, 1986:22).

Some 30 years after Hammett's experiment, Otto Weininger (1954) intentionally explored what Hammett had discovered by accident. He exposed rats to 'stressful stimuli' — in this case immobilisation and total food and water deprivation. Needless to say, there occurred a 100% death rate among his rat subjects. At autopsy Weininger found that rats which had been gentled during their lives displayed significantly less damage to their cardiovascular and gastrointestinal systems than non-gentled rats. He suggested that the reason for this was their ability to remain relatively calm within the stressful situation, which resulted in decreased secretion of the stress hormone ACTH (adrenocortico-tropic hormone) and — since an excess of stress hormones in the body causes damage — in less consequent degeneration of the internal organs.

Touch and newborn mammals

The newborn mammal depends on touch for its very survival. Nearly all mammalian mothers provide their newborns with tactile stimulation by assiduously licking them after birth, hereby kick-starting their physiological functioning. Licking of the genitals and perineum is particularly important since it activates the newborn's digestive and urinary systems. Infants that are unlicked for any reason are likely to die through a failure to eliminate urine and faeces. However, this fate is averted if a human carer simulates maternal licking by lightly stroking the infant's genital and perineal areas.

Newborn lambs usually cannot stand, and subsequently die, if unlicked by their mothers — although a few hardier lambs do have sufficient strength to hoist themselves upright without these maternal blandishments. As observed by workers at the Cornell Behavior Farm in New York, offspring who are precocious in this respect frequently elicit a matronly, firm-to-be-kind wisdom from their mothers; if her lamb attempts to stand before she has administered a thorough enough licking, the ewe will often keep it down with her foot until she has completed the procedure to her satisfaction (Montagu, 1986:33).

Goat-kids too are empowered by maternal licking to embrace life at the vertical. Barron (1955) studied twin goats born by caesarean section. The one newborn twin was left wet and in a warm room; the other was completely dried and well cleaned with a towel. The latter was able to stand sooner than its sibling, which led Barron to suggest that the cutaneous stimulation provided naturally by the mother goat's licking and grooming (and simulated in this case by towel-drying) was carried via nerves to the central nervous system. This raised the newborn kid's general 'neural excitability', including that of its respiratory centre. As a result 'the depth of the respiratory effort' and consequent oxygen levels in its blood increased, which in turn enhanced the muscular strength it required to stand (Montagu, 1986:66).

Not only are the offspring of mammals imperilled by lack of tactile input; their mothers also are thrown into disorganisation. Among both sheep (Liddell, 1956:116) and goats (Blauvelt, 1956:116), if the mother is separated from her newborn for even a few hours so that she cannot lick it, she fails to care for it when they are reunited.

Touch and physical growth

One of Weininger's (1954) contributions to physiology was to show that the gentle handling of animals could increase their physical growth. After weaning male rats at 23 days he then 'gentled' them daily for three weeks. On measuring them at 44 days, he found that their growth was greater and their average weight 20 grams heavier than that of non-gentled rats.

Conversely, failure of growth has been strongly associated with lack of touch; monkey and rat infants that are separated from their mothers and thus deprived of touch are smaller and lighter than their non-separated peers (for monkeys see Harlow & Zimmerman, 1959; Hinde & Spencer-Booth, 1971; Suomi et al., 1976; for rats, Hofer, 1984; Kuhn et al., 1979; Schanberg & Field, 1987).

A chain of physiological mechanisms underlies this phenomenon: growth in animals cannot occur without the creation of protein in the body — which cannot proceed without the activity of the enzyme ornithine decarboxilase (ODC) — which is in turn dependent upon *growth hormone* secreted from the pituitary gland.

An experiment by Saul Schanberg and Tiffany Field (1987:1433) showed that when rat pups were separated from their mothers they underwent a notable and immediate reduction of ODC activity in all the tissues examined by the researchers, including liver, heart, kidney, spleen and several brain regions. Soon after the pups were returned to their mothers their ODC activity returned to normal.

The decline in the rat pups' ODC function was found to be due exclusively to the absence of normal tactile stimulation (licking/

grooming) from their mothers; it was not attributable to any other maternal or nonmaternal stimulus, such as change in body temperature, unfamiliar environment (Butler & Schanberg, 1977), or interrupted feeding patterns (Butler et al., 1978) (even though rat pups feed about every ten minutes in their first two and a half weeks (Lincoln & Wakerly, 1974) which presumably makes feeding highly meaningful in mother-pup interaction). Nor was ODC functioning affected by other, non-tactile forms of stimulation whether auditory, visual, olfactory (Schanberg & Kuhn, 1980), kinaesthetic or vestibular (Pauk et al., 1986; Schanberg & Field, 1987:1434).

Along with the decrease in the pups' ODC activity there occurred a drop in growth hormone secretion. In their attempts to pinpoint the specific aspects of maternal contact that kept the pups' ODC and growth hormone operating normally, Schanberg and Field (1987:1434) spent months in 'behavioral observations and experimental failures with different forms of intervention'. They finally hit upon the solution of stroking the pups with a wet paint brush in imitation of the mother rat's customary tongue-licking movements. This form of stimulation and no other restored the pups' growth function to normal.

Schanberg and Field's experiment is particularly significant in that it pares down the possible influencing variables — it wasn't the personage of that specific mother which was the critical factor, or the rat pup's familiarity with and attachment to her; it didn't even need to be a rat providing the tactile stimulation; it was simply the type of touch naturally provided by the mother per se that regulated the pups' functioning.

In view of these findings it is not surprising that if animals are deprived of tactile stimulation over a period of time they fall short of the norm with respect to their physical growth.

Touch and immunity

Early mother-infant separation damages the animal immune system. Baby animals express grief in much the same way as human babies, for example by crying, or 'vocalising'. Reite and Field (1985) found that if infant monkeys were reunited with their mothers after a relatively brief separation their grief symptoms disappeared. However, their immune deficiencies persisted and as a result they were more vulnerable to disease than their normally reared counterparts. Further experiments have confirmed that mother-infant separation decreases activation of the lymphocytes (cells that fight infection), and increases the rate at which animals succumb to illness (Capitanio et al., 1998; Kanitz et al., 2004; Laudenslager & Boccia, 1996; Laudenslager et al., 1985; Montagu, 1986:27,198,239). Moreover, studies indicate that *touch deprivation is the major cause of this separation-damage* (Mitchell, 1979; Seay & Harlow, 1965; Seay et al., 1962; Suomi, 1984; Suomi et al., 1976). Baby mammals separated from their mothers but gentled by humans show significantly greater ability to withstand physiological damage and disease than non-gentled mammals (Montagu, 1986:28). In fact, all of the many studies showing the injurious effects of mother-infant separation (e.g. Harlow & Harlow, 1962) can be approached from the opposite direction, that is, as evidence that maternal touch builds and safeguards immune health when mother-infant physical contact is allowed to proceed naturally.

Physiological effects of gentling on succeeding generations

The physiological effects of gentle touch are passed on to at least one succeeding generation, sometimes with most dramatic effect. Werboff and colleagues (1968), for example, found that mice handled by humans throughout their pregnancies gave birth to a greater number of live foetuses than non-handled mice, and more of their pups survived infancy.

Summarising the effects of gentle touch on animals Ashley Montagu (1986:33) concluded that,

> Ungentled animals ... are ... in all respects less able to meet the assaults and insults of the environment', whereas 'Gentled animals respond with an increased functional efficiency in the organisation of *all systems of the body* (my italics).

Psychological effects of gentling on animals

Tactile experience is essential not only to the physiological, but also to the mental, emotional and social development of animals. Like Hammett, Weininger (1954) found that gentled rats were less fearful than non-gentled ones. When he illuminated the centre of his rats' environment with brilliant light the non-gentled rats held back timidly whereas the gentled ones, Mighty Mouse style, ventured significantly closer to the light. (Beware human parents who fear that treating children with tenderness will render them weak or cowardly; animal and human emotional systems are sufficiently similar for Weininger's experiment to serve as a cautionary tale.) As is generally the case, the rats' behaviours in this study had physiological correlates; the rectal temperatures of the braver rats were found to be substantially higher than those of the timid rats, which could indicate a difference in their metabolic rates (Montagu, 1986:32).

Even proverbially cool feline independence has proved susceptible to tender touch. Cat-enthusiast Eileen Karsh (1983) conducted an experiment in which 26 kittens were randomly divided into three groups. Two of the groups were housed in a laboratory and handled by experimenters, the first group for 40 minutes a day, the second for only 15 minutes a day. The third group of kittens was reared at home and petted frequently. Karsh found that amount of touch correlated with degree of sociability; the home-reared kittens turned out to be the most sociable as adults, those gentled for 40 minutes a day ranked second in sociability, while the least sociable of the three were those handled for 15 minutes a day.

Psychological effects of touch on succeeding generations

The psychological effects of touch, like the physical, are passed from parent to infant. In an experiment by Ader and Conklin (1963), rats handled by humans during their pregnancy produced offspring that were significantly calmer than the offspring of non-handled rats. This held true whether the rat infants remained with their biological mothers or were fostered by other females. And in Denenberg and Whimbey's study (1963), the impacts of touch were seen to be even more far-reaching: when the rats were gently handled *during their own infancy* their *offspring* were calmer than pups reared by mothers who had not been handled during infancy. (They were also heavier at weaning and defecated more, thus revealing more efficient gastrointestinal systems.)

Touch and animal mental ability

Interestingly, touch also stimulates animals' cognitive ability — their learning and memory (Montagu, 1986:238). Lewis Bernstein's rats, for instance, displayed impressively superior cognitive aptitude if they were handled and petted by an experimenter for ten minutes a day — they were more skilful at problem-solving, learned more quickly, and made fewer errors (for example in maze tests) (Bernstein, 1957). Similarly, rats gentled by Denenberg and Karas (1959,1960) during the first ten days of life were abler pupils than non-gentled rats. In addition, they weighed more *and lived longer.*

Ashley Montagu

Ashley Montagu (1905–1999), the remarkable anthropologist, thinker and humanist, is an outstanding figure in the field of touch research. Anyone interested in tactile matters — or simply in a marvellous book — could do no better than start with Montagu's *Touching: The Human Significance of the Skin* (1986, 3rd edition; original 1971). It is a rare mixture of inspiring humanity, outstanding scholarship, and a delightful literary style. We have Montagu to thank for collating the wealth of early research into touch, including the pioneering experiments mentioned thus far.

Current animal research

Later investigators have amply replicated the findings reported by Montagu. A number of studies have compared two strains of rodents (mice or rats) in which the rodent mothers conveniently display different qualities of maternal care. In the one — the high-touch strain — mothers provide their pups with copious tactile stimulation in the form of licking and grooming; in the other, low-touch strain, pups receive far less maternal licking and grooming. Individuals from the two strains develop significant personality differences. The abundantly licked/groomed pups grow up calm and fearless. In contrast, pups reared by low-level licking/grooming mothers exhibit fear, anxiety and an exaggerated response to stress throughout adulthood: they are more faint-hearted when facing bright light, show greater reluctance to step down from the safety of a small platform, and are less likely to strike out into the open centre of a field (Wei et al., 2012).

Various physiological factors undergird their fearful personalities; these include significantly increased production of stress hormones, and the impairment of chemical processes and brain organs (the hippocampus, amygdala, medial prefrontal cortex, locus coeruleus...) involved in the expression of fear (Caldji et al., 2003,2004; Francis et al., 1999:1156,1157; Liu et al., 1997; Wei et al., 2012:573; Zhang et al., 2005).

Ingenious cross-fostering of pups between low- and high-touch strains has established that *these psychophysiological differences are due to maternal care and not to inherited genetic factors*. Francis and colleagues (1999), for example, found that when the newborn pups of low-touch rats were placed for adoption with high-touch mothers they developed the brain characteristics, body chemistry and fearless personalities of the high-level lickers and groomers. Conversely, pups born of high-touch and adopted by low-touch mothers acquired the physiological and personality profiles of their adoptive low-touch community.

Francis and team took the experiment further; they allowed female offspring of both low- and high-touch mothers to mate and give birth with a view to observing their maternal behaviour. These second-generation offspring repeated the mothering patterns of the dam who had reared them and not their biological mother (that is, the low-touch pups that had been reared by high-touch mothers reproduced their foster mothers' high-level licking/grooming behaviour when they themselves became mothers, while foster-parent influence was equally strong in the high-touch pups reared by low-touch mothers).

Francis and colleagues (1999:1156) found also that when female rat pups from the low-touch strain were handled by a human experimenter, their subsequent licking/grooming behaviour towards their own offspring increased to the extent that there was no difference between the touch they provided and that provided by mothers of the high-touch strain. As in Schanberg and Field's experiment above (p.9–10), it didn't need a mother rat, or any rat, to produce the change in behaviour; rather it was the touch per se, in this case provided by a human, that was the catalyst of change.

Researchers are unpacking increasing layers of complex mechanisms that operate behind the scenes to shape these more immediately accessible signs of touch-provision and -deprivation. For instance, in response to lack of physical contact the bodily content of certain proteins decreases[1] (Andersen & Teicher, 2004; Wei et al., 2012), and neurotransmitter activity deteriorates (such as that of the 'feelgood' chemicals dopamine (Zhang et al., 2005), GABA (Caldji et al., 2003,2004) and serotonin[2] (Law et al., 2009)).

Other facets of touch confirmed by recent animal experiments are its beneficial effects on both cognitive ability and immunity. In the cognitive field, Wei and colleagues (2012) found that adult mice which had received much licking/grooming as pups showed superior ability in water maze tests and object recognition compared with mice that had received little touch (see also Aisa et al., 2007; Fabricius et al., 2008). In the area of immunity not only rodents and monkeys, but cats (Gourkow et al., 2014), lambs (Caroprese et al., 2006) and even parrots (Collette et al., 1999) that are gentled show superior immunity compared with ungentled control groups.

Harlow

No study of touch is complete without mention of Harry Harlow, groundbreaking scientist extraordinaire. Harlow's experiments with rhesus monkeys, conducted between 1957 and 1979, constitute a beacon in the advance of psychological knowledge (although, as in previous experiments described, they involved cruelty to the animals used). Before Harlow, the prevailing view of human motivation was the Freudian one which posits that our motives are dictated by 'primary drives' such as hunger, thirst and sex, and that love and affection are 'derived or secondary drives'. According to this theory, infants learn to love their mothers because they associate her with the reduction of their primary drives — a sort of primal 'cupboard-love' arrangement (Bowlby, 1958:350).

Harlow irrefutably disproved this thesis, certainly with respect to monkeys. He constructed two surrogate monkey mothers out of wire mesh. The wire skeleton of the one was left uncovered and hard to the touch. However, she had the attraction of a nipple that secreted milk when activated by the suckling of a monkey infant. The second surrogate mother provided no food but was covered with soft terry cloth. According to the received wisdom of the period, the monkeys should have passed their time with the wire-mesh mother because she reduced their hunger drive. However, quite the opposite happened — the monkeys spent as little time as possible with the wire-mesh mother and as much as possible clinging to the terry-cloth mother to whom they formed a lasting attachment (Harlow, 1958; Suomi, 1984,1990). In one instance a monkey had to be rescued from starvation because it refused to leave the terry mother to feed at all. In another, a particularly artful and agile monkey managed to cling to the terry mother with its legs while stretching its upper half over to the wire-mesh mother to suckle.

This finding — that 'contact-comfort' or 'love' (Harlow, 1958, 1974) was more emotionally important to the monkey infants than food — caused a furore in the world of psychology and beyond.

In the words of Stephen Suomi, a younger contemporary, Harlow 'stunned his audience' when reporting a series of his experiments to the American Psychological Association in 1958:

> Harlow's presentation immediately attracted the attention of the national and international news media. Soon pictures of rhesus monkey infants cuddling cloth surrogates and avoiding wire-covered ones flashed on television screens across the country and even graced the cover of *Life* magazine. The effect on developmental theorists and researchers was immediate and widespread across several disciplines, and the change in professional perception of the early importance of social contact in the socialization process has been maintained to this day.
>
> Suomi (1990:130)

The experiments in which Harlow separated monkey infants from their mothers and reared them in isolation had devastating effects on the infants. They developed abnormal psychological responses and behaviours, such as self-clutching, self-mouthing (oral contact with their own body-parts), huddling (for example, in little belly-down bundles on the floor) (Harlow, 1958:13), and stereotypy (identical, rhythmically repeated body movements). Unlike their healthy peers these monkeys were both fearful and hyperaggressive (Harlow & Harlow, 1962,1969; Mitchell, 1970,1979; Sackett, 1968); they showed no interest in exploring their surroundings, and shunned physical contact (Seay et al., 1962). At times they were found 'sitting and staring fixedly into space' (Harlow & Harlow, 1962:217) and some of the monkeys self-harmed by tearing at parts of their bodies with their teeth.

As adults they displayed aberrant sexual behaviours, as though the mother-infant separation had disrupted their entire instinctual systems. For example, they could not put themselves in normal sexual positions so were unable to copulate (Goy et al., 1974; Harlow & Harlow, 1962:217; Mitchell, 1979). If the females did become pregnant — through the persistence and motor skills of psychologically healthy males rather than by their own intention (Harlow & Harlow, 1962:218) — they turned out to be neglectful or cruelly abusive mothers; they 'struck and beat their babies, mouthed them roughly, and pushed their faces into the wire-mesh floor' (Harlow & Harlow, 1962:222). The effects of inadequate nurturing were thus passed on to succeeding generations.

Importantly, touch-deprived monkeys displayed these abnormal behaviours even if visual, auditory and olfactory contact with their mothers was permitted. This was discovered when researchers placed baby monkeys and their mothers in adjacent cages — close enough for the babies to smell, see and hear their mothers; the only deprived sense normally gratified by the mother was that of touch. Nevertheless, the babies displayed the same abnormal behaviours as monkeys that had been wholly severed from parental contact (Mitchell, 1979; Seay & Harlow, 1965; Seay et al., 1962).

As in Karsh's kitten experiment (p.12), some studies suggest a graded correlation between monkeys' behaviour and the amount of touch they receive. Suomi and colleagues placed mother monkeys and their infants in adjacent cages whose separating wall was constructed from wide-gauge mesh. By poking their paws through the mesh the infants could gain limited access to their mothers' touch. In these monkeys the 'separation reaction' was less pronounced than in monkeys that had been completely touch-deprived (Suomi, 1984; Suomi et al., 1976b).

Except in the case of one noteworthy study, none of the monkeys in these experiments recovered from the disorganising effects of being in isolation for the first six months of their lives. Their non-isolated peers had by then achieved complex social development, including the ability to engage in vigorous and aggressive play. Monkey newcomers introduced into such a group are first attacked and then accepted only if they return the aggression. However, isolates have not developed a normal repertoire of play responses and are unable to fight back. They therefore fail to gain acceptance into the group and continue to be the butt of aggression (Suomi & Harlow, 1972).

The heartening exception to this sequence of events was achieved in an imaginative experiment by Suomi and Harlow (1972). Having reared infant monkeys in isolation for their first six months they then placed them with three- and four-month-old monkeys. The younger monkeys were chosen as 'therapists' for the isolates because 'at this age clinging responses still form an integral part of their social repertoire, play is in the primary stage of development, and aggressive behavior has not yet matured' (Suomi & Harlow, 1972:488). By dint of these characteristics — their 'clinging' touch and lack of aggression — the younger monkeys returned the isolates to normality within six months (that is, the latter were behaving normally at one year).

It is perhaps worth speculating as to whether this has implications for human therapy — whether kindly touch may be the only method that will help some clients towards recovery, possibly child clients in particular. This idea may have occurred to child-care worker Meredith Leavitt-Teare who conducted an experiment with children which is reminiscent of Suomi and Harlow's monkey experiment; she taught Down syndrome children in her care to hug their autistic classmates. Typically, autistic children are averse to any human contact, including touch (Bennett et al., 2014; Grandin, 1992; Voos et al., 2013) while Down syndrome children are quite often highly affectionate and tactile. The autistic children who could not tolerate touch from adults were able to accept it from 'these same-size huggers' (Older, 1982:79).

Leavitt-Teare's work ushers us from the animal into the human world, and perhaps to the question,

What has all this animal research got to do with anything?

There are striking parallels between animal and human responses to touch and to the lack of it. In his outstanding book, *Affective Neuroscience*, Jaak Panksepp (1998) points out that in both non-human and human mammals the part of the brain that deals with basic emotions is the *limbic system* which is homologous (the same or very similar) in both structure and function across different species of mammal. The emotional systems of *all* mammals, including that relating to touch, are therefore the same or very similar — all mammals experience fear and the accompanying stress response when faced with danger; all infant mammals cry (or 'vocalise') when separated from their mothers; and all show comparable physical and psychological responses to touch.

The difference in humans lies in our possession of a new or 'neo'cortex, a later evolutionary development that grew up around and covers the older, limbic brain. It is the neocortex (in particular its prefrontal region) that enables us to regulate and modify the emotional and instinctual impulses that we share with animals.

The work of Panksepp and others has given animal research such as Harlow's renewed importance in our investigation of human need. The fact that many animal experiments could not have been conducted with human subjects (humans usually having more power to resist exploitation than animals) perhaps makes them all the more valuable as pointers to our emotional and behavioural responses.

Summary

Touch is essential for the physical and psychological well-being — and for the very survival — of animal mammals. In contrast, touch deprivation can result in ill-health and, particularly in the case of very young animals, in death. These findings have important implications for human touch-needs.

Notes

1 '... **in response to lack of physical contact the bodily content of certain proteins decreases...**'
Following mother-infant separation a significant decrease of the two proteins synaptophysin (Andersen & Teicher, 2004) and LBP (lipopolysaccharide binding protein) has been found in the rodent hippocampus. (The absence of sufficient LBP also causes spinal abnormalities) (Wei et al., 2012).

2 '... **neurotransmitter activity deteriorates (such as that of the "feelgood" chemicals dopamine..., GABA... and serotonin...)**'.
In rats deprived of touch, dopamine activity has been found to alter in the medial prefrontal cortex of the brain where it would normally optimise the operation of neurons and the functions they subserve. This alteration intensifies stress reactions (Zhang et al., 2005).
The neurotransmitter GABA (gamma-aminobutyric acid) controls the release of the stress hormone corticotropin-releasing factor (CRF) and has a calming, relaxing effect. With lack of physical contact the activity of GABA declines in the amygdala and locus coeruleus of the mouse brain (Caldji et al., 2003,2004).
Similarly with monkeys: marmoset monkeys subjected to maternal separation show decreased levels of a growth-associated protein (GAP-43), and changes in their serotonin and GABA systems (Law et al., 2009).

Chapter 2

Human touch research

There is heart-rending evidence for the critical role of touch in human development and well-being, and for the physical and psychological damage — even death — caused by touch deprivation (Cohen, 1987; Montagu, 1986; Older, 1982).

During the 19th century large numbers[1] of American infants died within their first year as a result of 'infantile atrophy' or 'marasmus' (from a Greek root meaning 'wasting away') (Montagu, 1986:97–98). This was particularly the case in foundling homes and orphanages; as late as 1915 the rate of infant marasmus casualties in these establishments could reach 100% (Chapin, 1915; Montagu, 1986:97–98) and it was commonly understood that once children had passed through their doors they were unlikely ever to be seen again.

Around the time of the Second World War researchers turned their attention to the cause of the condition. Curiously, they found that it quite often occurred in the 'best' homes and institutions where hygiene and nutrition were exemplary, whereas in poor and unhygienic environments children with good mothers often flourished (Bakwin, 1942,1949; Bender & Yarnell, 1941; Goldfarb, 1943a,b, 1945; Montagu, 1986:99; Spitz, 1945,1946a,1946b). The common denominator in the marasmus-free environments turned out to be 'mother love', central to which was loving touch — holding, hugging, cuddling.

Rather than denoting emotional-tactile deprivation, the term 'marasmus' is now generally used to describe the wasting away due to severe malnutrition in poverty-stricken parts of the world. Its former meaning is often assumed by the term 'failure to thrive' (FTT) (Money et al., 1976; Venkateshwar & Raman, 2000).

The following case of FTT was related by a hospital nurse into whose ward a poorly baby girl was admitted. Despite the latter's loss of weight and listlessness, none of the tests she underwent identified any specific illness. Fortunately this was an enlightened hospital ward and during the baby's stay the nurses lovingly held, cuddled and spoke to her. 'Miraculously' the child started gaining weight, became livelier, and within two weeks had cast off all adverse symptoms. During this time her parents did not once visit her. The hospital contacted them after the fortnight to inform them that their baby was now recovered. When they collected the child their behaviour towards her was indifferent and perfunctory.

It is easy to see how in a 19th-century American foundling home where there was little possibility of positive intervention, such a child could have continued fading away and eventually died through neglect.

Kangaroo care

While mammals, human and animal, can die from lack of touch, the corollary of this fortunately also holds true — lives can be saved through touch provision. This was graphically demonstrated in the early 1980s by innovative neonatologists Edgar Rey and Hector Martínez. The hospital in which they worked in Bogotá, Colombia, was hopelessly rundown, ill-equipped and (albeit on a cold plain in the Andes mountains) without heating. In this environment the death rate among premature infants in their care was 70%.

With little to lose, Rey and Martínez (1983) overturned the accepted policy of keeping the infants in hospital. Instead they instructed the mothers of preterm infants to tie their babies to their bare chests by means of shawls so that they were held in skin-to-skin contact for 24 hours a day. The result was a drop in preterm mortality from 70% to 30%. Because of the shawl-pouches in which the mothers carried their babies, this system of treating premature infants came to be called 'Kangaroo Care' (Anderson et al., 1986) (or 'Kangaroo Mother Care' — World Health Organisation, 2003a).

Continuing the work of Rey and Martínez in the very different setting of well-equipped American hospitals, Susan Ludlington-Hoe and colleagues discovered widespread benefits of touch to their tiny charges. Parents are invited into high-tech intensive care units and encouraged to hold their premature babies, often despite the latter being wreathed in a plethora of tubes and monitors. Through the physical contact, parent-infant bonding amplifies, to the pleasure and benefit of both parties; the infants' growth rate and weight increase; their cardiac and thermoregulatory systems normalise; and their respiratory functions improve, as shown by increased 'oxygen saturation' (oxygen in the blood), decreased carbon dioxide levels, and reduced likelihood of apnoea (cessation of breathing) (Ludlington-Hoe & Golant, 1993; Ludlington-Hoe et al., 1991; see Charpak et al., 2005).

Kangaroo Care was not immediately embraced with universal enthusiasm. In 1992 Dr Gene Anderson requested permission of the Hospital Universitario del Valle, Cali, in Colombia, to apply Kangaroo Care to their premature infants. In working with newborn sheep Anderson had found that if a lamb with breathing difficulties was allowed to nestle against its mother and was licked by her, its breathing recovered. Human premature babies also sometimes experience respiratory problems, a sign of which can be audible, laboured breathing called 'grunting respirations'. Anderson suggested that premature infants in the hospital be held by their mothers to find out whether the warm contact had similar effects on babies as on lambs.

The hospital's chairman of paediatrics, although initially reluctant, allowed Anderson to demonstrate the method with one baby. When he and his staff observed 'how the infant warmed, how his oxygen saturation improved, and how peaceful and at rest he was' they were converted to Anderson's idea and she was given leave to try it with a premature infant who had grunting respirations. After six hours all symptoms of respiratory affliction had disappeared and the infant thereafter flourished (Ludlington-Hoe, 1993:72).

A considerable number of studies have confirmed these and other salutary effects of touch on premature babies (e.g. Diego et al., 2007, 2009; Feldman et al., 2014; Ferber et al., 2002; Field et al., 2008a, 2010a; Lawn et al., 2010; Mendes & Procianoy, 2008). Smith (1989:199), for example, found that preterm babies who received gentle massage gained weight 45% faster than infants left on their own in incubators (even though both groups of infants ate the same amount). In studies by Tiffany Field and colleagues a group of preterm infants was provided with tactile and kinaesthetic stimulation in the form of body-stroking and movement of limbs. Compared with preterm infants receiving standard care, the stimulated preterms gained 47% more weight per day; were more alert and active during waking hours; showed more developed cognitive, motor and emotional behaviours; and left hospital six days earlier (at a saving of about 3,000 dollars per infant in 1986 currency) (Field et al., 1986b; Scafidi et al., 1986).

A later experiment by Field and colleagues (2008b) found that premature infants who were massaged had higher levels of insulin and of IGF-1 (insulin-like growth factor 1), a hormone important to childhood growth. The higher volume of these hormones correlated significantly with the infants' greater weight gain. In contrast, unmassaged infants had lower insulin and IGF-1, and commensurately lower weight gain.

The effects of massage on healthy, full-term infants have not been as thoroughly researched as those on preterm infants, but the results are encouraging: compared with control groups, massaged full-termers have cried less, slept better and shown reduced stress hormone levels (Field et al., 1996a; Goldstein Ferber et al., 2001), while massaged full-termers of postnatally depressed mothers were livelier, more attentive and happier, and mother-infant interactions improved significantly (Onozawa et al., 2001).

Effects of touch on adults in hospital settings

Touch provision in medical settings has produced effects on adults that are comparable to those found in juvenile patients: in different studies it has improved blood pressure scores, heart rate, respiratory rate (Hernandez-Reif et al., 2000a; Jamali et al., 2016; McNamara et al., 2003; Meek, 1993) and circulation (Henricson, 2008; see Krieger, 1975). A further panoply of positive touch-effects on both ill and healthy individuals, adults and children, has been discovered by Field and colleagues. Since their work constitutes the apotheosis of current touch research, I have reserved it for the grand finale of this chapter!

Principles underlying the effects of touch and touch deprivation

Before proceeding further, it might be useful to look briefly at two psychophysiological principles that underlie the effects of touch and touch deprivation described above, and that apply to all the tactual information in this book:

1) The crucial importance of meeting needs

Humans are born with fundamental needs. If these needs are met, especially during childhood, we are likely to be happy and successful in life and our baseline emotional state will probably be happy and relatively unstressed. This will be reflected in our biochemical functioning, that is, our bodies will be producing advantageous amounts of health-related 'happiness hormones' such as *endorphins, serotonin* and *dopamine* (Gerhardt, 2004; Schore, 1994).

If our needs are unmet we are far less likely to be happy and successful and our biochemical composition will then contain a greater preponderance of 'unhappiness hormones', or *stress hormones,* such as *cortisol, adrenalin* and *noradrenalin*. This is due to another highly significant mammalian characteristic, one that involves every cell, organ and function of our bodies and that profoundly affects our health and development, namely,

2) The 'stress response'

— that is, our biological response to stress (Cannon, 1929; Selye, 1936,1956; McEwen, 2017; Taylor, 2006). When we experience stress the body increases its production of the stress hormones. The purpose of these hormones is to energise us and enhance our ability to deal with the present emergency. Ideally the overtaxing situation resolves, our stress hormone levels subside, and we return to relative calm and the production of the health-boosting 'happiness hormones'.

However, when the disturbing situation does not resolve and the stress is ongoing, the body continues to produce heightened levels of stress hormones. Whereas normal amounts of these hormones in the body are essential for well-being — indeed, for survival — excess amounts of them as produced during stress-overload can cause widespread damage to the human organism.

Most people are aware of at least some of the physical symptoms produced by the stress response — muscular tension; racing, pounding heart; dry mouth; a 'knot' or 'butterflies' in the stomach; emotional agitation; sweating; disturbed (held, shallow or rapid) breathing; yawning; the need to urinate or defecate ...

The two principles above intersect: the denial of our essential needs is a major stressor and can therefore result in all the ill effects of surplus stress hormones. And both these principles are highly relevant to touch; as will probably be clear by now, touch is a fundamental mammalian need and, like all such needs, must be met if we are to avoid the psychophysiological damage caused by excessive stress.

Lack of sufficient caring touch at any stage of life can cause such stress, but it is particularly dangerous during childhood when it constitutes a severely *adverse childhood experience (ACE)* (Felitti et al., 1998). Barak Morgan and colleagues (2011), for example, found that the stress of being left alone in their hospital cots raised the heart rates of newborn babies by 176% and decreased their quiet sleep time (essential for early brain development) by 86%. Newborns who were held in skin-to-skin contact with their mothers showed neither of these stress signals.

The damaging impacts of adverse childhood experiences do not confine themselves to childhood; on the contrary they may continue throughout life (e.g. Felitti et al., 1998). Therefore, although not all individuals who undergo extreme touch deprivation suffer the ultimate fate of the foundling home orphans described above, those who do survive beyond childhood can be left with severe and lifelong physical, psychological and behavioural problems. The arch villain behind these problems is the stress hormone *cortisol* which, produced in excess, can cause grievous bodily harm. The following are a few of the deleterious effects of excess cortisol, all of which are likely to apply to the stressful effects of insufficient caring touch.

The effects of excess stress/cortisol on human immunity

Excess stress/cortisol weakens the immune system (Cohen & Crnic, 1982; Gatti et al., 1987; Glaser & Kiecolt-Glaser, 2005; Herbert & Cohen, 1993; Hussain, 2010; Kemeny & Schedlowski, 2007; Morey et al., 2015). One way it does this is by negatively affecting the white blood cells, such as the lymphocytes, which fight infection (Carlsson et al., 2014; Fauci & Dale, 1973; Gerhardt, 2004:102).

Indeed, the cortisol imbalance produced by environmental stress can so incapacitate the immune system that our ability to fight illness can be seriously degraded. This explains why excessive stress has been associated with increased incidence of ill-health, such as heart disease, stroke (Vogelzangs et al., 2010); cancer (Keinan-Boker et al., 2009; Kruk & Aboul-Enein, 2004; Pudrovska et al., 2013); diabetes (Lloyd et al., 2005); autoimmune diseases (Dube et al., 2009; Stojanovich & Marisavljevich, 2008); asthma (Wainright et al., 2007); gastrointestinal disorders, for example inflammatory bowel disease (IBD), irritable bowel syndrome (IBS), peptic ulcers and reflux disease (Konturek et al., 2011); reproductive problems such as miscarriage (Nepomnaschy et al., 2006; Wainstock et al., 2013), retarded foetal growth, stillbirth, premature birth, and low birthweight

(Field & Diego, 2008b; Relier, 2001); bone loss (Altindag et al., 2007) and osteoporosis (Azuma et al., 2015); muscle wasting (Poornima et al., 2014); poor wound healing (Ebrecht et al., 2004); skin conditions such as acne, psoriasis and urticaria (Kim & Park 2011); both general and abdominal obesity, which in themselves carry grave health risks; ageing of body-cells (Epel, 2009; see Humphreys et al., 2012), and premature death (Aldwin et al., 2011; Epel, 2009).

In babies, immune functioning is not only compromised by superfluous cortisol as it is in adults, but the baby's immune system can be prevented from forming properly to begin with. Its essential organs — the thymus, lymph nodes and spleen — would normally continue developing postnatally. However, in the absence of a loving primary carer who soothes away the baby's stress, such development is impaired (Schore, 1994:433,437).

Nurturing touch, on the other hand, safeguards against stress damage; it boosts immune function, for example, raises antibody levels (Gerhardt, 2004:97), and thus strengthens our ability to defend against disease (see Field et al., 2001; Hernandez-Reif et al., 2005a; Ironson et al., 1996). In babies, physical contact — holding, cuddling, stroking, kissing — keeps cortisol levels low (Dozier et al., 2008; Feldman et al., 2010; Hofer, 1995) and so prevents the erosion of immunity associated with surplus cortisol.

Stress and brain function

Excessive stress negatively affects the brain organs, thus impoverishing our cognitive abilities (McEwen, 2008, 2017; McEwen & Morrison, 2013; Money et al., 1983; Sapolsky, 1996; Shonkoff & Garner, 2012). As Sue Gerhardt (2004:62) has said, 'Stress makes you stupid'. The hippocampus — a brain area central to memory and learning — is a case in point. Too much cortisol in the body can lead to a rise in the brain's glutamate levels, and too much glutamate damages the hippocampus, causing it to lose some of its neurons (known colloquially and mysteriously as 'marbles') (Moghaddam et al., 1994). In consequence the afflicted individual eventually becomes forgetful and finds it more difficult to 'think straight'.

As a result of this hippocampal reaction to the stress mechanism, adults who have experienced severe stress in childhood have lower-volume hippocampi than normal (Dannlowski et al., 2012; Stein et al., 1997; Teicher et al., 2012; Vythilingam et al., 2002; Woon & Hedges, 2008).

Robert Hatfield (1994:5), commenting on the biochemical and neurological disarray caused by touch-deprivation stress, notes that

... with chronic imbalances of plasma cortisol and other hormones and neurochemicals there results abnormal brain tissue development as well as the destruction of previously normal brain tissue...', and while 'chronic touch deprivation or trauma results in measurable significant brain damage, ... frequent pleasurable touch results in positive changes in brain tissue.

Both long- and short-term cognitive improvements are wrought by pleasurable touch. Field and colleagues (1996c) found that after massage, adults' maths calculations increased in speed and accuracy; preschoolers (Hart et al., 1998) and four-month-olds (Cigales et al., 1997) performed better in cognitive tests; and, compared with unmassaged premature infants, pretermers who were massaged had significantly higher mental scores at two years 'corrected age' (that is, the time they would have been two had they been born full-term) (Procianoy et al., 2010).

The effects of excess cortisol on emotional state

Excess cortisol is directly associated with depression and anxiety. At the same time it inhibits production of 'happiness hormones' such as endorphins (Muñoz-Hoyos et al., 2011), dopamine (Moriam & Sobhani, 2013; Pani et al., 2000) and serotonin (Lanzenberger et al., 2010; Sunderland, 2006; Tafet et al., 2001). These hormones are chemical expressions of happiness and pleasure (that is, if we are feeling good they are present in our systems in advantageous amounts). Depressive and anxious states are thus accompanied by both an excess of cortisol and a deficiency of pleasure hormones in the body (Field et al., 2005).

Touch and human growth

As in animals, touch plays a salient role in human growth, a phenomenon recorded by Dr Elsie Widdowson in 1951. Widdowson noticed that children from an orphanage ruled by a stern, punitive woman were shorter than same-aged children from a second orphanage run by a warm-hearted, cheerful woman who felt genuine affection for children.

Her interest piqued, Widdowson embarked on an innovative yearlong experiment in the two orphanages: the first six months she spent in observation which confirmed the restricted height and weight of the children in the unhappy orphanage — with the exception of a small group of orphans who were the severe matron's favourites and whose growth surpassed that of their peers. Unequal nutrition was not the answer to this curious circumstance since the children in both establishments were being fed the same post-war food rations.

At the beginning of the second six-month period the two matrons of the orphanages swapped places — the cold, punitive one along with her coterie of favourites moved to the orphanage previously run by the warm-hearted, kindly matron, and vice versa. In addition, it was arranged that extra food rations be given to the children under the care of the unpleasant matron.

Both women took with them to their new posts the power to influence their charges' growth rates; despite the increase in their calorie intake, the children who had been developing relatively normally under the auspices of the kindly matron showed a drop in growth rate when they were supervised by the cheerless matron — although her group of favourites continued to do comparatively well — whereas the children previously under the unpleasant matron rapidly gained height and weight in the care of the warm, kindly head (Widdowson, 1951).

This connection between lack of nurturing and growth failure has since been called by many labels, among them 'psychosocial dwarfism', 'maternal deprivation syndrome' and 'psychosocial growth failure' (Johnson & Gunnar, 2011). Aside from decreased height and weight, symptoms of the condition include strange behaviours, physiological deficiencies, cognitive dysfunction, and speech impairments (Blizzard & Bulatovic, 1996; Johnson & Gunnar, 2011; Money, 1992; Powell et al., 1967a, 1967b). When the affected children are removed from their inhospitable milieux and placed in welcoming environments they show excellent powers of recovery (Money et al., 1976, 1983; Reinhart & Drash, 1969; Skuse et al., 1996), including 'spectacular' growth spurts (Montagu, 1986:244). If they are then returned to unfavourable surroundings their symptoms recur (Older, 1982:56).

Psychological and behavioural effects of touch deprivation

Some of the abnormal behaviours in Harlow's monkeys (p.16) might have struck a chord as being similar to disturbed human behaviour, for one of the many animal-human parallels is the response to the absence or loss of a tactually loving primary carer (or 'secure personal base', e.g. Bowlby, 1988:46; Rutter, 1980:269). In studies by Mary Ainsworth and colleagues (1978), human infants who had been inadequately mothered, like Harlow's monkeys, expressed anger, aggression and fear without apparent reason; they were uncooperative; and displayed unusual behaviours indicative of psychological disorder, such as stereotypy (e.g. rocking), hand-flapping, and trance-like states (comparable to the 'staring into space' described by Harlow). A number of the dysfunctional monkey behaviours are recognisable in troubled older humans, for example the self-harming (Fox & Hawton, 2004; Saunders & Smith, 2016), disadvantageous sexual behaviour (Hatfield, 1994; Montagu, 1986:206), and inability to parent successfully (e.g. Belsky et al., 2009; Gerhardt, 2004; Madden et al., 2015).

Spitz

René Spitz was one of the earliest researchers to document the effects of human touch deprivation. His work was widely influential — in fact sparked the subsequent spate of studies on animal touch deprivation. In 1945 Spitz began a study in which he compared infants in a foundling home with those in a prison nursery. The latter group of children received daily affectionate care from their mothers and developed healthily. In contrast, even though physical conditions in the foundling home were superior to those of the prison — the home was warm, hygienic and provided adequate nutrition — its infants were not touched or held by staff and lacked any form of stimulation. Their illness and mortality rates were higher than among the prison children, and those who survived developed severe emotional and behavioural disturbances:[2] they were depressed and fearful; engaged in 'bizarre' finger movements, sometimes for hours at a time; and when anyone approached they cried and shook their heads from side to side (as if saying 'no'), while the older infants tended to hide their faces in their blankets or clothes (Spitz, 1945).

In a follow-up study of the children when they were aged between two and four, Spitz found that most of them were not only unable to relate to others, but could not accomplish age-appropriate physical tasks, such as walking, talking, or eating unaided (Spitz, 1946a,b).

Personality distortion

A number of studies mentioned so far show the destructive effects on children of general neglect rather than of touch-neglect alone. However, as in various of the animal experiments described, some human research has isolated the touch component from overall nurturance levels and has indicated that touch deprivation is a critical factor in the distress and disturbed development of neglected children. Louise Biggar (1984), for example, studied the effects on children of touch aversion in their mothers and found that if the mothers refused physical contact with their infants during the first three months after birth, the infants were angry and aggressive at one year. Moreover, the severity of the children's psychological problems corresponded with the extent of their mothers' antipathy to touch — the greater her antipathy the more often her child either hit or angrily threatened to hit her during play, that is, 'in relatively stress-free situations' when there was no particular present-time cause for aggression. Monitoring these children again when they were six years old, Biggar (1984:69,70) found them verbally unresponsive and withdrawn, or antagonistic and rejecting (see also Ainsworth et al., 1978; Main, 1990).

Personality repair

The child psychologist, Viola Brody, demonstrated that touch can reverse developmental distortions such as those of the children in Biggar's studies. Brody (1997) created *developmental play therapy*, the central curative principle of which is 'caring touch'. A film recording her work with a severely disordered girl of almost five years is one of the most dramatic and moving examples of psychological repair I have encountered. At her first therapy session the girl was frenetically hyperactive and lacking in concentration — she spent much of the time running from wall to wall of the therapy room — and she was unable to form personal relationships or to tolerate the briefest touch.

Through play, Brody gradually, skilfully, eroded her touch aversion until in her final therapy session the child lay in her arms wholly relaxed and at peace. Brody regarded this ability of young children to let go and relax completely in the arms of someone they trust — to 'tune in and bliss out' (my colloquialisms, not hers) — as a kind of meditation essential to well-being. The girl's acceptance and enjoyment of caring physical contact went hand in hand with overall personality transformation; she gained the ability to trust, to relate to others, to love, also to concentrate and fully absorb herself in an activity.

Touch and self-esteem

Nurturing touch is essential for building and maintaining high self-esteem (Andersen et al., 1987; Holroyd & Brodsky, 1980:443; see Koole et al., 2014), particularly in childhood; children who do not receive sufficient loving touch feel rejected and unlovable, which significantly, and often permanently, damages their self-esteem.

This connection between touch and self-esteem is two-way — individuals with high self-esteem tend to have positive attitudes towards touch (Jourard, 1966; Silverman et al., 1973).

Body image

Tactile nurturance is also instrumental in creating positive body image, a phenomenon closely related to self-esteem (Gupta & Shork, 1995:185,188; Hunter & Struve, 1998:22; Jourard, 1966:228). Jean Wilson (1982:65) found that touching adult medical patients in her care fostered an improved acceptance of their own bodies and that this was 'an integral part of ... physical and emotional health'. She suggested that 'to disregard all physical contact between therapist and client may deter psychological growth'.

By contrast, insufficient touch can produce negative body image (Burgoon et al., 1996:73; Mahler et al., 1975; Pines, 1980). In his insightful book *Body self and psychological self* (1989), Krueger observes that young children whose physical boundaries are not continually delineated by touch — by holding and caresses — grow up to perceive their bodies as ill-shaped and excessively large.

Touch and emotional state

Well-intentioned touch generally has 'feelgood' properties; it can evoke contentment, love and security (Hollender, 1970), that is, feelings which bolster well-being and quality of life. Where troublesome feelings exist, physical contact can allay them — depression (Hollender & Mercer, 1976), fear, anxiety (Knable, 1981:1106) and panic (Older, 1982:182) can dissolve through caring touch, as can isolation and loneliness (McNeely, 1987:10).

In the words of Bertram Forer (1969:230),

> ... contact with others is reassuring that one is a bounded person but not alone. Verbal contact alone leaves one in a limbo of isolation from one's own body and from other persons.

The social value of touch

These personally advantageous feelings engendered by physical contact have social value; secure, contented, loving individuals are more likely to exert a benign social influence than not-so-loving, discontented ones, the more so since we are highly influenced by the emotions of those around us (Fowler & Christakis, 2008). (I am referring here to the discontent generated by love-deprivation in families and not that which results from social and political injustice; people in the same socioeconomic circumstances can be contented or dissatisfied depending on whether or not their childhood needs have been met, which filters their perception into brighter or darker hues respectively.)

The connection between touch and societal harmony was discovered in the 1970s by the developmental neurophysiologist James Prescott and a colleague when they studied 49 non-literate cultures around the world. In all except one of these cultures they found a highly significant correlation between tactile deprivation and aggression on the one hand, and between tactile interaction and non-violence on the other. This work, in combination with contemporaneous laboratory studies, convinced Prescott that lack of tactile pleasure was a major cause of physical violence, drug abuse, depression and sexual aberration (Prescott, 1971,1975; Prescott & Wallace, 1976). His views were sometimes dismissed at the time as claiming too much for the benefits of touch (see Hatfield, 1994; Montagu, 1986:226). However, in the light of later research they make perfect sense. There is now sound evidence that neglected children are at risk of becoming adults with a propensity for violence — that the touch-deprived six-year-olds in Biggar's study (p.30), unless 'therapied' and reparented, are likely to continue on their angry, disruptive path into adulthood (e.g. Huesmann et al., 1984; Weiler & Widom, 1996). They may also crave the high of natural opiates produced by parental cuddling (for example, endorphins and serotonin) and with harmful, sometimes tragic, consequences, try to fill the hole in their experience with the high of drugs (Gerhardt, 2004:105, 110; Miller, 1983:109–129).

Prescott's findings may apply generally to human societies whether non-literate or literate. They were more recently replicated by Tiffany Field (1999a) when she observed French and American preschoolers interacting with their parents and peers in a playground. The American children played with, talked with and touched their parents less than their French counterparts and were more aggressive towards both parents and peers. Field (1999a) found similarly when observing teenagers from Paris and Miami in MacDonald's restaurants; compared with the French teenagers the American youngsters 'spent less time leaning against, stroking, kissing and hugging their peers'. They instead engaged in greater verbal and physical aggression towards them, and in more self-touching.

As with negative personality development in younger children, aggression in adolescence can be reversible. Insufficient touch can cause it, and tactile input reduce it, as Diego and colleagues (2002b) demonstrated when they provided troubled teenagers with massage and thereby lowered their aggression, hostility and anxiety levels (see also Batmanghelidjh, p.36–37 in this text; and Field, 2002).

Touch, cooperation and goodwill

A number of studies have found that touch engenders specific feeling-thought states and behaviours — such as cooperation — that directly encourage social amity and cohesion (Kraus et al., 2010; Linden, 2015:14–21). Unwitting subjects were approached by a stranger who lightly touched them on the upper arm and asked them to help with a time-consuming task, such as picking up papers scattered on the floor. Control groups were simply asked for help and not touched. Those who had received the brief touch were more likely to help than those who had not, regardless of the gender of the interacting pair (Goldman & Fordyce, 1983; Willis & Hamm, 1980: but see Dolinski, 2010).

This increase in goodwill is linked to the finding that physical contact tends to foster positive attitudes towards the environment in which it occurs. For example, in an experiment by Fisher and colleagues (1976), a librarian deliberately touched some book borrowers on the hand as they returned their books, and omitted to touch others. Even though the physical contact lasted for less than a second (about half a second, in fact), those who had experienced it were more favourably disposed towards the library and its staff than the untouched borrowers.

As Byrne and Clore (1970) maintained, we evaluate the stimuli we receive according to our affective state — if we're feeling happy we are more likely to approve of the people around us, the wallpaper we see or the music we hear ... than if we are feeling miserable or disgruntled. It seems likely that the book borrowers who had been touched in Fisher's library exemplified this, that they felt happier — perhaps more welcomed, included — than the untouched borrowers, and that these feelings spilled over to their surroundings.

The same principle is probably at work in Guéguen and Jacob's (2005) experiment in which restaurant waiters increased the tips they received by briefly touching their customers (see also Crusco & Wetzel, 1984; Eaton et al., 1986; Gallace & Spence, 2010; Hornik, 1992; Joule & Guéguen, 2007; Kleinke, 1977).

Summarising the psychological impacts of touch, Forer (1969:229) concluded that

> Physical contact is essential ... to ... the development of a sense of self, realistic perception of self and others, ability to establish long-term relationships and to love.

Touch throughout life

Caring physical contact is needed for optimal health throughout life (Gerhardt, 2004:40; Hertenstein et al., 2006; Hollander & Mercer, 1976:49; Huss, 1977:12; Montagu, 1986:28; Morris, 1971).

In infancy and childhood

(see also much of this chapter, most of Chapter 3, some of Chapter 4, etc.)

Touch is particularly crucial in infancy (e.g. Burgoon et al., 1996:71–75; Feldman, 2011; Field, 2001a; Hertenstein et al., 2006; Stack & Jean, 2011). Babies know they are loved and cared for first and foremost through their skins, since the skin is the baby's most highly developed sensory organ. The primary way of communicating love to a baby is therefore through touch — holding, cuddling, stroking, caressing, kissing (Hofer, 1995; Montagu, 1986).

'**Being lovingly held is the greatest spur to development,**' says Gerhardt (2004:40, my emphasis) — and not being lovingly held its greatest impediment.

More than other baby mammals such as calves and puppies, the human infant's development is incomplete at birth. Ashley Montagu's (1986:53) perception of this state of affairs brings home the baby's total dependence on her carer(s) during her first years of life. Montagu considered that human babies are born halfway through the gestation period — because otherwise their heads would grow too big to pass through the mother's birth canal — and that the second half of gestation continues outside the mother's body (see 'obstetric dilemma': Rosenberg & Trevathan, 1995; Wittman & Wall, 2007). If the baby's development is to proceed healthily she needs the warm, enveloping circle of her caregiver's arms to create an external equivalent to the snugly enclosing internal womb.

Touch is at the heart of the life-sustaining bond (or 'attachment') between children and their carers (Barnard & Brazelton, 1990; Brazelton & Cramer, 1991; Montagu, 1986); and the amount and quality of the touch received in childhood are key components of the template that shapes all future relationship patterns (Frank, 1957:239; Gerhardt, 2004; Huss, 1977:12; Jourard, 1968:137; Peloquin, 1989:305; Takeuchi et al., 2010).

Babies and children who do *not* receive sufficient loving touch are tense, insecure, and prone to fears, anxieties, low self-esteem and other psychophysiological difficulties which may dog them throughout their lives.

In adolescence

During adolescence tactility is notably subject to social influence. In contrast to some non-Anglo cultures in which physical contact continues as a natural expression of affection at all stages of life (see Chapter 5), Anglo teenagers, and sometimes preteens, often become too embarrassed to accept a hug from parents or other family members. As a result they can be somewhat touch starved. Depending on tactile norms in the adolescent's particular social group, this lack may or may not be redressed to an extent by an increase in exchanges of touch between peers.

Some touch-shy teenagers may accept a massage from a family member on account of its slightly medicinal associations, and because it can be viewed as a purely physical matter rather than an expression of affection. (The latter may elicit reactions of disgust and embarrassment from the adolescent.)

Even if constrained by social pressures to forgo tactile satisfaction, if the teenager has received much tender touch during childhood, she need not be driven to veer from a healthy life-course by a temporary spell of tactual famine. However, this is not so of teenagers who have been deprived of childhood touch. Such adolescents run the risk of falling into sexual relationships as a way of fulfilling their non-erotic touch needs, hence the link between touch deprivation and teenage pregnancy.

During the 'liberated sixties' when it became more acceptable to discuss sex, a number of researchers revealed this link (Blinder, 1966; Hollender, 1961,1970; Hollender et al., 1969) — which is of course still relevant today (Office for National Statistics, 2016). In my own clinical practice a number of women have confided that they had embarked on early sexual relationships in order to satisfy their longing for affectionate touch rather than for sexual satisfaction, that 'sexual activity for them was a price to be paid for being cuddled and held' (Malmquist et al., 1966:481).

Camila Batmanghelidjh has had many detractors since the charity she founded, 'Kids Company', was closed in 2015 amid allegations of financial mismanagement. I have no idea of the logistical operations of Kids Company. Whatever they were, Batmanghelidjh's achievements in the psychological sphere are remarkable. The Company worked with vulnerable children and teenagers who were often victims of abuse, exploitation, neglect, hunger, drug addiction, homelessness and gang involvement. Their parents had been unable to fulfil their parenting roles since they themselves had often suffered years of abuse and neglect (Batmanghelidjh, 2012, personal correspondence).

Batmanghelidjh and her team 'reparented' the teenagers — gave them love, care, support, encouragement — and loving touch. They functioned

> towards vulnerable children like an additional parental figure. In this context, appropriate levels of touch are encouraged, provided they are not about meeting the worker's needs but they are about responding to the child's needs ... We allow our workers to do play-fighting with the children and also lots of sporting activities. Workers and children do art, clay work, fashion, performing arts, all of which have a natural physical contact transaction. Children who feel comfortable can make use of our complementary health treatments. We have osteopaths,

massage therapists, reflexologists, beauty therapists and other forms of touch therapies at Kids Company. We believe that traumatised children hold cellular memories of adversity and need to be helped to release these tensions appropriately.

Batmanghelidjh (2013, personal correspondence)

Batmanghelidjh and co-workers turned around the lives of over 85% of the youngsters with whom they worked — an unusually high rate of success in work with severely disadvantaged adolescents (Gaskell, 2008; Gow, 2012; Hillman & Wainwright, 2012; Jovchelovitch & Concha, 2013; Lemma, 2010).

During pregnancy

A pregnant woman who is tenderly touched or massaged by her partner feels supported, loved and loving. Caring touch releases the hormone oxytocin, popularly known as the 'love' or 'cuddle' hormone, into the systems of both mother and father. Oxytocin is associated with relaxation, bonding, love, caring, trust and altruism (MacGill, 2017; Neumann, 2007; Schneiderman et al., 2012; Uvnäs-Moberg et al., 2014).

Other 'happiness hormones' are released through touch, such as endorphins (Dunbar, 2010; Khajehei & Behroozpour, 2018), serotonin and dopamine (Field et al., 2005). Endorphins are endogenous opiates; they are associated with euphoria and with the easing of anxiety, stress and pain. Serotonin, as a natural antidepressant, is associated with gladness and with emotional calm and stability. Dopamine too is associated with pleasure, and with reward. In addition, each of these 'feelgood' chemicals plays further essential roles in maintaining health (e.g. Frazer & Hensler, 1999; Rokade, 2011; Tóth et al., 2012), and they pass to the foetus through the placenta in the same way as stress hormones do.

Through interparental touch, therefore, the mother's love for her partner and baby blooms, deepens, becomes a consciously expressed and tangible entity; the father similarly is more bonded with mother and baby and more involved in the birth; the foetus is bathed in love which aids her development; and family closeness is affirmed.

In the postpartum period

Postpartum parents continue to experience mutual touching as nourishing and supportive. Where postnatal depression occurs, physical contact can alleviate it. This is important for both the afflicted parents and their offspring since sufferers of postnatal depression find it more difficult to care for their children adequately (Field, 2010; Field et al., 2007a; Gordon & Feldman, 2015; Mantis et al., 2019; Muzik & Borovska, 2010).

In a study by Field and colleagues (2009), severely depressed women were prescribed a 12-week massage course administered during and after their pregnancy by a significant male partner. The results of this intervention were startling. Unlike the unmassaged control group, the massaged women experienced less depression, their cortisol levels lowered, they had fewer preterm or low-birthweight babies, and their babies had lower cortisol levels and scored higher in a newborn behavioural assessment test.

In single parenthood

Touch can ease the stresses of single parenthood. Psychologist Steve Biddulph advises single mothers to arrange a weekly massage in order to experience tactile caring and relaxation. They are hereby more able to remain calm and happy, to the benefit of both themselves and their children (Biddulph, 2015, personal communication).

In middle age

The life-enhancing effects of physical contact persist into middle age and beyond (Burgoon et al., 1996; Hertenstein et al., 2006:24; Jakubiak & Feeney, 2017) — loving touch relaxes, affirms, increases well-being, helps to keep relationships alive, and boosts coping skills in the face of vicissitude (see Morrison, 2016).

Touch and the elderly

Older persons are particularly prone to isolation and loneliness and sometimes long for the antidote of affectionate touch (Hollinger, 1986; Langland & Panicucci, 1982; McCorkle, 1974; McNeely, 1987:10; Montagu, 1986:396; Peloquin, 1989:305). This is poignantly expressed in Donna Swanson's poem *Minnie Remembers* (1977), written when she had been a widow for 20 years, during which time she had been

>'Respected.
>Smiled at.

But never touched.
Never held so close that loneliness
was blotted out…'

Research suggests that Donna Swanson's last years would have been far happier and richer had she crossed paths with health professionals such as Gineste and Marescotti (2008), or Dawn Nelson (1994, 2006), in whose treatment of elderly patients loving touch is a cardinal feature.

Besides the simple 'human' touch to which Swanson refers — a hand gently held, a hug that blots out loneliness – more structured touch in the form of massage bestows many benefits on elderly recipients: it induces relaxation (Harris & Richards, 2010), lowers anxiety and depression, reduces cortisol levels (Field et al., 1998b), relieves loneliness, calms irritability, warms and enlivens, revives interest in life (Nelson, 1994,2006), ameliorates pain, increases the range of motion (ROM) in joints, improves blood circulation, lessens the likelihood of pressure sores, and grounds Alzheimer patients in physical reality. So desirable are the effects of massage on the elderly that geriatric massage has become a specialty (Puszko, 2009).

Touch and the dying

In the late 1950s, the pioneering doctor and psychiatrist Elisabeth Kübler-Ross became concerned about how terminally ill patients were treated in the medical profession, which led her to challenge the non-acceptance of death within Western culture (Kübler-Ross, 1969; see Gawande, 2014). Contrary to medical practice at the time, she discussed death openly, and sensitively, with dying patients. The large majority greatly welcomed such open discussion, and all appreciated her unfailing empathy and support. Since touch is an ideal medium for conveying these qualities it was often part of conversations between Kübler-Ross and patients during the different stages of the dying process (Kübler-Ross, 1969:22,57,59,99–100,124). When patients were mourning the impending loss of life and loved ones, there was sometimes

> no or little need for words. It is much more a feeling that can be mutually expressed and is often done better with a touch of a hand, a stroking of the hair, or just a silent sitting together.
> Kübler-Ross (1969:99–100)

Doctor Dame Cicely Saunders' approach had much in common with that of Kübler-Ross. In 1967 Saunders founded the hospice movement in which the words she addressed to dying patients have become a motto:

> You matter because you are you. You matter to the last moment of your life and we will do all we can not only to help you die peacefully, but also to live until you die.
> https://www.stchristophers.org.uk/about/
> damecicelysaunders/tributes

Both 'human' touch and, increasingly, massage are used in hospice and palliative care as a means of fulfilling Saunders' pledge. Tender 'human' touch in these settings engenders calm, peace, a sense of security and well-being, and it eases the fear and loneliness sometimes experienced by patients at the end of life. Gentle massage similarly has been found to lessen pain, anxiety, depression (Falkensteiner et al., 2011), stressful feelings and stress hormone levels (Osaka et al., 2009), blood pressure and heart rate (Meek, 1993).

* * *

Touch in the teaching profession

> Three broad touch categories exist: good touch, bad touch and absent touch ...
> Green (2017:774)

The current government policy on touch within the UK teaching profession is aberrated, harmful and arguably — since touch is a fundamental need — contravenes children's human rights. The government has ruled that in general pupils should not be touched by their teachers. As a result, many preschool and primary children are sent into a haptic desert for large parts of their waking week.

In children particularly, the need for physical contact has no substitute, just as there is no substitute for food or drink if they are hungry or thirsty. It is natural and healthy for a small child to want to hold his teacher's hand or snuggle into her lap and be held, particularly when he needs reassurance, comfort, rest or re-energising (see Anderson, 1985,1986). Nursery and primary schoolteachers have told me with frustration and regret, occasionally with self-congratulation, that they 'find a way to put the child off or distract them from wanting touch'. The messages children are likely to receive if someone 'puts them off' is that their innate need for touch is in some way bad and shameful, and that they are not lovable enough to be touched (Horner, 1968; Imes, 1998:182; Lewis & Streitfeld, 1972:210). If adults absorb such messages — and they do — children, who have less ability to rationalise and to seek alternative, healthier company, will do so far more acutely. They are unlikely to be fully relaxed and contented which can prevent them from maximising their educational and social potential. Such touch avoidance on the part of teachers moreover provides an undesirable model of stilted, unresponsive behaviour rather than a healthy model of empathy, kindness and emotional warmth.

This is all the more regrettable since legally and morally teachers officiate *in loco parentis* (Children Act, 1989), and young children in particular will look to the teacher to fulfil this quasi-parental role. Teachers are less likely to succeed in this respect if enjoined to withhold a parental behaviour as fundamental as touching.

Furthermore, many young children, when first placed in the strange situation of the school classroom, experience the temporary loss of their parents and familiar home environment as anxiogenic and distressing. It is the teacher's responsibility to alleviate these feelings by making the classroom as safe and warmly inviting as possible. Fortunately most children will touch each other and to an extent meet their touch needs in that way. However, this does not satisfy the need for a loving, accepting parent-substitute who responds with reassuring hugs or hand-holding when required. And if badly handled, the transition from home to school can cause long-lasting social anxiety.

For the above reasons some wise heads of schools disregard the government injunction prohibiting teacher-pupil touch. One independent London school I know of sends out a brochure to prospective parents saying: if your child falls over we will pick him up and cuddle him because that is what he needs at that moment.

Anecdotal evidence from teachers indicates that children function less well in schools that heed government policy on touch. Jennifer, a primary schoolteacher, had worked in two establishments — one in which the policy was adhered to, and a second in which the headteacher rejected it on the grounds that it was harmful and ludicrous. Jennifer found that at the school in which touch exchange was allowed to occur naturally the children were happier, calmer, far less aggressive, and concentrated better.

Iona, who was nearing retirement and had taught both junior and senior children in tough inner London schools, discovered early on in her career that touch can be a useful disciplinary method:

> '*I was working in a school whose head thought that children should sit silently at their desks all day. I didn't believe in that – I liked the children to be lively and engaged, but as a junior teacher I didn't have the clout to change things. Every now and then the head teacher did a round of classroom inspections and one day she warned me that she'd be dropping in. It so happened that my class became involved in a particularly boisterous discussion just before she was due to appear. Panic!*
>
> *I HAD to get those 15- and 16-year-olds to quieten down.*
>
> '*Without thinking — instinctively — I put my hand gently on the heads of the noisiest of them and they immediately, magically, calmed down. When the head appeared the class was sitting in total peace and silence. I've used touch in this way ever since.*'

No fear is more justified than a fear of child abuse. However, the muddled thinking apparently engendered by this fear among policy makers is counterproductive. With more rationality brought to the table, and with recourse to the large volume of information now available about physical and sexual abuse (see Chapter 3), it should be perfectly possible to thrash out the distinctions between positive and negative touch.

The two forms of touch, caring and uncaring, are opposite in their effects. The first should be encouraged since it is essential to young children's health; it strongly influences their ability to develop personally and socially, and to learn. The second is severely harmful. It is as daft and deleterious to ban both negative and positive touch in schools as it is to ban good books and excellent teaching because their bad versions exist, or healthy school lunches along with the unhealthy sugary, fatty ones.

* * *

Touch in the nursing profession

Aside from physical therapies which by definition entail touch (for example massage and body psychotherapies — see pp.207–208), the nursing profession was for a time alone in recognising the remedial power of physical contact and consistently allowing space for touch research in its journals (Older, 1982:184; several articles cited in this text emanate from nursing scholarship).

Nurses are daily faced with the exigencies of relieving physical and emotional suffering and, according to Sayre-Adams and Wright (1995:vii),

> It is intuitively apparent to those who work within the healthcare field that caring and touching are immutably bound together with the healing process.

A number of authors make a clear distinction between 'instrumental/procedural' touch (that required for nursing and medical procedures) and 'empathic' touch (Gadow, 1984:67; Goodykoontz, 1979:5; LeMay, 1986:28; O'Hearne, 1972:453; Weiss, 1986:496). It is the latter, often in the form of hand-holding, that nurses have used to convey caring and understanding (Schmahl, 1964:74), to comfort (Gleeson & Timmins, 2005), and to break down barriers and establish rapport. Patients moaning in discomfort have experienced relief for as long as 30 minutes after having their hand held (Knable, 1981:1109); and for those who are intensely stressed, vulnerable and isolated, touch has been found incomparable in producing immediate reassurance (Rubin, 1963:828). Indeed, in the experience of Lianne Mercer (1966:20) who cared for psychiatric patients, physical contact has the capacity to reach patients when all else fails.

The following narrative movingly illustrates these contentions. It relates the experience of a patient in two London hospitals and was written by the patient's mother:

RUTH'S STORY

by Barbara Berkeley-Hill

This is a difficult story to tell, even after 22 years, and I will have to be the one to tell it rather than Ruth herself, who still doesn't want to feel that she is tempting fate by talking about an illness that came from nowhere and might return some dreadful day. However it is a story that needs to be told because it celebrates the wonderful people who literally saved her life, and who did this, not through conventional medical interventions (though these of course played an enormous part), but through reaching out to touch her with their love.

My daughter Ruth had led a fairly charmed life up until the age of 19. She was a bouncy, funny, passionate girl who loved life and was delighted to have gained a place at Bart's and the Royal London Hospital to study medicine. But in her second term, on 28th January 1998, her life changed for ever. There had been some worrying signs: a flu-like virus had made her really ill over the Christmas holidays. She was beginning to feel increasingly worried about frequent headaches and an inability to find the right words when speaking or writing. On the morning of the 28th she had a massive fit in one of her lectures and was rushed to hospital. At first there seemed nothing too serious to worry about and she was discharged, but four days and several fits later she was diagnosed with viral encephalitis and admitted to King's College Hospital where she remained for three months in a critical condition. And it was the care she received there, particularly at the hands of two exceptional nurses, that brought her back to us.

Although whatever virus it was (and we will never know) had long departed by the time Ruth was admitted to King's, it had penetrated her brain and done serious damage. She could not speak, all her cognitive skills had gone, she did not recognise us or know how to relate to her surroundings, she had even forgotten how to eat, so was in danger of literally starving to death. The only skills which were intact were her motor skills, so she could run. And run she did, through the wards, and on one memorable day, up onto the roof. Managing a patient like her was obviously extremely difficult, but King's had nursed people with encephalitis before (even though it is a very rare condition affecting one in 10,000 people). From experience they knew that they had to play the waiting game and let the brain heal. They therefore did not sedate her even though this would have been by far the easiest solution in a busy neurological ward, but they somehow managed her very challenging behaviour. And they did much more than this — they loved her. If she wanted to curl up under their desk during the night shift, they would build her a nest of blankets and keep her close to them. If she was very restless and distressed at night they would stroke and soothe and sing to her. Rather than give her painkillers if she had a headache, one of the sisters who was trained in a variety of alternative therapies and was a practising craniosacral therapist, would massage her. Every day I would come into the ward and try and build on their good work, holding her, massaging her, combing her hair, talking gently to her, coaxing her to eat, and gradually, very gradually she came back.

The whole medical team worked with us to help us deal with our distress and give us the confidence to take her out to the park, to the local Chinese restaurant, to try and take the first steps to helping her rebuild her life, but she was very bewildered and afraid and often my husband would have to carry her back to the hospital in his arms. Our strong, confident, sociable daughter had become a frightened child again. But at least she was still with us, at least there was some hope of recovery although we were gently but firmly told that a brain injury of this severity would probably lead to significant disabilities, and that her life, and ours, would never be the same again.

Even though this critical period had been devastating, with such a strong medical team around us we felt supported and hopeful. However this exceptional level of care brought its own problems. She could not stay at King's indefinitely; where could and should she go next? She was very frail both physically and emotionally but had to be assessed to determine the level of neurological damage. It was decided to move her to a special unit within another London hospital dealing with the aftermath of serious brain injury. Here the regime was completely different and it nearly broke her. Gone was the hands-on approach. Here the regime was cold and clinical. The cognitive behaviour therapy approach was designed to get Ruth to re-establish her boundaries, to modify her behaviour and start the long, hard journey of relearning her social as well as her cognitive skills. This was all very necessary and commendable but the transition from one type of care to another was too sudden and too shocking. We visited every day, but here the doors of the unit were locked, the behaviour of some of the patients was very bizarre and frightening and we never felt part of the medical team as we had done before. After two weeks of being left in her own room for long periods she became so withdrawn and distressed that we decided to discharge her. However with the help of her consultant we reached a compromise whereby she stayed in the unit for three days and nights with much increased levels of attention and a clear structure and routine to her days, and slept at home for the remaining four days and nights, attending daily therapy sessions. This worked well and after an intensive eight-week programme she was finally allowed home. At this stage her IQ was assessed as being well below average and we were encouraged to give up all hope of her ever returning to medical school.

During the next nine months Ruth embarked on a difficult and demanding rehabilitation programme. She was lucky enough to gain a place on a special programme for young people suffering serious brain injury run by a charity called Rehab UK. She also completed a part-time art foundation course at Ravensbourne College of Art and Design. She had been a talented artist and dancer before her illness and these creative skills were some of the first to return. At times she was completely exhausted by the demands placed upon her but through sheer determination on her part and careful monitoring by the clinicians working with her it became clear that the brain was reconnecting, that skills were coming back, that perhaps a return to medical school was not impossible. During this very testing time Ruth received enormous support from her friends who came to sit with her when she was too tired to go out, who did her nails and hair when she lost faith in her appearance, who stayed in frequent contact despite being away at university, who never gave her the feeling that she had been abandoned or forgotten. But despite all this progress and the knowledge that she was in the thoughts and prayers of so many people she suffered from recurrent nightmares in these early months of recovery and I often slept with her until the worst had passed. She would curl up in 'spoon' position with her back to me and I would wrap myself around her, reassuring her with my touch that there was someone there for her throughout the night. Alongside all the cognitive input she continued to have craniosacral therapy from the same nurse who had originally cared for her in King's. This had a profound effect on her, enabling her to find the peace and calm and strength she so desperately needed to carry on.

Miraculously she did return to medical school nearly two years after she had been taken ill. We were very apprehensive about her taking on so much but she was determined. How will I ever know if I could have done it if I don't try? was her argument and the medics agreed. With hindsight she did go back too soon, but the friends who had started out with her two years previously insisted that she come and live with them even though they were now in their third year and she was having to start again. They too pushed her and encouraged her and were there to catch her when she fell or faltered. In her five years at medical school she did not fail one exam and she has now been a practising doctor for ten years. Of course the most important person in this story is Ruth herself; without her courage and determination such a wonderful outcome would not have been possible. But I know that the exceptional care she received in those first few critical weeks made the rest of the journey possible and I can never thank those doctors and nurses enough for what they did.

* * *

Contemporary touch research; Field and colleagues

Contemporary touch research has culminated in the exceptional work of Tiffany Field and colleagues. In over 200 controlled experiments, from 1982 onwards, they have demonstrated that touch in the form of massage therapy improves health and well-being in a wondrous array of physical and psychological conditions. The breadth of this array suggests that, *like other fundamental needs such as sleep and exercise, touch has a regulatory and health-enhancing impact on the human organism as a whole* — that, as Montagu found in the case of animals, caring physical contact promotes

> an increased functional efficiency in organisation of all systems of the body.
>
> Montagu (1986:33)

Below is a brief mention of some of Field and colleagues' experiments, along with a few studies by other researchers who entered the arena of touch research more recently. In each of these experiments the unmassaged control groups showed no improvement or deteriorated. Conversely, in the massaged groups, blood sugar levels of children with diabetes dropped to within normal range (from 159 to 121) (Field et al., 1997b; Sajedi et al., 2011); and multiple sclerosis patients experienced a decrease in spasticity, paraesthesia (abnormal sensations such as pins and needles/pricking/burning) and urinary symptoms (Siev-Ner et al., 2003), while their self-esteem, body image and social functioning improved (Hernandez-Reif et al., 1998b).

Migraine sufferers who received massage had less severe and fewer headaches, a smaller number of distress symptoms and sleep disturbances, lower use of painkillers, and higher serotonin levels (Hernandez-Reif et al., 1998a; see Lawler & Cameron, 2006). And cancer patients found that massage therapy reduced their pain

(Forchuk et al., 2004; Wilkie et al., 2000), nausea (Grealish et al., 2000), symptom distress (Smith et al., 2002), anxiety (Stephenson et al., 2000), depression (Hernandez-Reif et al., 2004), the nausea and vomiting associated with chemotherapy (Shin et al., 2004), and it improved their quality of sleep (Kashani & Kashani, 2014).

In Ecuador, one of the developing world countries where diarrhoea is the second leading cause of death, infant orphans who were not massaged had a 50% greater chance of diarrhoea than massaged infants and an 11% greater chance of succumbing to illness of any kind (Jump et al., 2006).

Effects of massage therapy on immunity

One of the many significant findings in Field and colleagues' research is that massage strengthens the immune system by boosting cells that fight disease; in breast cancer patients it increased the number of natural killer cells and lymphocytes (Hernandez-Reif et al., 2004, 2005a), and decreased the degeneration of natural killer cell activity that normally accompanies radiation therapy (Billhult et al., 2009).

In children with leukaemia, massage raised the children's white blood cell and neutrophil counts (Field et al., 2001); while in HIV patients natural killer cell and CD8 T cell numbers were significantly increased, and natural killer cell activity was improved (Ironson et al., 1996; see also Diego et al., 2001; Shor-Posner et al., 2006).

Parents as massage therapists

In some studies, as in the two above on child diabetes and leukaemia, parents were taught to administer massage therapy to their children, to the benefit of both. For example, in children with asthma, peak air flow and lung function were enhanced, cortisol levels were reduced, and both the children's and parents' anxiety decreased (Field et al., 1998a).

Pain, anxiety and depression

Pain, anxiety and depression — either singly or together — are integral to a wide range of clinical conditions. Looking at the work of Field et al. it becomes clear that in addition to producing the measurable physiological improvements to specific medical conditions, massage is a primary, drug-free method of reducing all three of these complaints. Pain, for instance, yielded to massage therapy across a large number of assorted ailments including accident and emergency (A&E) conditions (Kubsch et al., 2000), cancer (Falkensteiner et al., 2011; Hernandez-Reif et al., 2005a; Stephenson et al., 2000) and cardiac surgery (Bauer et al., 2010; Wentworth et al., 2010). Where other symptoms accompanied the pain these were simultaneously reduced, for instance in shoulder-pain patients the reduction in pain was accompanied by significantly increased range of motion (ROM) in the affected shoulder (Van den Dolder & Roberts, 2003).

Similarly, depression (e.g. Field, 1998; Field et al., 2009; Hou et al., 2010) and anxiety (Black et al., 2010; Field et al., 1996b; Wentworth et al., 2009) have been relieved by massage therapy in people of different ages and health status. One example are patients who received massage of the hand after cataract surgery and who as a result had significantly decreased anxiety, blood pressure, pulse rate, and levels of the stress hormones adrenalin and noradrenalin — whereas in the non-massaged control group adrenalin, noradrenalin and cortisol levels rose (Kim et al., 2001).

Depression and anxiety often occur and are relieved together (Feijo et al., 2006; Field et al., 1992). Children in the United States who developed severe posttraumatic stress in the wake of Hurricane Andrew and who received massage were less anxious and depressed, and had lower cortisol levels than unmassaged children (Field et al., 1996e).

Where pain, depression and anxiety were all three present they were simultaneously relieved by massage (Field, 2014) — as in low back pain sufferers who also slept better, experienced improved flexibility (including increased trunk flexion), had higher serotonin and dopamine levels (Field et al., 2007b; see Preyde, 2000), and lower painkiller intake (Ginsberg & Famaey, 1987).

The list of ailments alleviated by massage therapy continues at length but there is not space to present more of it here. For readers who wish to explore further, abstracts of all of Field and colleagues' experiments with fuller details may be found at www6.miami.edu/touch-research, the website of Florida's Touch Research Institute which Field founded in 1992.

Massage therapy with healthy participants

Field and team have found also that massage provides a host of benefits to healthy individuals. For example, it lowered workplace anxiety (Shulman & Jones, 1996), job stress (Cady & Jones, 1997; Katz et al., 1999), heart rate and blood pressure (Boone et al., 2001; Delaney et al., 2002), and it improved emotional state and sleep (e.g. Field & Hernandez-Reif, 2001; Field et al., 1996d).

Elderly retired volunteers who were depressed and were taught to massage infants experienced less depression and anxiety, their stress hormones (cortisol, adrenalin and noradrenalin) decreased, and their life-style and health improved (Field et al., 1998b).

Fathers taught to massage their babies showed more enjoyment, warmth and expressiveness when interacting with them, to the enhancement of father-infant relations (Cullen et al., 2000).

Massage alleviated women's reproductive difficulties: it reduced premenstrual symptoms — pain, depressed mood, anxiety and water retention (Hernandez-Reif et al., 2000b); shortened labour time (Bolbol-Haghighi et al., 2016); diminished labour pain (Chang et al., 2002; Field et al., 1997c); prevented laceration during delivery (Davidson et al., 2000; see Labrecque et al., 2001); curtailed hospital stays; heightened mothers' positive feelings, decreased anxiety and postnatal depression (Field et al., 1997c); and improved the quality of breast milk (Foda et al., 2004; Jones et al., 2001).

Massage has long been a boon also to professional and amateur exercisers (sportspersons, athletes, dancers...) since it decreases delayed onset muscle soreness (DOMS), that is, the pain and stiffness experienced after unaccustomed or strenuous exercise (Hilbert et al., 2003; Mancinelli et al., 2006; Zainuddin et al., 2005). Following arm exercises, for example, untrained participants who were massaged showed reduced DOMS, cortisol, and creatine kinase (an enzyme in the blood associated with muscle damage), and also elevated neutrophil counts, compared with unmassaged participants (Smith et al., 1994).

Finally, as stated earlier (p.27), massage has produced improvements in the cognitive performance of healthy children and adults (Cigales et al., 1997; Field et al., 1996c; Hart et al., 1998; Procianoy et al., 2010).

Purely 'human' touch and more structured touch

Although the type of touch on which I am focusing is primarily of the everyday 'human' variety rather than structured techniques as in massage, the experiments of Field and others are eminently relevant, since caring touch of all kinds produces cutaneous stimulation and its accompanying psychophysiological phenomena (generally the release of oxytocin, endorphins and serotonin ...; the reduction of stress hormones and negative feelings; and the increase of relaxation, positive feelings and well-being).

Some instances of 'human' touch lie within a grey area between spontaneous tactile expression and structured techniques; a mother who has never studied massage will rub a sore tummy or stroke her child's hair or back in a regular, soothing rhythm akin to 'effleurage' (a long, smooth massage stroke); or someone trying to massage away a friend's headache will instinctively use a mixture of effleurage and some form of 'petrissage' (a kneading action, for example, a circular, more or less on-the-spot movement pressing into the muscle). In certain massage therapies the practitioner will simply hold a body-part for a few moments, as all the world over people hold a hand or shoulder to express caring and to comfort. Indeed, massage therapy most probably originated with movements such as these that were performed instinctively in everyday life and were extended and formalised into massage techniques when they were seen to be effective.

Summary and conclusions

Physical contact contributes to optimal well-being throughout the human lifespan. It is particularly critical in childhood when sufficient loving touch is essential for healthy development and for happiness and success in life. In contrast, touch deprivation can cause psychophysiological ill-health, unhappiness, and in extreme cases, death.

Since unanswered need — especially in childhood — causes acute stress, cortisol overload and impaired health; and since love is a paramount human need; and because babies know they are loved primarily through their skins, it follows that loving touch in infancy is the principal determinant of healthy development, and that the paramount cause of early developmental problems — the impairment of major brain organs, chemical imbalances, personality distortions and unhappiness — is likely to be a lack of loving touch. It follows too that a number of the problems that drive people to therapy — depression, anxiety, inability to cope, rage, aggression, antisocial behaviour, drug abuse, eating disorders, absence of happiness/pleasure... — are caused by inadequate childhood nurturing, of which touch is the central pillar.

If the reader baulks at the enormity of this claim for touch (as I did initially when I saw it standing baldly there on the page), let us not embark on a pointless discussion on quantity — on whether it is *the* most important factor, or by how much. Enough to be aware that it is a sine qua non in the establishment of human health and in its optimal maintenance throughout life.

Notes

1 **'In 19th century America large numbers of infants died within their first year as a result of "infantile atrophy" or "marasmus".'**
The numbers of infant deaths in foundling homes and orphanages are well documented (Cohen, 1987; Hunter & Struve, 1998:13; Montagu, 1986:97). The death rate from marasmus for American infants generally is more difficult to ascertain. The figure of over 50% has been suggested (Montagu, 1986:97). Whatever the exact number, several sources agree that it was of significant magnitude (Cohen, 1987; Hunter & Struve, 1998; Older, 1982; Zur & Nordmarken, 2011:e4).

2 **'... those who survived developed severe emotional and behavioural disturbances...'**
Spitz's institutionalised children pre-echo the condition of children consigned to the shockingly inhumane orphanages of Caeușescu's totalitarian regime in Romania (1967–1989). When Caeușescu was overthrown and the orphans' plight became known outside Romania, thousands of the children were adopted by parents in Britain, America and Canada. Those adopted before they were six months old have recovered to the extent that there is no or little detectable difference between them and the control groups of children reared in families from birth. Other orphans adopted from six months onwards have never completely recovered, and the later they were adopted the more severe their developmental difficulties (e.g. Sonuga-Barke et al. 2017).

Chapter 3

Negative touch

Touch is powerful (Peloquin, 1989:301,302). When misused its destructive effects can be as far-reaching as its positive effects when used caringly. The most egregious forms of inhumane touch are physical and sexual abuse. They are inflicted on females and males of all ages, and particularly on children who are easiest prey to adult maltreatment. I focus mainly on child abuse in this chapter since it is the most clear-cut violation of tactility. However, physical and sexual abuse of adults, for example between marital partners or in war zones, can devastate lives and produce many of the same effects as those outlined below (see Barnett et al., 2011).

Child physical abuse (CPA) has been defined as

> The intentional use of physical force against a child that results in, or has the potential to result in, physical injury.
> Centers for Disease Control and Prevention (2008:14)

It includes punching, kicking, whipping, shaking, scratching, biting and burning (with boiling water, cigarette, lighter, stove, hot iron ...). Other torments range from twisting, painful squeezing, pinching, grabbing, pushing, throwing, binding, to strangling, drowning, poisoning, and to beating either with the hand or with an object, such as a switch, belt, cord or brush (e.g. Barnett et al., 2011:141,150).

Child sexual abuse (CSA) has been variously defined as, for example,

> The involvement of dependent, developmentally immature children and adolescents in sexual activities they do not fully comprehend and to which they are unable to give informed consent ... [and] that violate the social taboos of family roles.
> Schechter and Roberge (1976:129)

and

> Contacts or interactions between a child and an adult when the child is being used for sexual stimulation of the perpetrator or another person when the perpetrator or another person is in a position of power or control over the victim.
> cited by Faller (1993)

The latter is one of several definitions highlighting the abuser's use of power to coerce or manipulate his* victim.

Sexual abuse includes 'anal or vaginal penetration by the penis or another object, oral-genital and oral-anal contact, touching of intimate body parts whether clothed or unclothed...' (Barnett et al., 2011:199). In addition, normal caregiving behaviours can be distorted so as to become sexually abusive, for example, if an adult subjects a child to repeated, unnecessary genital examinations or cleaning (Berson & Herman-Giddens, 1994). (Unlike these forms of sexual abuse, other forms do not involve physical contact, for example, a father or another male discomforting a teenaged girl by watching her undress or shower; exposing his genitals or masturbating in her presence; or using sexual language or innuendo when addressing her.*)

All forms of child abuse and neglect evoke negative affect in the victims, such as fear/terror, anxiety, sadness/grief, confusion, shame, humiliation, self-blame, guilt, self-loathing, a sense of betrayal, lack of trust, helplessness, hopelessness, disgust, anger/rage, hatred.

All forms of child abuse and neglect cause stress which affects the body's stress response mechanisms, sometimes to the extent that biochemical functioning is permanently damaged (for example, that of hormones and neurotransmitters) (Barnett et al., 2011:159; see Veenema, 2009).

All forms of child abuse and neglect can produce negative alterations in brain structure or, in very young children who are still

---

* The pronouns at the two asterisks above do not by any means imply that abusers are invariably male — although a collation of current statistics across all forms of abuse shows that the majority are — nor that victims are always female – although, by the same computation, most are (Barnett et al., 2011:165,167,211; Sedlak et al., 2010:17).

undergoing brain development, can prevent parts of the brain from forming satisfactorily in the first place (Andersen et al., 2008; Arnsten, 2009; Bremner, 2003, 2006; Cohen et al., 2006; Dannlowski et al., 2012; Davidson & McEwen, 2012; De Bellis et al., 1999,2002; De Bellis & Kuchibhatla, 2006; Edmiston et al., 2011; Eluvathingal et al., 2006; Everaerd et al., 2015; Gee et al., 2013; Hanson et al., 2010; Kumari et al., 2014; McCrory et al., 2010; McEwen & Morrison, 2013; Richert et al., 2006; Teicher, 2002; Teicher et al., 2003,2004, 2012; Woon & Hedges, 2009; see Gerhardt, 2004; Schore, 1994).

These effects of abuse and neglect can last well into adulthood and throughout life (e.g. Banyard et al., 2001; Draper et al., 2008; Felitti et al., 1998; Greenfield, 2010:2; Kendall-Tackett, 2003), and they may manifest in any or all personality domains — emotional, mental, physical, behavioural, sexual, interpersonal and social.

Until otherwise stated, the consequences of abuse mentioned below are caused by both physical and sexual abuse.

Effects of child abuse on mental health and personality

Compared with the non-abused population, survivors of CPA or CSA are significantly more likely to suffer mental health problems (Barnett et al., 2011:152–155,225–227; Briere & Elliott, 2003; Herrenkohl et al., 2013; Kolko & Kolko, 2010; Scott et al., 2010; Widom, 2000). These can manifest as depression (Barnett et al., 2011:153,226; Negele et al., 2015); dysthymia (a relatively mild but chronic form of depression associated with low mood or 'flat affect') (Barnett et al., 2011:155; De Bellis et al., 1994); anxiety; panic disorder (Goodwin et al., 2005; Herringa et al., 2013; Safren et al., 2002); attention deficit hyperactivity disorder (ADHD) (Fuller-Thomson et al., 2014; Stern et al., 2018); posttraumatic stress disorder (PTSD), symptoms of which can include sleeplessness, nightmares and flashbacks (Cohen et al., 2004; Widom, 1999); suicidality (suicidal thoughts, attempted and completed suicide) (Angelakis et al., 2019); self-harm (Liu et al., 2018: Santa Mina & Gallop, 1998); and accidental fatal overdose (Cutajar et al., 2010b).

Low self-esteem is a common sequel of maltreatment (Kaufman & Cicchetti, 1989; Romano & De Luca, 2001); also, as mentioned earlier, feelings of helplessness (Farber & Joseph, 1985; Summit, 1983; see Seligman, 1972), hopelessness (Allen & Tarnowski, 1989; Spokas et al., 2009), aggression (Moe et al., 2004, Verril, 2018), and anger (Barnett et al., 2011:155,225,224,226; Springer et al., 2007) (for example, survivors may perceive offence and react angrily where offence is neither present nor intended). The last two effects of maltreatment can give rise to 'externalising' disorders (El-Baz et al., 2016), that is, when the abuse victim's anger, aggression and distress are taken out on others, sometimes in the form of physical violence.

There are other personality disorders associated with abuse. They include borderline personality disorder (Johnson et al., 2009:145–146; Widom et al., 2009); and psychiatric disorders such as obsessions and compulsions (Mathews et al., 2008), hallucinations, delusions (Bendall et al., 2008; Read et al., 2003), bipolar disorder (Liu, 2010; Maniglio, 2013), and schizophrenia (Cutajar et al., 2010a).

Relationship difficulties

The psychological consequences of sexual and physical abuse include serious relationship difficulties, among them irrational, disturbed interpersonal behaviour; low levels of intimacy; trouble forming and sustaining friendships and long-term intimate relationships; and higher rates of marital conflict, domestic violence, 'walking out on' partners, divorce and sexual infidelity (Barnett et al., 2011:153; Child Family Community Australia, 2019; Colman & Widom, 2004).

Some survivors may be unable comfortably to tolerate any form of physical contact even in its nonsexual, nurturing form — they may stiffen, flinch or recoil when touched, which impedes closeness in relationships.

Self-destructive behaviours

Suicidality is not the only way in which abuse victims attempt to obliterate their pain; another, usually less direct route to self-destruction is that of substance use and abuse, which can give rise to dependence on/addictions to alcohol (World Health Organisation, 2019), cigarette smoking (Chartier et al., 2009; Roberts et al., 2008) and illicit drugs (Dube et al., 2003; Moran et al., 2004). A study by Widom and colleagues (2006), for instance, found that in middle adulthood (mean age 40), survivors of child abuse and neglect used illicit drugs far more — marijuana in particular, also cocaine, heroin, and to a small extent psychedelics — and had more problems related to substance use than a matched group of individuals who had not been maltreated. Abuse survivors are more likely than non-abused individuals to struggle with eating disorders (Jonas et al., 2011; Rayworth et al., 2004), obesity (Boynton-Jarrett et al., 2012; Felitti, 1991; Rohde et al., 2008) and physical inactivity (Bellis et al., 2014; Springer et al., 2003:e4). They are also more liable to engage in risky sexual behaviours (Barnett et al., 2011:153; Senn & Carey, 2010) which increase the prevalence of unwanted teenage pregnancy (Anda et al., 2002; Noll et al., 2009) and sexually transmitted diseases (Wilson & Sathiyasusuman, 2015; Wilson & Widom, 2009) including HIV/AIDS (Center for AIDS Information and Advocacy, 2012; Wilson & Widom, 2008).

Effects of child abuse on cognitive ability

Partly because of the stress-related brain changes caused by childhood abuse, survivors are at higher risk than non-abused individuals of cognitive deficits (Gould et al., 2012; Irigaray et al., 2013), which result in poorer academic achievement (Green & Messman-Moore, 2015; Jacob & Ryan, 2018) and failure to finish school (Diette et al., 2017; Porche et al., 2011).

The physical effects of child abuse

Abuse survivors are more prone to physical ill health than the non-abused population (Felitti et al., 1998; Irish et al., 2010; Springer et al., 2007) — they are more likely to suffer heart/cardiovascular disease (Dong et al., 2004; Fuller-Thomson et al., 2010); chronic lung disease (Anda et al., 2008; Shields et al., 2016a); cancer (Brown et al., 2013; Fuller-Thomson & Brennenstuhl, 2009; Ports et al., 2018); liver disease (Dong et al., 2003; Hughes et al., 2017); diabetes (Kendall-Tackett & Marshall, 1999; Shields et al., 2016b); gastrointestinal disorders (Drossman, 1995; Leserman & Drossman, 2007); ulcers (Fuller-Thompson et al., 2011a; Kamiya et al., 2016); chronic pain syndromes (Sansone et al., 2013); fibromyalgia (Boisset-Pioro et al., 1995; Häuser et al., 2011); headaches/migraine (Tietjen & Peterlin, 2011); arthritis (Badley et al., 2018; Fuller-Thomson, 2009); asthma (Bhan et al., 2014; Cohen et al., 2008; Coogan et al., 2013); chronic fatigue syndrome (Fuller-Thomson et al., 2011b; Heim et al., 2009); skin disorders (Erfanian, 2018; Gupta, 2006); menstrual problems (Koci & Strickland, 2007; Soydas et al., 2014); physical symptoms with unknown cause (Nelson et al., 2012; Springer et al, 2003); high inflammation levels, and 'metabolic syndrome', that is, a 'cluster' of physiological characteristics that present together and are recognised risk factors for serious disease. They include overweight, particularly in the abdominal area; high blood pressure; low HDL ('good') cholesterol; high blood sugar; and low oxygen consumption (the rate at which oxygen is used by the body tissues) (Buameister et al., 2016; Danese et al., 2009).

Social effects of child abuse

The social effects of child abuse are far-reaching — compared with non-abused individuals, survivors have a higher probability of being unemployed or underemployed (Liu et al., 2013); entering into prostitution (Widom & Kuhns, 1996); being involved in intimate partner violence (IPV) (Fang & Corso, 2007; White & Widom, 2003); and committing crime, including violent, sex, drug and property crime (Widom, 1989,1995; Widom & Maxfield, 2001). This leads them to incur a higher-than-average number of arrests and gaol sentences. Ogloff and colleagues (2012), for example, found that CSA survivors have on average a five times greater chance than the general population of being charged with an offence.

Abuse of own children — the 'sorry-go-round'

Parenting styles and behaviours are passed from one generation to the next, for better and worse (e.g. Kovan et al., 2009). This process of *intergenerational transmission* applies as much to child abuse and neglect as to any other behaviour. Therefore, although most survivors of abuse do *not* go on to abuse their own and other children (Cashmore & Shackel, 2013:e17) — research suggests that approximately two thirds do *not* (Hunter, 2014; Kaufman & Zigler, 1987; Oliver, 1993) — there is still the remaining third who do, and certainly, individuals who have been abused are more likely to abuse others than those who have not themselves been abused (Bijleveld et al., 2016; Jesperson et al., 2009; Yang et al., 2018). According to Murray Straus (1991b), who did much valuable work in this area, the rate of child abuse is about 13 times higher among abused than among non-abused parents.

Moreover, abused individuals tend to commit the *type* of abuse they have suffered in their own childhoods (Felson & Lane, 2009).

A study by Jinseok Kim (2008) found that parents who had been neglected during childhood, compared with those who had not, were 2.6 times more likely to neglect their own children and two times more likely to physically abuse their own children, while parents who had been physically abused during childhood compared with those who had not were five times more likely to physically abuse their own children and 1.4 times more likely to neglect them — and so the sorry-go-round spins on with the sad legacy being passed from one generation to the next.

There are countless other manifestations of this sorry-go-round mechanism in the lives of abuse survivors whether or not they go on to maltreat their own children. *Revictimisation* is one example — survivors are in greater danger than the non-abused population of being abused again as adults, for example raped, sexually assaulted or beaten (Arata, 2002; Desai et al., 2002; Widom et al., 2008).

Not surprisingly, the effects of CSA and CPA are similar to the extent that these two forms of abuse are similar; to the extent that they differ, each will have its own distinctive impact.

Specific effects of physical abuse

Victims of CPA typically show bodily signs of the abuse — bruises, black eyes, welts, rope marks, open wounds, cuts, punctures, untreated injuries at different stages of healing, fractured or broken bones, and dislocation of joints. Some signs of CPA, however, such as skull and other bone fractures, organ compression, organ rupture and internal haemorrhaging are visible only through X-rays and scans and may therefore go undetected.

CPA can have shocking consequences, including permanent disfigurement; disability in the form of irreversible brain damage, blindness, deafness, seizures, tremor, and paralysis; coma; and death (e.g. Gluck, 2016).

Cognitive damage inflicted by CPA may manifest as learning difficulties, for example, deficits in concentration, reading, verbal ability, maths skills, memory, problem-solving and general intelligence. The academic performance of CPA survivors can therefore be far poorer than average, and their special education needs greater (Barnett et al., 2011:152,153,159; Halambie & Klapper, 2005).

One of the most serious causes of cognitive damage is 'abusive head injury' which occurs in infants who are shaken (National

Institute of Neurological Disorders and Stroke, 2019). One study of 11 children who had suffered 'shaken baby syndrome' found them to have significantly lower intelligence scores at seven to eight years of age than a matched group of non-abused children (Stipanicic et al., 2008).

Intergenerational transmission of physical abuse

In CPA, once again, there is robust evidence that childhood experience shapes adult behaviour — that violence experienced or witnessed in childhood is predictive of violence in adulthood (Kendall-Tackett, 2003) and thus infects families and societies. As Barnett and colleagues observe (2011:159),

> Physical aggression and antisocial behaviour are among the most common correlates of CPA.

The interpersonal relationships of CPA victims of all ages are often marked by aggression (Moe, King & Bailly, 2004; Verrill, 2018); hostility (Gluck, 2016); defiance; conflict; antisocial and abusive behaviours, and violence; by fighting in and outside the home (Barnett et al., 2011:152–153,160); violent delinquency (Lansford et al., 2007); violent juvenile and adult crime (Barnett et al., 2011:153,154; Widom & Maxfield, 2001); dating violence (that is, the perpetration of physical, sexual or emotional violence by one or both members of a dating couple) which CPA survivors both inflict and receive to a greater extent than non-abused individuals (Foshee et al., 2004); and the physical abuse of marital partners (Herrenkohl et al., 2004; McKinney et al., 2009).

Bullying — the 'use of power and aggression to distress a vulnerable person' (Barnett et al., 2011:160) — is a further behavioural problem associated with CPA, unsurprisingly, since the adult in any CPA incident is a perfect bully-model. Children who are physically abused by an adult have greater likelihood than non-abused children of perpetrating bullying at school, and also of *being* bullied (Dussich & Maekoya, 2007). If the antagonist in a conflict is weaker, the child may act out the bullying role modelled by her abusive parent; if stronger, she may slip into the victim role that she enacts habitually within her family.

As with other adverse childhood experiences (ACEs), victims of bullying suffer depression, anxiety, sadness, loneliness, hopelessness, social withdrawal, physical symptoms (e.g. Moore, 2017), and such sleep problems as insomnia (Fleming & Jacobsen, 2010), nightmares, night terrors, and sleepwalking (Wolke & Lereya, 2014). Their academic performance may deteriorate (Ladd et al., 2017), they may drop out of school (Cornell et al., 2013), and, compared with non-bullied children, they more often play truant, use drugs and alcohol, experience health problems, and engage in self-harm. In extreme cases bullied children may be driven to suicide (Wolke & Lereya, 2015). (Not only children but adults also are harmed by bullying: workplace bullying is associated with cardiovascular disease, fibromyalgia, depression and PTSD, while adult social phobia has been linked to teasing or bullying during childhood (Srabstein, 2009)).

Corporal punishment

> The trauma of harsh punishment is likely to cause permanent neurobiological changes.
>
> Barnett, Miller-Perrin and Perrin (2011:145)

Corporal punishment (CP) may be defined as 'the use of physical force with the intention of causing the child to experience bodily pain or discomfort so as to correct or punish the child's behavior' (Gershoff, 2008:9). Fierce controversy rages over the use of corporal punishment of children (Barnett et al., 2011:142–145).

Harsh corporal punishment is as much part of CPA as any other form of physical abuse; it gives rise to the same psychological and social problems (Afifi, 2012; Gershoff, 2002) including depression (Afifi et al., 2006); PTSD (Medina et al., 2001); suicidality (Straus & Kantor, 1994); aggression (Muller et al., 1995; Thompson et al., 2017); antisocial (Afifi et al., 2019; Grogan-Kaylor, 2005; Rebellon & Straus, 2017), abusive and violent behaviours; delinquency; adult crime: for example homicide, assault, and robbery (Straus, 1991a:133); family and marital violence (Swinford et al., 2004), such as 'wife beating' (Straus & Kantor, 1994); alcohol and substance abuse/dependence (Cheng et al., 2011); and the physical abuse of their own children by abuse survivors who become parents (Straus, 1991a:140; Straus & Kantor, 1994).

As with other forms of CPA, victims of harsh corporal punishment can suffer brain damage (e.g. Sheu et al., 2010) and academic failure (Alyahri & Goodman, 2008). In an experiment by Tomoda and colleagues (2009), 18 to 25-year-olds who had experienced harsh physical punishment as children showed significantly reduced grey matter in three brain areas[1] compared with non-abused participants, and their IQ scores were correspondingly lower.

Since harsh corporal punishment lies firmly within the domain of physical abuse it is not a central part of the corporal punishment controversy. What *is* hotly debated is the greyer area of spanking, paddling or slapping a child. On the one hand, many parents consider these punishments a normal and necessary part of parenting (Cuddy & Reeves, 2014; Gomba, 2015). On the other, anti-CP conviction has led 53 countries world-wide to ban corporal punishment in all its forms (Brilliant Maps, 2018).

Research for the most part comes out strongly in favour of the latter view. One reason for this is that spanking can escalate into behaviour that is clearly definable as CPA. This is particularly true of adults who employ frequent spanking, or who spank with an object rather than with the hand, and who are more likely to inflict other harsh punishments (Paige & McLain, 2019; Zolotor et al., 2008).

Even where this slide into unmistakeable CPA does not occur, childhood spanking has been linked to adult psychiatric disorders such as major depression, alcohol abuse/dependence, and externalising problems (see p.56) (Afifi et al., 2006).

There is moreover sound evidence that the consequences of physical punishment are contrary to its intended effects — that it in fact *fosters* defiance, disobedience, verbal and physical aggression (fighting, bullying…) and antisocial behaviours (Barnett et al., 2011:144; Gershoff, 2002; Muller et al., 1995; Straus et al., 1997; Thompson et al., 2017). As George Holden (2002:592) asserts, '*Discipline* means to train, instruct, or educate' — to teach prosocial and constructive attitudes and behaviours so that they become part of the child's inner moral template — and this is often the stated aim of CP advocates. However, the literature shows that physical punishment miscarries also in this regard, for rather than internalising the adult's message in the long term, the child merely complies outwardly with the punisher's wishes out of fear and a short-term desire to avoid further anger and pain. At the same time CP endangers the child-parent bond (Gershoff, 2002), teaches that violence is an acceptable method of dealing with disagreement (Straus, 1991a:134; see Bandura et al., 1961) and fails to teach alternative problem-solving methods (Gershoff, 2008; Paige & McLain, 2019; Straus, 1991a).

In both families (e.g. Aha! Parenting, 2019; Gershoff, 2002, 2008, 2013; Gershoff & Grogan-Kaylor, 2016) and schools (Gershoff, 2017; Hyman, 1996), positive — nonviolent, loving — methods of discipline have proved more effective than corporal punishment.

Specific effects of sexual abuse

Child sexual abuse (CSA) is more likely than other forms of abuse and neglect to distort the sexual aspects of personality. One sign of CSA is 'sexualised' conduct where the child talks and behaves in ways that display a knowledge of adult sexual behaviour inappropriate for his age (World Health Organisation, 2003b:77–78); he may engage in genital exposure or masturbation to an unusual degree, or in sex play with others in which he acts out his sexual experiences, for example, by inserting objects into his own or another child's vagina or anus; or he may use sexual language, or show greater-than-normal preoccupation with sex (Barnett et al., 2011:222).

Physical signs of CSA are difficulty sitting and walking. In individuals of all ages the signs include bruises around genitals, breasts, or palate (as a result of oral rape); scarred or torn hymen; genital pain or itching; unexplained bleeding from vagina or anus; unexplained venereal disease; frequent urinary infections; and difficulties with urination (Barnett et al., 2011:223; Krajewski et al., 2016).

Women survivors of CSA face the risk of gynaecological/reproductive problems including pelvic pain (American College of Obstetricians and Gynecologists, 2011; Jamieson & Steege, 1997); pain during intercourse; and menstrual disturbances, such as heavy bleeding, severe menstrual pain (Kirkengen, 2010:217) and premenstrual syndrome (PMS) (Golding et al., 2000).

CSA can also give rise to adult sexual disorders such as anorgasmia (inability to achieve orgasm); absence of sexual desire or arousal; and sexual phobia/aversion (Barnett et al., 2011:226) in which survivors may feel fear, anxiety, revulsion, horror, discomfort or guilt in relation to sexual interaction, or to certain aspects of it that evoke memories for the abused partner. A CSA survivor who has been made to lie on her back while being abused may not be able to lie on her back during sexual intercourse with an adult partner because it may trigger extreme agitation and flashbacks of the past abuse. Or survivors may dissociate (be unable to stay mentally present) during sexual interaction, feel unprovoked anger or irritation towards their sexual partners, or experience general dissatisfaction with sexual relationships (Barnett et al., 2011:226; Hall, 2008; Polusny & Follette, 1995).

CSA can lead not only to sexual avoidance, but also to its behavioural opposite — to prostitution (Abramovich, 2005; Pereda, 2015), and to high-risk sexual activities such as promiscuity/multiple sexual partners and unprotected sex (Senn & Carey, 2010; Senn et al., 2008). As observed earlier, these activities increase the incidence of teenage pregnancy (Noll et al., 2009) and sexually transmitted diseases (Wilson & Widom, 2009), such as HIV/AIDS (Arriola et al., 2005; Mimiaga et al., 2009; Thornton & Veenema, 2015).

Aside from adolescent pregnancies, women survivors of CSA experience higher-than-average rates of premature birth (Trickett et al., 2011) and menstrual problems (Kirkengen, 2010:217). In addition, they tend to suffer psychological difficulties in relation to sexual and reproductive issues; pregnancy, childbirth and motherhood can evoke distress, anxiety, lack of confidence in the ability to parent (Sperlich & Seng, 2008), and a greater likelihood of postpartum depression (Buist & Janson, 2001) and posttraumatic stress (Lev-Wiesel et al., 2009) than in non-abused women. These factors render it more difficult for CSA survivors to care for their children (e.g. Bernard-Bonnin, 2004).

Sexual abuse victims generally feel deep shame, perceiving themselves to be bad, dirty, damaged, disgusting. They also frequently experience guilt (Dorahy & Clearwater, 2010; Kalra & Bhugra, 2013) and self-blame (e.g. Feiring et al., 2009; Romano & De Luca, 2001:60,74), even though abuse or neglect of any type is never, in any circumstances, the child's fault but always the adult's.

In the case of some survivors it seems that CSA can affect sexual orientation. This was Corrine's experience:

> *'I was so scared of men because of my father's anger and abuse that when sexual longings kicked in in my teens I had an affair with a woman — the sex had to go somewhere and I was prevented by terror from putting it into exploring relationships with men.*
>
> *I think my sexuality at that time was also shaped by the fact that my mother, although she was a good person, was a pretty*

useless mother. She didn't give me warm, loving attention. She didn't like physical contact much — no warm cuddles — so I grew up longing for a Mum and at the same time terrified of men. The two things together dug me into that hole.

But something inside me knew that I didn't want to remain in that state — that I was in transit; it wasn't my real path. So I gradually struggled out of it. Years of good therapy helped. But I still married a man who was extra kind, and malleable — without very firm boundaries — and who I knew wouldn't react aggressively if I vented my anger on him, which I'm ashamed to say I still do sometimes even though he doesn't deserve it.'

Understandably, the view that homosexuality/lesbianism has resulted from damaging childhood experience can be unacceptable to members of gay and lesbian communities. My own clinical experience has led me to believe that sexual orientation, like any other aspect of personality, can be distorted by childhood adversity and that this has occurred in some people (Roberts et al., 2013; Wilson & Widom, 2010). It of course goes without saying that in others homosexuality/lesbianism and its physiological underpinnings — such as amount of male and female hormones — are inborn (see Blanchard, 2001; Bogaert et al., 2017; Lousada, 2009:10). (To date I have not come across research on bisexual and transgender persons in relation to this question.)

Disclosure of sexual abuse

How the disclosure of sexual abuse is received is crucial to the CSA survivor's well-being. If she is believed and listened to with empathy and supportiveness by recipients of the disclosure — family members, teachers, representatives of institutions… — the traumatic effects of the abuse decrease. In contrast, being disbelieved becomes a trauma in itself and at the same time exacerbates the victim's experience of the original abuse trauma (Jacques-Tiura et al., 2010).

Twin studies

Latterly definitive studies on childhood sexual abuse have been conducted with twins (Dinwiddie et al., 2000; Kendler et al., 2000). Nelson and colleagues (2002), for example, studied 1,991 pairs of twins of whom one had been sexually abused and the other had not.

A significantly greater number of personal and social problems was found in the abused twins, including major depression, attempted suicide, alcohol and nicotine dependence, social anxiety, revictimisation in the form of rape, and divorce.

Summary and conclusion

The most injurious forms of negative touch are physical and sexual abuse which can carry devastating consequences for mental and physical health.

Combining the material in this and the previous chapter we find that loving touch builds and maintains healthy brains, bodies and personalities, while negative touch damages them.

The effects of both these forms of touch can last throughout life and be visited upon succeeding generations.

Note

1 '… **18 to 25-year-olds who had experienced harsh physical punishment as children showed significantly reduced grey matter in three brain areas…**'
— the right and left medial frontal gyri and right anterior cingulate gyrus.

Chapter 4

The tactility scale

In my bid to discover more about human responses to touch I interviewed 90 'ordinary' people, 'ordinary' in this context meaning that they were asked about their experiences of touch in everyday life, not in therapy — how they felt when they were touched and touched others, what meaning it held for them.

This group shall henceforth be called 'non-clients', for want of a more positive term. It included 33 non-British interviewees since I wished to explore the possible impact of culture on attitudes to touch, and perhaps to shed light on whether the widespread avoidance of physical contact within talking therapies is based on sound psychological principles — on human need and authentic processes of therapeutic change — or whether it instead reflects unexamined cultural norms. In addition, through hundreds of informal conversations with Britons and non-Britons I was able to garner further information on the subject and to check whether or not my interviewees were representative of their cultures with respect to tactual attitudes and behaviours.

I originally intended to interview 100 non-clients, but instead stopped after 90 since by then the questions I was asking of this group had been thoroughly answered; although interviewees' autobiographical details were unique, it was possible at this stage to predict the more general aspects of their attitudes to touch.

It was also often possible to tell by their body language before the verbal interview began — when they walked into the room and stood or sat — whether they would prove to be tactile or not. The non-tactile participants were more physically tense — their movements were less fluid and spontaneous, their facial expressions more fixed and they tended to smile less often than tactile participants (that is, than those who were comfortable with physical contact). I found subsequently that other researchers too had noted this association between body language and tactility (Andersen et al., 1987; Fromme et al., 1989; Hunter & Struve, 1998:9; Silverman et al., 1973).

The tactility scale

My attempt to make sense of the welter of non-clients' information gave rise to the 'tactility scale' (see diagram below) — to my surprise, since putting people into categories and scales is not my preferred mode of operation. In general I find it objectifying and therefore uncomfortable. However, despite my misgivings, creating the scale turned out to be worthwhile for the ideas that emerged; it clarified the fact that people's tactility takes different forms and that certain factors predictably influence these forms. Also, the scale may perhaps serve as a basis for other researchers who wish to tie down and quantify its elements more precisely.

The need for touch in humans is innate and universal[1] but the ways in which we express it are learned; whether we greet each other with hugs, kisses, handshakes, or with words alone, depends on the tactual mores of the people around us. The word 'tactility' can refer to both innate and learned aspects of touch, but for the purposes of the tactility scale it refers to the latter.

The non-clients in my sample fell into eight categories, mainly according to how frequently they experienced physical contact. Frequency of contact was in turn determined both by the extent to which participants enjoyed being touched and touching others, and by whether they had opportunities to do so.

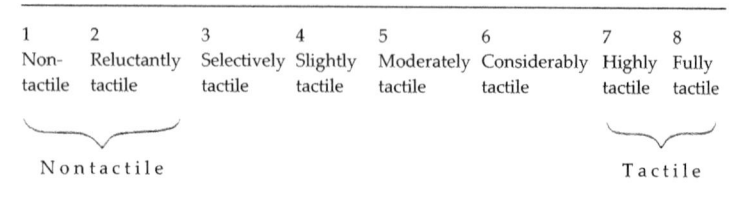

1	2	3	4	5	6	7	8
Non-tactile	Reluctantly tactile	Selectively tactile	Slightly tactile	Moderately tactile	Considerably tactile	Highly tactile	Fully tactile

Nontactile · Tactile

The tactility scale.

The eight categories on the scale form a continuum ranging from non-tactile at one end to 'fully' tactile at the other. They describe participants' tactility at the *beginning of adulthood*, once tactile habits have been securely formed. (The beginning of adulthood was a movable benchmark; according to interviewees' personal histories it ranged from 17 or 18 to about 25.) An exception to this rule were three child participants whose category labels describe pre-adult tactility. (A second exception is mentioned on p.70.)

Some interviewees had retained the same degree of tactility from early adulthood to the time of the interview, while others during that time had migrated across the scale to inhabit a different tactile zone.

There follows a brief description of the categories on the tactility scale and, in order to flesh them out, a few tactile profiles of some of the participants in the study (in boxes). Words used by participants themselves are in *'italics and inverted commas'*.

1) Non-tactile (*n* = 34)

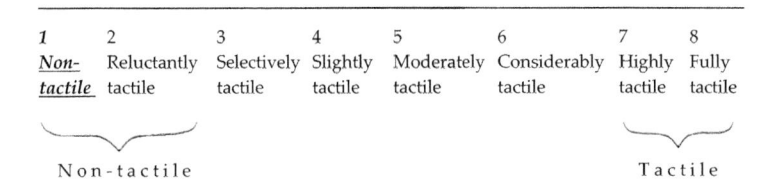

1	2	3	4	5	6	7	8
<u>Non-tactile</u>	Reluctantly tactile	Selectively tactile	Slightly tactile	Moderately tactile	Considerably tactile	Highly tactile	Fully tactile

Non-tactile ←⎯⎯⎯⎯⎯⎯⎯⎯⎯⎯⎯→   Tactile

Non-tactile interviewees had experienced extremely minimal nurturing touch during childhood or none at all. Ten of their number recalled having *'craved'* touch as children (9 of the 10 used the word *'craved'* and one used *'thirst'*). As adults all but two (94.1%) had travelled the scale to greater tactility since the beginning of adulthood. Betty and Robert were the two exceptions:

> Non-tactile in early adulthood, Betty and Robert had remained so into their 60s when they were interviewed. Both were strongly averse to physical contact and avoided it as far as possible. Robert had been with an unsatisfactory partner for two years and had no children, because of which he described himself as *'one of life's failures'*. Betty had not had partner or children. She too described herself as a *'failure'*, specifically because of her discomfort with touch. (This does NOT imply that everyone without partner or children feels a failure, simply that these two did, which means that this sentiment in comparable circumstances falls within the scope of possible human responses.)

2) Reluctantly tactile (*n* = 8)

1	2	3	4	5	6	7	8
Non-tactile	*Reluctantly tactile*	Selectively tactile	Slightly tactile	Moderately tactile	Considerably tactile	Highly tactile	Fully tactile

Non-tactile   Tactile

Reluctantly tactile participants were essentially non-tactile, although some time after the beginning of adulthood they had been goaded away from their non-tactile inclinations by exceptional life events, such as becoming close to a partner, or giving birth to and raising a child or children. In these circumstances they might be tactile to varying degrees with the partner or offspring. In all other situations they avoided touch, finding it at best uncomfortable and at worst *'disgusting'*, and they rated themselves unhesitatingly and vehemently as non-tactile.

This was the only category whose members had acquired their defining tactile character after the beginning of adulthood, since partners and children had appeared later in life.

> Mary's tactility was unwaveringly reluctant. Her family was of Irish Catholic culture which she considered to be *'very repressed'*. She found touching others *'disgusting'* and considered that since about 1990 *'things have gone disgusting in England'*. (Perhaps someone with historical inclinations might like to investigate the curious fact that two other interviewees also mentioned around 1990 as the time when English tactility began increasing.) Mary suggested that the reason for this regrettable development was the growing trend of travel to tactile cultures *'where English people pick up revolting foreign habits'*.
>
> She had become *'slightly more relaxed'* about touch through her involvement in theatre so that by the time she reached her 50s, instead of refusing a hug outright, she occasionally submitted to one with a humorous quip ('Oh, go on, if you must'). She accepted some sexual touch from a boyfriend but when it came to non-sexual, affectionate touch she remained staunchly anti-touch with him and with the rest of humanity.

Julia's childhood experience affords a rare opportunity to tease apart the effects of emotional love and tactile love. It also highlights the impact of tactile deprivation even when other, non-tactile aspects of a relationship are positive:

> '*I know my Mum loved me,*' she said, '*but she had a thing about touch. She was uncomfortable with it and uncomfortable with her own body — with bodies generally — and she was squeamish about natural bodily functions. She didn't hug or hold me much but when she did I could feel even as a small child that she wasn't relaxed. She didn't enjoy it; the uncomfortable feelings got in the way. So I felt rejected, as if there was something horrible, yucky, about me.*'

Julia was now in her early 50s. Her mother was still alive and, having travelled psychologically and feeling alone and vulnerable in her old age, felt the lack of nurturing physical contact. However, Julia had thoroughly internalised her mother's earlier attitudes to touch and could not bring herself to hug her mother. When the latter tried to hug her, Julia froze, and she endured her mother's occasional kisses on the cheek with reluctance. These attitudes persisted not only in relation to her mother but entered into other relationships — with one exception; in her late 30s she had met a partner with whom she had come to enjoy tactile affection.

Rosemary's mother had died early in Rosemary's childhood and her stepmother had been strictly non-tactile. Rosemary continued in non-tactile mode until the birth of her son catapulted her into moderate tactility with him alone. Her son was now in his 30s and still the only person with whom Rosemary was at all tactile. When anyone else touched her she recoiled as politely as possible.

Childhood sexual and physical abuse within non-tactile categories

In addition to tactile neglect, some participants in the first two categories on the scale had suffered much painful touch in the form of childhood sexual and/or physical abuse. Three of these interviewees had worked on abuse issues in therapy, had come to terms with their experience, and were ready to disclose it. A further 12 reported reactions to touch that were consistent with histories of abuse but did not offer outright disclosures. For example, Shirley *'used to jump a foot into the air'* when touched briefly and lightly, perhaps on the arm or hand; Meryl experienced *'unwelcome sexual attention'* from uncles; Vera's mother had been *'offensively, disgustingly'* tactile; Josie was extremely frightened of and averse to touch and her acceptance of it within a relationship was slow and tortuous.

3) Selectively tactile (*n* = 3)

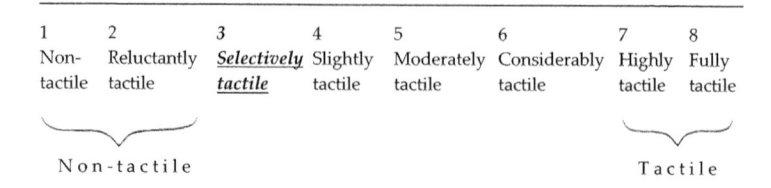

1	2	3	4	5	6	7	8
Non-tactile	Reluctantly tactile	*Selectively tactile*	Slightly tactile	Moderately tactile	Considerably tactile	Highly tactile	Fully tactile

Non-tactile {1, 2}   Tactile {7, 8}

Selectively tactile were similar to reluctantly tactile interviewees in that they exchanged touch to different degrees with selected others only, such as a sibling, or one parent because the other parent was non-tactile. In addition, the emphasis in both groups was on the *number* of others touched in contrast to *frequency* of touch as in the other categories (although number in this context could of course influence frequency). The difference between the two groups was the strong aversion to touch in reluctantly tactile individuals which was absent in the selectively tactile group.

The three participants in this category had retained the selectivity they had learned in childhood and had recreated it in their adult lives.

> Dara was from a fully tactile African culture. As a baby she was always carried on the back of her mother or another family member. During her childhood the streets of her neighbourhood became rough and dangerous as a result of political and social change. The family was thus forced in

upon itself; she and her six siblings became very close and tactile with each other but were non-tactile with people outside the family.

As an immigrant in England, Dara constructed a situation which was reminiscent of this formative experience — she was very tactile with the nursery children in her charge, and non-tactile with others.

Beri replicated her childhood tactile patterns even more precisely. Her family had lived in a fully tactile culture and torrid climate. Her mother was fully tactile with her own sister and with her children, including Beri, but thoroughly non-tactile with others. This was because in the heat *'people sweat and not everybody uses deodorant, so you don't want to touch'*. Even though Beri now lived in a relatively cold climate, she was fully tactile exclusively with her own children — and with her sister.

Joseph's mother was moderately tactile; his father and his English public school were strictly non-tactile. Joseph was now strictly non-tactile with everyone but his wife, with whom he was moderately tactile.

4) Slightly tactile (*n* = 6)

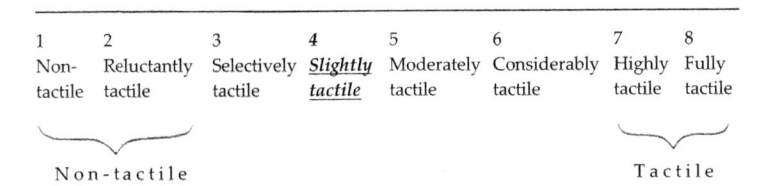

1	2	3	4	5	6	7	8
Non-tactile	Reluctantly tactile	Selectively tactile	*Slightly tactile*	Moderately tactile	Considerably tactile	Highly tactile	Fully tactile

Non-tactile　　　　　　　　　　　　　Tactile

Slightly tactile participants had experienced little touch during childhood so that whatever they did experience was highly significant; decades later a rare goodnight kiss or an adult stroking their hair shone out in their memories.

As with some of the non-tactile participants, two of the four in this group had 'craved' touch as children and actively sought it in adulthood. All four had moved along the scale to become more tactile.

> Dirk's mother had been 'not at all tactile'. She was silent about her past but Dirk had sensed that she was afraid of touch — 'she had her own story; maybe she had been abused.' His father had been 'a bit more tactile' but his older sister had received all their father's attention. Fortunately his was a fairly sociable family and the surrounding culture was tactile, so Dirk would eagerly anticipate the arrival of visitors to their house because they sometimes gave him affectionate touch.

> Tactile expression featured little in Gail's family life. Her father sometimes gave her playful, teasing touch but this did not make up for the fact that her mother was 'not that touchy. Mum liked cuddling babies but not much after that and it was a large family so there was always a young child who needed attention.'

> Fred's father had left his mother before he was born. Fred 'craved' cuddles as a child but his mother, as an impoverished single parent, was usually too rushed, tired or harassed to provide them.

5) Moderately tactile (*n* = 6) — around the middle of the tactile scale

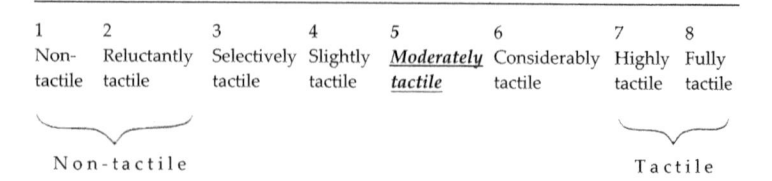

1	2	3	4	5	6	7	8
Non-tactile	Reluctantly tactile	Selectively tactile	Slightly tactile	*Moderately tactile*	Considerably tactile	Highly tactile	Fully tactile

Non-tactile   Tactile

Children in moderately tactile families were not cuddled every day as a matter of course but every now and then, perhaps a few times a week. I had the impression that in these particular participants the reason for this was family habit rather than any touch aversion on the part of parents or grandparents — 'touching a lot just wasn't our way'. Since there was no psychological barrier to touching among them, instrumental touch was freely given — carrying a baby from A to B, sitting a child on a lap if an elderly person needed her seat on the bus, or holding a child's hand while crossing the road — but there was less use of touch for the openly intentional expression of love and caring.

Two of the participants in this group were still moderately tactile. The remaining three had increased in tactility.

> Tim's parents were loving and moderately tactile but his father had fought in the Second World War and had thus been absent for a sizeable portion of Tim's childhood. The English boarding school he attended from the age of eight was thoroughly non-tactile.
>
> Tim experienced a conflict between his inner desire for tactile expression and his outward behaviour. *'I feel very tactile inside,'* he said, *'but the [English] culture has made me nervous.'* Because of *'fear of rebuff'* he generally behaved in a non- or slightly tactile manner, but if others initiated touch he was moderately tactile. He would *'cuddle animals happily'*. (As Anglo readers may have noticed, some people who are non-tactile towards humans are highly tactile towards animals, perhaps because this satisfies their touch-needs in social circles where interhuman physical contact is not the custom.)

Two participants in this moderately tactile group mentioned not only the *amount* of touch they had received as children but its *quality*, as though their touch-satisfaction was moderate in both respects:

> Ted's family was moderately tactile and he had continued in this mould. He had been hugged and kissed as a child, *'but with a sense of restraint about it, reserve, let's-be-careful — I'm*
>
> (Continued)

tactile, but I'm English.' He was now restrained, careful, with his stepdaughters lest they *'feel sexually threatened'*. However, he had moved to the right (more tactile) end of his moderately tactile category through the influence of *'new-age circles'* and because *'English people have become more touchy-feely.'*

Hristo's (English) mother was tactile with him only until he was five, and his grandmother until he reached puberty. His (middle European) father was highly tactile — lots of physical rough-and-tumble play, hugs and cuddles. Another form of touch Hristo experienced was the wrestling he did with his brother, so in all he received a good deal of physical contact as a child. However, he felt that *'there was not enough gentle touch'* in the mixture he had been fed, which he thought made him feel uneasy as a teenager; romantic fantasies he wreathed around girls involved tender, loving touch, but because this was not within his experiential repertoire he lacked the confidence to express it.

6) Considerably tactile (*n* = 2)

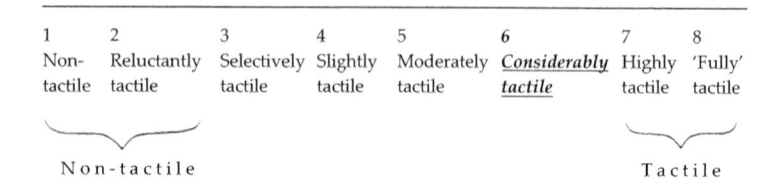

1	2	3	4	5	6	7	8
Non-tactile	Reluctantly tactile	Selectively tactile	Slightly tactile	Moderately tactile	*Considerably tactile*	Highly tactile	'Fully' tactile

Non-tactile ⟵⟶ Tactile

Physical contact features significantly in the lives of considerably tactile individuals; hugs are enjoyed frequently — daily or almost daily — although not quite as frequently or unreservedly as in the last two categories on the scale.

In the case of both participants in this category, tactility had been on the father's rather than on the mother's side of the family, and both had remained considerably tactile in adulthood.

> Tara's mother was moderately tactile in behaviour but Tara had always sensed her emotional discomfort with touch. In contrast, her father was *'very cuddly'*. As an actor he was often away on tour but actor friends of the family were continually visiting her childhood home. Tara had thus grown up in a highly tactile theatrical community which had showered her with cuddles and kisses. On the whole as an adult she was considerably tactile, particularly when in the company of theatre friends. However, every now and again she was surprised to feel the discomfort with touch that she associated with her mother. On these rare occasions she became non- or reluctantly tactile.

> Hannah's mother had been non-tactile but Hannah remembered being *'held close'* by her tactile father and paternal grandmother. Her father's family had been the stronger influence so that she herself was considerably tactile.

7 & 8) Tactile (*n* = 31)

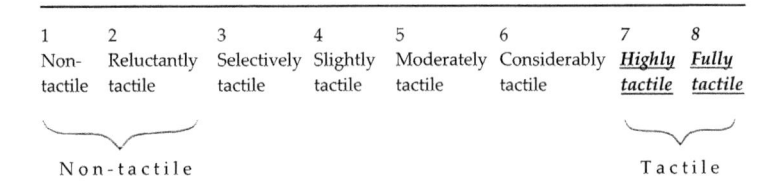

1	2	3	4	5	6	7	8
Non-tactile	Reluctantly tactile	Selectively tactile	Slightly tactile	Moderately tactile	Considerably tactile	*Highly tactile*	*Fully tactile*

Non-tactile   Tactile

7) Highly tactile (*n* = 24). Here daily hugs, kisses and conversational touch occur freely between family members and friends. Initially and to a small extent, these behaviours are more limited with people newly introduced into social circles. They are also expressed a little less openly (in the sense of publicly) and within a slightly more restricted social radius than in the final, 'fully' tactile category. The most tactile British participants belonged to this highly tactile group.

> Kirsty was the youngest of six siblings — seven years junior to the sibling immediately before her. As the baby of the family she was doted on by nuclear and extended family members including a full set of grandparents and numerous aunts, uncles and cousins who lived close to her family home. There was always someone to cuddle, play with and, if necessary, to comfort her. Memories of childhood were *'warm and happy'* and she grew up feeling *'loved ... confident'*.
>
> Early on she became aware that although hugging and kissing occurred often in her own family, non-family members were not hugged and kissed. As an adult she was still highly tactile within her own family but with non-family was more *'held in ... less relaxed and lively'*.

> Daisy fondly described a warmly physical mother who kept open house where friends were either tactile to begin with or were drawn into her mother's tactile ways. Daisy loved the freely expressed tactile affection she had experienced as a child. Now in adulthood she sought friendships with tactile others because she found that relationships which incorporated touch were *'more lively and fun, more spontaneous, warm ... natural'*. Since British people tended to be non-tactile her friendship networks were largely non-British.

8) **Fully tactile ($n = 7$),** characterised by the freest and most frequent physical contact — hugs, kisses, walking in public spaces arm in arm with family and friends, or with arm round shoulder or waist; hugs and kisses at greeting and parting, not only with familiar others but also with people met for the first time; frequent touch during conversation (on arms, shoulders, back); extremely warm, tactile behaviour with children. These forms of contact occur repeatedly throughout the day.

> Santiago had lived in two South American countries during childhood, both of which were fully tactile. His mother, father, siblings and extended family had embraced and kissed him unreservedly throughout his childhood and teenage years. They still did. At school he and his friends unselfconsciously held hands and exchanged hugs, and teachers and pupils too exchanged affectionate hugs. When someone new was introduced to his family, for example a colleague or associate of his parents, he or she was welcomed into the family with hugs and kisses; it would have been considered odd and unfriendly not to do so.

> Amira was born into a wealthy Indian family. The adults who looked after her throughout her childhood — her mother and 'ayahs' (nannies) — were all lovingly tactile. Within her family, both same and opposite gender family members kissed and embraced each other. In her social environment greeting and parting were accompanied by kisses and embraces, professional men such as bank managers held hands as they strolled down the pavement, and young men ambled along with arms around each other's shoulders.
> As a student in Tunisia, Amira experienced a similar level of tactility. When she visited the homes of fellow female students she found that they and their sisters all slept in the same room, cuddled each other, and fought over who would be allowed to cuddle her.

There were no British participants in this group nor members of other 'Anglo' cultures (in this study, White societies in America, Australia, Canada and South Africa).

In addition to the eight categories on the scale there was a further, ninth category:

9) Varyingly tactile (*n* = 50), denoting movement, a tactile journey

This group comprised individuals whose tactility had changed over the course of their lives (as in most of the participants mentioned above who had moved out of their original tactile category into another). Varyingly tactile participants could be either increasingly or decreasingly tactile.

9a) Increasingly tactile (*n* = 48)

These were participants who had been non- or less tactile initially but had moved towards the tactile end of the scale. Their shift in tactility had been set in train by various *environmental change-agents* and had begun at different times after early adulthood — in some participants soon after; in others, as late as their 40s; in one instance, 50s; and in another, early 60s.

Interviewees mentioned ten of these tactual change-agents:

1 Travel, that is, the influence of individuals from more tactile cultures whom participants had befriended either in Britain or while travelling abroad.
2 A relationship with a partner or spouse.
3 A relationship with their own child or children.
4 'Changing times', that is, the fact that British culture has become more tactile.
5 Arts trainings — drama/dance/music/art — and the tactile communities they create.
6 Boyfriends or girlfriends, that is, early exploratory relationships before settling with a longer-term partner or spouse.
7 Psychotherapy that included everyday 'human' touch (hugs, a hand held), except in the case of one participant whose therapy had not included touch but had made her *'more open'* and therefore more accepting of touch outside therapy.
8 'Body psychotherapy' — psychotherapy that incorporated massage and an emphasis on body awareness.
9 Massage/bodywork.
10 'New-age' groups and self-development programmes.

With two exceptions all the varyingly tactile participants (that is, 48 out of 50 = 96%) were in this increasingly tactile group.

The tactility scale 81

Movement from non-tactile to reluctantly tactile

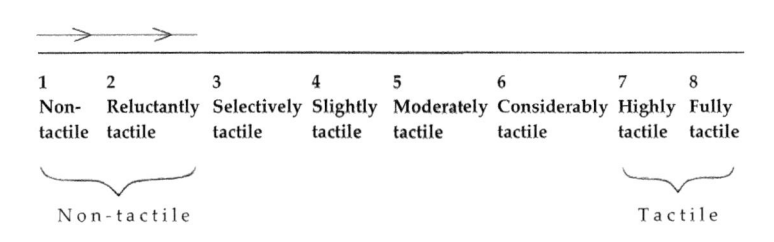

1	2	3	4	5	6	7	8
Non-tactile	Reluctantly tactile	Selectively tactile	Slightly tactile	Moderately tactile	Considerably tactile	Highly tactile	Fully tactile

Non-tactile   Tactile

When asked whether her childhood family had been tactile or not, Valerie exclaimed with abhorrence, *'NO! I come from the North — a hard, mining town'* where touch was considered *'wimpish, sissy. Ugh, I can hardly stand it* [touch, not the Northern attitude].' The change-agent for her had been moving to London and being exposed to *'different Southern habits'*. At her first experience of a London dinner party she had been appalled by the fact that people pecked each other — and her — on the cheek in greeting. She still found touch revolting, although living in London's more expressive tactile climate had slightly inured her to the horrible practice and as a result it was not *quite* as revolting as initially. Raising her own children had further loosened her cast-iron tactile boundaries so that she was slightly to moderately tactile towards them, and towards the under-fives with whom she worked. Even so, the thought of touching anyone else was highly unpleasant.

Shanti was born soon after her family arrived in England. Although as a rule the family was tactile, the strain of immigration had disrupted the normal tenor of their lives and Shanti had been *'forgotten in her cot'*. The experience had impaired her trust in others, which she thought was the source of her distaste for touch. During her adolescence and 20s, the one exception to this overall touch aversion was her relationship with her youngest sister. With her she felt comfortable

(Continued)

> enacting the tactile patterns of the rest of her family; they would cuddle together on the sofa to watch television and stroll down the street arm in arm.
>
> However, a change — a broadening out of her selectivity — had recently occurred through the person of her fiancé who had carefully, sensitively, melted her reluctance and little by little wooed her into the enjoyment of caring touch. At the time of the interview she was still selectively tactile since this change had not generalised into feeling comfortable about touching anyone other than her sister and fiancé.
>
> By the time we had a follow-up meeting two and a half years later, she was happily married to her former fiancé and had a baby. These experiences had wrought sufficient tactile magic to carry her into the further reaches of moderate tactility and she now enjoyed hugs with friends at greeting and parting.

> Belinda was one of the several non-client participants who had 'craved' touch as a child. She still did, but was usually too stiff and shy to accept it even when it was offered. Her touch aversion was expressed more as acute discomfort and fear rather than disgust as in the other reluctantly tactile participants. Many a battle raged within her small frame between touch craving and touch aversion. Over the years the craving had made some headway so that she was now slightly more tactile and would warily accept a hug or a brief massage on neck or shoulders from a few people whom she knew well.

From non-tactile to selectively tactile

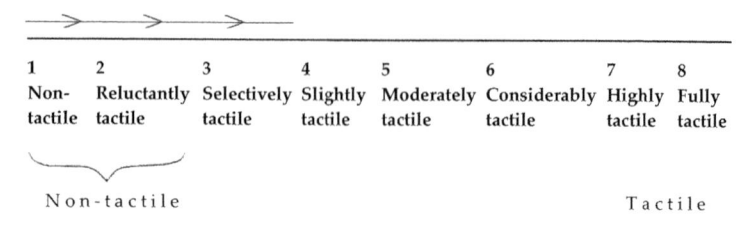

1	2	3	4	5	6	7	8
Non-tactile	Reluctantly tactile	Selectively tactile	Slightly tactile	Moderately tactile	Considerably tactile	Highly tactile	Fully tactile

Non-tactile   Tactile

The tactility scale

John's mother had been *'insecure, needy, ... smothering. Touch from her was distasteful.'* His father was *'very cold, separate'* and non-tactile. Being born to these parents had meant a difficult childhood for John. He had gradually become more emotionally organised and comfortable with touch through involvement with tactile *'new-agey groups'*. Now in his late 50s he was married for the first time and moderately tactile with his wife, but non- to slightly tactile with others.

Harriet was born to a non-tactile family and vividly remembered having *'craved'* bodily contact as a child. Despite the relative dearth of tactile nurturance there had been models of psychological caring in her childhood environment, and her tactile experience had not been so painful that she had shut down her touch needs. Still in contact with these when she had her own children she was able to empathise with their need for touch and be considerably tactile with them. With her husband she was slightly to moderately tactile but when touched otherwise was tense and uncomfortable. She paid for massage sessions *'as an uncomplicated way to satisfy touch-hunger'*.

Jen's had been a single-parent family. Her mother was *'absolutely not tactile'* and Jen was now making up for lost time with her husband *'because underneath you always crave touch'*. She was tactile with her husband only.

From non-tactile to slightly or moderately tactile

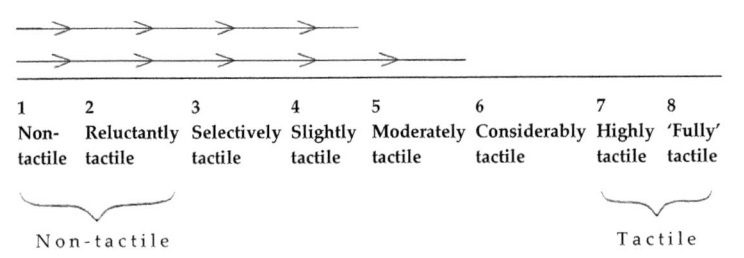

1	2	3	4	5	6	7	8
Non-tactile	Reluctantly tactile	Selectively tactile	Slightly tactile	Moderately tactile	Considerably tactile	Highly tactile	'Fully' tactile

Non-tactile   Tactile

Lucinda's mother had been thoroughly non-tactile and her father *'too tactile'*. Lucinda obviously did not wish to dwell on the latter aspect of her story. Whatever the details of her experience, it had left her extremely frightened and rejecting of touch, and emotionally fragile in general.

Change for her had come about through psychotherapy which had included very sensitive, minimal touch, and thereafter through dance therapies involving much touch. She was now non-tactile with most people, and slightly to moderately tactile with those whom she knew well. However, her progression to the latter, more tactile category within a relationship needed to be very slow and careful for her to feel safe.

Beth's father, like Tim's (p.75), had fought in the Second World War and Beth had seen little of him while growing up. Her mother was rejecting and strictly non-tactile; so were the horror-film nuns at her Catholic boarding school, the memory of whose maltreatment caused her (literally) to sweat decades later. Letters to her mother begging to be allowed to leave the school were ignored — the 'discipline' (canings and verbal cruelty) was good for her.

In common with several other interviewees, Beth was saved by a *'cuddly'* grandmother whose *'warm, safe lap'* she recalled as a haven. With this taste of nurturing warmth in her experience she was open to the increased tactility afforded by *'changing times'*, that is, by the relative relaxation of strict non-tactility in England. (Beth was one of the three participants who considered this change to have occurred from about 1990.) Her increased tactility was further spurred through working with extremely tactile mixed-race children in South Africa who were *'always touching, holding hands, kissing, leaning up against me and each other'*.

Beth now enjoyed touch. However, when in England her behaviour was non- to slightly or moderately tactile in accordance with the habits of whatever the current company.

Adam had been non-tactile through lack of opportunity in a non-tactile family and a non-tactile (English) culture. In his mid-30s he had been softened into freer tactile expression by the touch needs of his own children. He was now moderately tactile with them and slightly tactile with others, including his wife.

Josephine answered the question about her family's tactility or lack thereof in no uncertain terms. '*Absolutely not. No-one touched anyone in the immediate or extended family. Not at school either.*' She thought this was responsible for the fact that she had never had a physical love-relationship or children.

The catalyst of change for her were the classes of a '*huggy*' Tai Chi teacher into whose circle of friends she had been welcomed. Her tactility had then further expanded through Circle Dance classes. (As its name implies, Circle Dance is mostly done in a circle, holding hands. Participants learn folk dances from all over the world to appropriate world music. In addition to the hand-holding, Circle Dance culture in general is moderately to considerably tactile, with affectionate hugs sometimes exchanged at greeting and parting.)

Josephine now veered between relapses into her old, non-tactile mode when '*feeling cut-off*', and excursions into moderate tactility when at her most outgoing, and when the surrounding company sanctioned it.

Ellen's parents were '*not at all tactile*'. Shortly before her 40th birthday, Ellen had embarked on a personal growth course whose loving, spiritual orientation was often expressed in touch (hugs, hand-holding). Through continued contact with such groups she had settled into moderate tactility. However, she considered that this change had come too late for her to create a relationship with a partner and bear children — she had '*missed the boat*'.

From non-tactile to considerably tactile

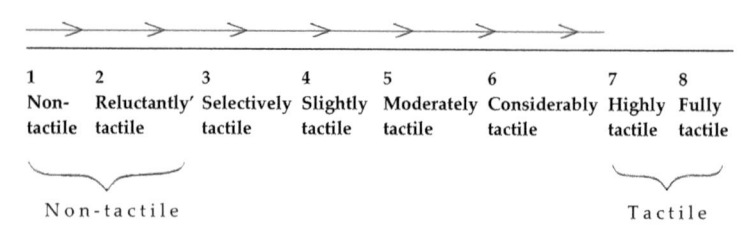

1	2	3	4	5	6	7	8
Non-tactile	Reluctantly tactile	Selectively tactile	Slightly tactile	Moderately tactile	Considerably tactile	Highly tactile	Fully tactile

Non-tactile   Tactile

> In Jim's opinion the reason his childhood had been non-tactile was because *'we're English.'* When well into middle age, he and his wife discovered Circle Dance (see p.85) through which they became considerably tactile (hugs, kisses) with their Circle Dance friends. They were both still non-tactile with previous, English friends who were themselves all non-tactile. Their newfound tactility through Circle Dance had the added effect of bringing them closer together as a couple.

From non-tactile to highly tactile

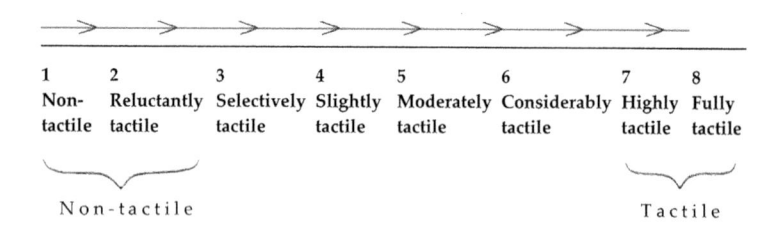

1	2	3	4	5	6	7	8
Non-tactile	Reluctantly tactile	Selectively tactile	Slightly tactile	Moderately tactile	Considerably tactile	Highly tactile	Fully tactile

Non-tactile   Tactile

> Steve's relationship with touch had been one of extreme discomfort ever since he could remember. In his family, at school and in the surrounding culture — the rough, scary streets in which he played as a child — affectionate touch was considered *'sissy, wimpish, soft, weak'*. He still exuded fear at the thought of being labelled in these terms.
>
> Through psychotherapy which included hugs at the ends of sessions he had come to feel more comfortable with caring

physical contact. Towards the end of his therapy the therapist had recommended Biodanza (a form of dance/movement to music created by Rolando Toro. Its aim is to enhance happiness, pleasure and health, partly by revitalising emotions and instincts that may have been dimmed by family and cultural prohibitions. Tender, loving and respectful touch is one of its principal elements).

Steve was now slightly tactile generally, and highly tactile during Biodanza classes. Through the influence of these classes he had become acutely aware at the age of 40 that his personal life was devoid of sensual pleasure, and he was actively seeking a close relationship that incorporated the tactility he experienced at Biodanza.

Jurgen had been non-tactile through lack of opportunity only and not at all through touch aversion. His mother rarely touched him — she was overworked and always busy — and he had never known his father. He was one of the 12 interviewees who mentioned having '*craved*' touch as a child, and the craving had persisted into adulthood.

His love of both touch and movement had drawn him to Contact Improvisation (an improvisatory form of dance done usually with a partner, sometimes with a group, of which physical contact is a major feature). Because he had no emotional barriers to touching, simply a need to satisfy, Jurgen fell naturally into the tactility entailed in this dance form.

Later he discovered Biodanza (see above) in which he could wholly satisfy his desire for tactile expression. He was now fully tactile with his Biodanza friends both during and between classes, and with other tactile individuals. However, he felt uncomfortable with the '*stand-offishness*' that non-tactility signified for him; he therefore behaved cautiously with typically English people and avoided befriending them.

From moderately to considerably tactile

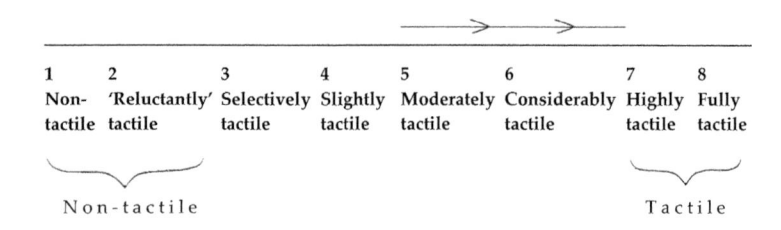

1	2	3	4	5	6	7	8
Non-tactile	'Reluctantly' tactile	Selectively tactile	Slightly tactile	Moderately tactile	Considerably tactile	Highly tactile	Fully tactile

Non-tactile   Tactile

> Charlotte's family were moderately tactile, *'But,'* she said when trying to explain the limitations of their tactile expression, *'We are British.'*
>
> A landmark holiday in Brazil had shown Charlotte a different way of being which she felt was the realisation of an internal emotional-tactile map, one that had been awaiting expression all her life. In Brazil people were wholeheartedly and unselfconsciously tactile, which she felt gave her permission to behave similarly. The demonstrative way in which children were treated struck her in particular as joyous and healthy — they were constantly being picked up, cuddled and delighted in. Charlotte now periodically visited Brazil where she was highly tactile, a state in which she felt most alive and happiest. Once back in England she often *'withdrew'* because she felt that in general *'English people don't really like touch.'*

9b) Decreasingly tactile (*n* = 2)

The two (out of 50) participants in the 'varyingly tactile' category who had become less rather than more tactile had done so through reduced opportunity for touch and not through choice — one due to the death of her husband, and the other as a result of immigration from a fully tactile to a non-tactile culture.

> Penny had been consigned to diminished tactility at the age of 76 on the death of her husband. Despite a full social life she found the lack of affectionate physical contact — cuddles, a supportive hand on her shoulder — the cause of painful loneliness.

Although Penny happened to be the only participant in this situation, she represents many others for whom the death of a spouse or partner removes, or much reduces, opportunities for affectionate touch.

Individuals experiencing separation or divorce may also feel the loss of tactile nurturance keenly, although in their case it may be temporary. Indeed, a longing for the warmth and cosiness of non-erotic physical contact can sometimes be a spur to seeking a new relationship.

Shanaz was the second decreasingly tactile participant:

> Having lived in a fully tactile Middle Eastern culture until the age of 20, Shanaz then immigrated to non-tactile England. Here, through work and marriage, she had fallen into mainly English, non-tactile social networks. As a result she lacked opportunity to exercise her initial tactility and over time had lost some of it.

In contrast to Shanaz, four other participants from tactile, non-Anglo cultures who now lived in England still frequently saw members of their cultures of origin and their tactility had thus survived more or less intact. They considered the non-tactile behaviour they had learned in Britain to be a transient and relatively superficial adaptation assumed in order to fit in and avoid offending — their 'real selves' were as tactile as ever.

Some conclusions

An idea which I think emerges from the tactile profiles above is that tactility is the natural and healthy state of human beings. Once independent and freer of family constraints, the large majority of participants in the non- or less tactile groups had gravitated towards greater tactility. With their new tactile status had come closer interpersonal connections and improved life satisfaction.

Non-tactility, on the other hand, tended to be associated with less functional psychological states — with low self-esteem, interpersonal difficulties, and more unwanted feelings such as discomfort, fear and dissatisfaction. At the extreme end of non-tactility was touch aversion which in some cases was linked to histories of child abuse and/or neglect.

It is interesting to speculate on the survival or otherwise of the human race if non-tactility were the behavioural norm. In the present study the incidence of childlessness was greater among non-tactile than among tactile participants — which brings to mind Montagu's observation that nurturing, *non-sexual* touch during childhood is a prerequisite for successful *sexual* relationships later in life (Montagu, 1986:206–207; also Hatfield, 1994:e4). Of 19 non-tactile women participants who were past childbearing age, nine had not had children and the average birth rate among the 19 was less than one child per woman. If this figure represented the stable birth rate in a society its population would gradually dwindle into extinction, since the birth rate required to sustain a population in the industrialised world is 2.1 children per woman (United Nations, 2007:15). Among the same-aged women on the tactile end of the scale ($n = 9$) the birth rate was at least 2.1. If this finding is more generally applicable, then from an evolutionary point of view insufficient loving touch cannot be overly advantageous for the continuation of the species (although some might say that the population explosion and competition for resources turns this principle on its head. However, extremely grave as these problems are, I do not think that unfulfilled tactile-emotional needs and the individual and societal stress they cause is a satisfactory solution to them.)

Four non- or less tactile participants corroborated this hypothesis from a subjective point of view in that they blamed their lack of a partner and children on their non-tactility.

A further conclusion suggested by the touch profiles above concerns the origins of our attitudes to touch. This is so salient to the present enquiry that it warrants a chapter of its own.

Note

1 '**The need for touch in humans is innate and universal...**' although in rare instances of abnormal skin sensitivity, usually through damage to the peripheral nerves, this need falls by the wayside because of the pain that accompanies physical contact.

Chapter 5

The origins of attitudes to touch; how tactile habits are formed

Note: By *Anglo cultures* I refer to English-speaking cultures in Britain and in areas of the world influenced by British colonisation, such as parts of Australia, Canada, North America and South Africa. A common thread runs through these cultures regarding attitudes to touch (Hunter & Struve, 1998:85; Jourard, 1966).

By *British culture* I mean England, Ireland (North and South), Scotland and Wales.

* * *

As is to be expected of any learned human trait, the two potent influences that determined tactility within my sample of 90 turned out to be those of the family, and of culture (that is, the wider social context in which families live).

The effects of family on tactility

In most cases participants' tactility had been formed by the tactile habits of their childhood families. Thus at early adulthood (my designated benchmark of tactility) 85 of the 90 participants (94.4%) belonged to the same tactile category as their families of origin.

Some had had their touch needs met during childhood — they had been sufficiently held and cuddled in a warm, loving, relaxed way by at least one primary carer. These individuals had continued to want touch in adulthood and considered it a natural part of communication.

In contrast, participants whose touch needs had been inadequately met reacted to the lack in one of two ways: one group had remained in contact with their innate need for touch and had sought out tactile experiences in life so as to 'catch up on' the fulfilment of that need. A second group had rejected physical contact because of its painful associations with childhood sexual or physical abuse, or with the neglect or rejection of their natural drive to receive and give affectionate touch (see Hunter & Struve, 1998:33). Jessica, for example, behaved in the mode of her loving and moderately tactile family until she was sexually abused by a babysitter at the age of nine. The experience froze her innate tactile impulses; from then on she was averse to physical contact and, to the mystification of her family, became a 'difficult' child — contrary and distant — whereas previously she had been friendly and cooperative.

Steve had been instilled with a fear of affectionate physical contact by his family and neighbourhood culture which considered that touch was *'sissy, wimpish, soft, weak'* (see p.86–87); people suspected of these attributes were ostracised and violently bullied. Steve's internalised environmental beliefs contributed significantly to the touch-related discomfort he experienced. It was not until middle age that he was able to battle through his conditioning in order to satisfy a longing for tender touch.

Individual versus family tactility

Jessica (above) was one of a minority of people I have met whose tactility in early adulthood was different from that of their families. In all there were only five such participants in the sample of 90 (5.55%). One was Mina whose older brother had developed a life-threatening disease. This had caused her parents acute anxiety and necessitated spending much time with her brother in hospitals. The experience had lasted several years during which Mina was emotionally and tactually ignored. As a result she felt deeply rejected, sad, angry and, in turn, rejecting of others. Her normal process of acculturation into family tactile norms was thus disrupted and she became the only non-tactile member of her highly tactile family.

For four non-clients the difference between individual and family tactility took the opposite direction — although born into non-tactile families in the UK, they were nevertheless tactile in early adulthood through the influence of the non-British, tactile cultures into which their families had been transplanted. Two of the four had been abundantly held, hugged and kissed by local nannies during childhood, and all four had received affectionate touch from non-family members in the highly tactile surrounding culture — which brings into focus a central issue in the touch discourse, namely:

The effects of culture on tactility

Culture is a highly potent determinant of tactility. My findings tally with other studies that have found similarly (e.g. Anderson et al., 1987; Frank, 1957:237).

I imagine that some readers will share my discomfort with cultural generalisations since they can stray into stereotyping and prejudice. However, the evidence seems indisputable that touch norms are culture-specific and come within the bracket of other culture-specific customs, such as type of clothing worn (loincloth and beads, or jeans and T-shirt...) and ceremonial traditions (marriage and funeral rituals...).

Similarities and discrepancies between familial and cultural tactility

In matters of tactility the family is the culture bearer, culture's teaching instrument. Most often, therefore, the tactile attitudes and behaviours it perpetuates are those of the surrounding culture. Thus in the case of 71 participants (78.9%), the customs of their families with respect to touch were more or less identical to those of the wider environment.

The remaining 19 participants (21.1%) reported a discrepancy between familial and cultural tactility. A link emerged here between rigid non-tactility and childhood abuse, as though they sometimes (not always) operated as twin aberrations. Tania for instance had grown up in Greece, a fully tactile culture in which her parents were anomalously non-tactile — they provided no tender, loving touch — but her father inflicted severely abusive touch on her, both sexual and physical, and her mother was physically abusive. Tania emerged from her painful childhood with an intense aversion to touch, in contrast to the full, warm tactility of mainstream Greek culture which surrounded her.

In a more normal course of events — without the distorting effects of abuse and neglect — there might be a haptic interplay between the two forces of family and culture. Either could prevail or else they could gently meld, depending on a number of variables, for example, the age of the individual when exposed to tactual customs that contradicted those of her family; the length of such exposure; whether religious ideology was involved; the closeness of family ties; the strength of family values, and the firmness, sometimes tyranny, with which parents and possibly the extended family insisted upon them.

The origins of attitudes to touch 95

Paula's experience was of the melding kind, in which differing family and cultural norms seemed to have influenced each other equally. Her mother was Greek, her father Italian, and both were fully tactile. They had immigrated to Australia where Paula was born. Paula herself was more tactile than White Australians were in general, but less so than her parents' generation because *'being brought up in an Anglo-Saxon environment erodes some of it'*.

Just as tactility can be whittled away, so non-tactility may thaw through cultural counterinfluence. Tabitha's family was imbued with English non-tactile customs that were removed to a fully tactile culture when her father's work took him to South America. Tabitha quickly learned the ways of her schoolfellows and initially led a double life tactually speaking; she was non-tactile with her English parents and their friends, and tactile with her peers. If by chance her English and South American social groups met, she felt uncomfortably self-conscious about her behaviour with both. The discomfort gradually resolved as she became aware that her mother's tactility was increasing through the influence of South American women who had welcomed her into their friendship network.

First-generation children of immigrants into societies with different tactile habits, such as Tabitha, may experience tension between family and cultural pressures particularly acutely. If we step back chronologically and look at the bigger picture, however, it becomes evident that the fundamental tussle here is between two tactually different cultures — English and South American in Tabitha's case — and that in general the touch-related family/culture opposition obtaining at any time is born of these cultural differences.

Touch in Anglo and non-Anglo cultures

Tabitha's experience raises a further aspect of my findings that accords with other studies: Anglo cultures in general are less tactile than non-Anglo cultures (Andersen & Leibowitz, 1978:105; Andersen et al., 1986,1987; Argyle, 1988:60,215; Burgoon et al., 1996:230; Field, 1999a,1999b; Remland et al., 1995). And among the Anglo cultures in my sample, British culture was the least tactile (Jourard, 1966). This is certainly changing, at least in some areas; I daily see throngs of London teenagers freely hugging each other in greeting and parting and it is possible that when they are adults researchers will not be able to draw the comparison between Anglo and non-Anglo touch norms. However, minimal Anglo tactility was still vividly in evidence in my interviewees' material, and particularly so in the case of those who had lived in two societies with contrasting attitudes to touch.

Rosa for example was Spanish, that is, from a fully tactile culture, but she had worked in England for nine years. During this time she felt her tactility had decreased:

> 'Here in England people don't approach you, people don't touch you. There is distance, rigidity. I think how sad it is that the culture has given this rigidity, this buffer – people going with bubbles around [them]. If I'm here I'm more suspicious – here you think the touch usually comes with something – if it's from a British person, something sexual.
>
> After nine years in the UK I became British in that way. When I go back to Spain on holidays I really notice now when people come so close and I surprise myself that it bothers me now. Then after a few days I get back into my culture and realise how good it is. It makes you feel part of something, that you're another person. It's a signal of normality, and humanity. In Spain if the touch is sexual you get a message very clearly. In Spain it [non-sexual touch] doesn't have any connotation; it doesn't mean anything [ulterior]. It makes you feel good. It's warmth, contact, togetherness. You feel a connection, the value of having that rapport with someone.'

In Rosa's experience, touch strengthened both individual identity *and* her connection with others:

> 'You feel relaxed. If you're more relaxed it means you are happy with, more comfortable with yourself, because it's not [about whether] you deserve to be touched, because everybody does it and you do it to anybody, any shape, any colour, but your body becomes much more visible, much more part of who you are ... You're more aware of your body; the touch reminds you that it's there. The identity thing is stronger because you get reminded all the time.
>
> And it's not just who you are, but also what connects you to the other person who touches you.'

Pierre, like Rosa, had lived in two cultures — his childhood in France, a relatively tactile society, and his mid-20s onwards in

England. He described his discomfort at encountering English tactile customs:

> *'It's as if I was holding something back – something which feels natural; I was containing my natural flow of energy, of welcoming someone, of greeting someone. By doing that it seems like I protect myself from rejection. I don't feel good. I don't feel as alive as if I were able to express myself as I want to. There's more tension.'*

Natalia was eight when, to her confusion, her family emigrated from fully tactile Uruguay to non-tactile England. On her first day at her English school she reached out her arms and kissed her teacher in greeting as was customary in Uruguay. However, she swiftly learned English ways in order to fit in. Now as an adult Natalia was fully tactile with Latin and non-tactile with English people — a behavioural disjunction commonly experienced by dual-cultural participants.

After the British interviewees, two cultures more or less tied for second place in non-tactility: firstly, non-British Anglo cultures (White societies in Australia, Canada, North America and South Africa (see p.92); secondly, German culture. Charlie was an example of the former. His family had emigrated from Britain to Australia several generations previously. Although moderately tactile, that is, not as tactile as most non-Anglo individuals, Charlie was nevertheless aware that he was more comfortable with touch than his English friends. He attributed this to the Australian way of life — sunshine, treks in the outback, and the relaxation induced by a slower, more laid-back life-style into which his family had been acculturated.

The four German participants in my sample had all had unsatisfactory tactile experiences as children: three had suffered tactile neglect, and one of these had in addition been subjected to severe sexual and physical abuse. The fourth had received a moderate amount of touch but had experienced it as a burden since it was the product of her mother's need and little to do with her. These participants could of course be atypical. My ad hoc, wider exploration of German tactility reveals a mixed picture. Certainly in some parts of Germany tactual attitudes have greatly changed in recent years — kindergarten children are now lovingly hugged, cuddled on laps and introduced to massage, and primary school children continue to exchange much affectionate physical contact with their teachers. However, there is evidence that before these changes German culture was generally on the non-tactile side of the haptic spectrum (Garreau, 1981; Older, 1977:198).

Bicultural upbringing

Some participants had grown up in two different cultures from birth rather than happened upon a second culture in later life. Janine's mother and her mother's family were Iranian and fully tactile, while her father and his family were English and non-tactile. Janine considered herself to be fully tactile like her mother but expressed this in her behaviour exclusively with the Iranian side of the family, and with Iranians generally. She animatedly described the tactile part of her life as warm, rich and colourful — her eyes shone, her cheeks were slightly flushed and many lively hand gestures accompanied her narrative. In comparison the description of her English family sounded cool and flat — the extra sparkle in her eyes disappeared, her cheeks were paler and her hands more or less immobile. She felt her English family were less concerned about one another. (However, she had found a plus-side to this — there was more individual freedom within British culture because people did not take such a personal interest in the activities of their family members.)

A comparison of participants at the extreme ends of the tactility scale provides an immediate thumbnail impression that cultural factors are at play in the shaping of tactility. In the non-tactile category, 31 of the 34 participants (91.2%) were from Anglo cultures, and only 3 (8.8%) from non-Anglo cultures. By contrast, the fully tactile category consisted entirely of non-Anglo participants.

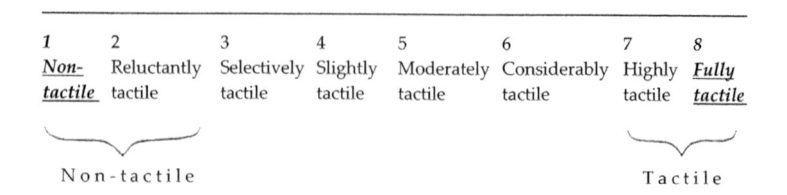

1	2	3	4	5	6	7	8
Non-tactile	Reluctantly tactile	Selectively tactile	Slightly tactile	Moderately tactile	Considerably tactile	Highly tactile	*Fully tactile*

Non-tactile   Tactile

The categories above in bold italics are those compared in the table below.

Anglo (mainly English) participants			Non-Anglo participants		
	%	number		%	number
Fully tactile:	0	0	Fully tactile:	100	7
Non-tactile:	91.2	31	Non-tactile:	8.8	3

Comparison of participants in the non-tactile and fully tactile categories on the tactility scale.

These Anglo and non-Anglo differences remained in evidence throughout the scale, although they were not always as immediately apparent; 17 Anglo (mainly English) participants were highly tactile in early adulthood, that is, more tactile than the Anglo norm. I did not attempt to trace long-term influences on their tactility by enquiring too far into their histories, but eight of them appeared to be bona fide exceptions — they had been raised by British parents and lived in Britain throughout their childhoods. In all cases their mothers set the tactual tone of the family — they were highly tactile with their children who continued the tradition. One of these interviewees, in her mid-20s, had just returned from a visit home during which she had snuggled up to her mother on the sofa and found it *'bliss'*. Another came from a family whose members often hugged and kissed each other on the lips, behaviour that she gradually realised was not typically English. In three of the families the father was also highly tactile; in the other five he was less tactile than the mother.

In the remaining 9 of the 17 highly tactile Anglo interviewees, appearance was deceptive. Isobel and Ros were both British but touched others more often than their British peers, and their tactility had a non-British flavour — a fluid, spontaneous warmth and freedom. The mystery was explained when it emerged that both their fathers had been posted abroad to work which meant that they had spent their childhoods in more tactile cultures, one in Holland, the other in Cyprus. When they returned to Britain the effects of their overseas experience stayed with them. Isobel now worked with children where her tactility was a boon to her charges (fortunately in a nursery whose head rejected the current appallingly misguided idea that children should not be lovingly touched (see p.40–42).

Ros worked for an English company in which she raised spirits, goodwill and motivation through her tactility. In the general ethos of the company, tactile behaviour was a breach of 'professionalism'. However, through undeniable bodily experience Ros knew from within that touch was valuable, and she had the confidence in it and in herself to change workplace customs. As manager of a team she touched others during conversation — perhaps on an arm or shoulder — and dispensed hugs to those who were comfortable with them. In consequence the team cohered more, the atmosphere in her section of the organisation improved noticeably and work became a brighter, happier place. (It is worth noting that Ros was an attractive woman and that perhaps not everyone would have been as successful as she was.)

Paula (p.95) and Janine (p.98) were the third and fourth members of this group of Anglo participants whose high tactility was the result of non-Anglo influence. The other five interviewees in the group were to all appearances British but turned out to be members of a more tactile minority culture (see below).

Religion in relation to tactility

The participants in this study had been raised either in non-religious families, or in one of a wide variety of faiths — Buddhist, Christian (Catholic, various Protestant denominations, Christian Scientist, Jehovah's Witness, Unitarian), Hindu, Jewish, Muslim, Sufi and Zoroastrian. Of those who had been raised in a faith, the large majority had ceased to regard religion as relevant to their lives and did not consider it to have influenced their tactility either way.

Among the few exceptions to this were one British Presbyterian and four British Catholic participants who perceived a connection between religious ideology and tactility — in their case religion seemed to have colluded with culture in consolidating the touch taboo. (By contrast, in the fully tactile cultures of South America, Catholicism did not impede tactile behaviour.)

A second group of exceptions demonstrated that, while national culture is generally the major determinant of tactility, a strong, closely knit minority community may have tactile traditions strong enough to supersede the norms of the dominant culture. The group comprised five Anglo-Jewish participants (four British, one American) who were more tactile than average Anglo participants and who attributed this to their Jewish upbringings. Four of the five were not at all religious but were nevertheless rooted in the culture surrounding their religion. (It was chance that these particular interviewees were included in my sample; from subsequent investigation I found that the same principle applied in a number of other closely knit and tactile religious minorities such as Albanian Muslim, Greek Orthodox and South American Catholic.)

As with English-Iranian Janine (p.98), the upbringing of these five Anglo-Jewish interviewees was as bicultural as that of participants who had lived in two tactually different countries. Danielle, for example, from a highly tactile English-Jewish family, experienced a conflict between family and cultural tactile norms:

> '*I am naturally physical but I have trained myself to hold back. I learnt, I don't know when — possibly as an adolescent — that I was really freaking people out, especially boys ... so I stopped doing it; I reined in my natural way and became a prim and proper English girl.*'

In common with other bicultural individuals, Danielle had two modes of tactile behaviour — she was tactile with Jewish family and friends and with tactile associates, and non-tactile with most English people.

As in the earlier example of Tabitha (p.95) the tension between family and culture experienced by Danielle and the four other Anglo-Jewish participants may actually have arisen from opposition between two different cultures; four of the five had Russian and one had Polish parents or grandparents, that is, antecedents from cultures that are more tactile than British culture. Possibly their Russian and Polish tactility was preserved by the closeness of Jewish family and community ties. Four other participants in the sample of 90 had grown away from their original Jewish culture and their attitudes to touch in early adulthood were no different from those of their Anglo counterparts.

Among the five non-Anglo participants who were uncharacteristically non-tactile, there was one instance of deceptive appearance — Ailene had been born into a fully tactile African culture but turned out to have been fostered from earliest babyhood by a strictly non-tactile British-Catholic family (see p.145–147). (Of the other four interviewees in this group, two had become touch-averse through childhood sexual abuse and one through childhood neglect. The fourth was born and raised in Germany which at the time had a tradition of non-tactility.)

Not only was culture the major force determining participants' initial tactile status; it was also the most powerful change-agent of tactile behaviour during adulthood. Tilly, for example, was English and initially slightly to moderately tactile. Like several Anglo participants she had progressed along the tactility scale through contact with more tactile, non-Anglo cultures. While holidaying in Italy she met her Italian future husband on a beach and was introduced to the whole of his large family. Tilly loved the warmth they expressed through their frequent hugs and kisses and was soon joining in with enthusiasm.

Subcultures

> We are raised in a plurality of cultural subgroups, each exerting a multiplicity of influences upon us ... We are molded by the subjective culture of our reference subgroup.
>
> Howard (1991:192), drawing on the work of Triandis (1972) on 'subjective culture'

So far the subcultures that have emerged as influential in shaping tactility are certain minority ethnic and religious groups living within the majority culture. However, these are not the only minority cultures whose tactility differs from the mainstream. Subcultures may also be created through trainings and professions, a notable example being that of the arts. Eighteen non- or slightly tactile British participants in my sample had become far more tactile through the influence of arts trainings which encourage tactility, such as drama, dance/movement, music and art. Perhaps because freedom of expression is important to artistic endeavour, students and graduates of these trainings form tactually expressive communities within which hugs, kisses and conversational touch occur to a far greater extent than within mainstream British society. (As will be evident later, this capacity of trainings to create distinctive subcultural groups has a bearing on attitudes to touch in therapy.)

Summary and conclusions

Culture is the most powerful determinant of tactual attitudes and behaviours, and the family is the culture bearer. Most families therefore transmit the tactile norms of the society in which they live, which usually means that familial and cultural tactile influences are mutually reinforcing and more or less inseparable.

There are exceptions to this rule. In my sample these were most often due to the pull of societal tactile customs that were different from those of the family and which influenced its children. Further exceptions occurred as a result of childhood abuse and/or neglect which disrupted the survivor's normal acculturation into familial and societal haptic norms.

Of the cultural forces that shaped tactility, the majority culture of a country was most potent. Less often, minority subcultures within the predominant culture also determined tactility. Among these were ethnic and religious groups whose tactile customs differed from those of the mainstream.

In addition, subcultures are created by certain trainings and activities. For example, students and graduates of arts trainings such as drama and dance form communities in which touch occurs far more freely than in most of Britain.

Chapter 6

Touch in everyday life; what 'ordinary people' (non-clients) said about touch

Most of the 90 non-clients I interviewed expressed a rosy view of touch (80%, $n = 72$). Some had held this attitude from the start and others had acquired it by the time of the interview.

A minority of non-clients expressed an unequivocally negative view of physical contact (5.6%, $n = 5$), and the remaining participants in the sample had mixed responses, that is, tactile interaction might evoke either positive or negative feelings and thoughts (14.4%, $n = 13$).

NON-CLIENTS WHOSE EXPERIENCES OF TOUCH HAD BEEN POSITIVE (80%, $n = 72$)

Three overarching themes emerged from the interviews with participants whose attitude towards touch was positive:

Touch

1) *satisfies fundamental human needs;*
2) *promotes positive relationships;* and
3) *produces beneficial changes in people's lives.*

These main themes broke down into discrete but interrelated concepts; a client might say that when experiencing touch she felt *'loved'*, which might in turn increase her *'happiness'* and *'vitality'*, and at the same time have a physiological impact, perhaps of *'relaxation'* or *'energy'*. Because of this capacity of touch to affect the whole person, I have described participants' touch-descriptions according to the personality domain in which a quality is principally (rather than exclusively) based. For example, I have labelled 'relaxation' a 'physically-*based*' rather than a purely 'physical' need because its effects radiate out from the physical to the other aspects of personhood — the emotional, cognitive, and transcendent or 'spiritual'. (This last facet of personality is relevant only to those who perceive the existence of a spiritual dimension; some do not, or are more comfortable conceptualising 'transcendent' feelings as part of emotional experience.)

In the following summary of non-clients' interviews the three main themes are presented in **BOLD CAPITALS**; theme-words not actually mentioned by clients but which summarise what they expressed are in **bold**; theme-words mentioned repeatedly by clients themselves are in ***'bold italics and inverted commas'***; and verbatim quotations from clients' narratives are in *'italics and inverted commas'*. In a few cases, these words in italics and inverted commas were not mentioned by one participant only but are a composite of several participants' touch-descriptions.

1) TOUCH SATISFIES FUNDAMENTAL HUMAN NEEDS

— both for physical contact in its own right and for the qualities and meanings it communicates, such as warmth, acceptance, love, safety, comfort ...

a) Physically-based needs satisfied by touch

Relaxation

An intriguing finding emerged here:

Over a third of non-clients (38 out of the 90, 42.2%) mentioned *'relaxation'* as an effect of touch —

when I'm touched *'I relax immediately', 'I feel my whole body relax'...*

A further third (*n* = 30, 33.3%) mentioned synonyms for or states implying relaxation — touch was *'calming', 'de-stressing', 'letting go', 'melting', 'meld (I meld into the hug)', 'mellow', 'peace', 'it makes me sleep better'...'*

The total number of participants who mentioned the concept of 'relaxation' was therefore 68 (75.6%) which made it by far the most frequently cited effect of touch.

This was the more striking since only open questions were used in the interviews such as,

> How do you feel when you are touched or touch others/when you exchange touch? What does it mean to you?

No Likert-type scales or tick-box questioning were used.

(A Likert scale asks respondents to grade their responses on a continuum, for example:

Please mark where you are on the scale:

When I'm touched I feel:

Extremely relaxed	Relaxed	Fairly relaxed	A bit tense	Tense	Extremely tense

A 'tick box' question might be:

Tick the words that describe how you feel when you are touched:

Relaxed
Tense
Loved
Glowing
Irritated
Happy
Angry
[etc.]

The above two methods of 'closed questioning' suggest words and concepts to the interviewee, whereas in the 'open questioning' used in this research, interviewees come up with their own thoughts without outside influence. They therefore might not mention even important aspects of an issue, for example because these do not enter into their train of thought on that particular day or because the interview might end before they have reached the point of considering or being ready to mention them. Both closed and open methods of questioning have their value.)

Without exception, touch-induced relaxation was regarded by participants as desirable and concomitant with an increase of positive feelings such as *'happiness', 'pleasure'* and *'well-being'*.

This is an important finding in view of the thriving literature on stress which links relaxation and positive affect with health, and excessive tension and negative affect with ill health (e.g. Alkadhi, 2013; Humphreys et al., 2012; Mariotti, 2015; McEwen, 2017; Seib et al., 2014; Yaribeygi et al., 2017).

Embodiment

Touch produced the experience of embodiment — of 'being in' one's body:

'Touch brings me into my body. It grounds me, earths me.'

In all, 15 participants mentioned that the sense of well-being accompanying touch had this specifically physical orientation.

b) Physically- and emotionally-based needs satisfied by touch

'Warmth'

After relaxation, *'warmth'* was the most commonly cited effect of touch (mentioned by 37 participants — 41.1%). This accords with the contention of some researchers that warmth is a primary characteristic of touch,[1] and a fundamental feature of interpersonal bonding (Argyle, 1988; Major & Heslin, 1982).

A number of participants expressed appreciation of the link between physical and *'emotional/inner warmth'* (Linden, 2015:9–11; Williams & Bargh, 2008).

As with relaxation, all who mentioned the warmth received via touch found it a positive experience.

Vitality

When I'm touched I feel *'energised', 'alive', 'vital', 'watered like a flower', 'as if I'm coming into life'*. Touch is *'refreshing', 'invigorating', 'strengthening', 'it infuses me with extra spirit'*. *'I wither without touch.'*

Physical contact also elicited and heightened emotions, which further enhanced the sense of *'aliveness'* it engendered.

Pleasure

Touch is *'pleasurable', 'it feels great', 'gorgeous', 'lush', 'wonderful', 'good', 'really nice', 'yummy'*.

Stacey's rhapsodic evaluation of touch could have issued from a pop song: *'It's like a glow from the tip of your head to the tip of your toe.'*

c) Emotionally-based needs satisfied by touch

'Love', and related qualities

When touched I feel *'loved', '[held in] affection', 'liked', 'welcome', 'appreciated', 'accepted', 'empathised with', 'understood'*.

For some participants physical contact brought an *'unconditional'* dimension to the communication of these qualities; they felt *'unconditional love'* or *'unconditional acceptance'* from the toucher.

'Happiness'

When I'm touched I feel *'happy', 'joyful', 'positive', 'carefree', 'bliss', 'great', 'optimistic', 'I beam inside'* ... Touch arouses the expectation that *'something good's going to happen', 'it gives me extra enthusiasm for', 'increases my enjoyment of life'*.

These effects applied across the lifespan. According to 12-year-old Jonathan,

> *'Touch makes you feel happy if you're down in the dumps or even better if you're feeling good. Jolly. I dunno, I can't really explain happy — a sort of happy feeling in your body. A sort of rush of — yeah, happiness — that just fills your body, which is nice, that feel.'*

Twenty-five-year-old Ros thought that

> *'Touch lifts, like sunshine; it's the same unexplainable thing; I can't explain why sunshine makes me happy either!'*

And 82-year-old Janey radiated joy at the thought of being touched:

> *'When I'm touched I feel happy! Happiness!'*

Nurturance
I feel *'cared for'*, *'looked after'*, *'nurtured'*, *'nourished'*, *'comforted'*, *'supported'* when I'm touched.

Safety
I feel *'safe'*, *'secure'*, *'reassured'* when touched.

Alleviation of negative feelings
In its capacity to elevate our emotional state towards the lighthearted end of the unhappiness-happiness spectrum, touch not only evoked positive feelings but alleviated negative ones such as *'anxiety'*, *'fear'*, *'worry'*, *'panic'*, *'depression'*, *'loneliness'*.

A number of participants raised this point in relation to medical settings. For example, Louise had found that touch was the sole antidote to the dread and horror aroused by her dentist's ministrations:

> *'The only way I can bear to have the dentist do anything in my mouth is if the nurse holds my hand. And not in those nasty, clammy rubber gloves; she has to take her glove off so that I can feel SKIN. As soon as I feel her hand it's as if I suddenly go into another country — from being in a dark, scary place where I'm knotted up inside, everything is brighter, I'm calm, stable, relaxed, and the dentist can get on with her job.'*

c) Cognitively- and emotionally-based needs satisfied by touch

'Self-esteem'
Touch increased and maintained participants' *'self-esteem'*, *'self-worth'*, *'confidence'*, *'body image'*, *'self-respect'*; they felt more *'lovable'*, *'better about myself'*, *'valued'*, *'affirmed'*, *'empowered'*, *'congratulated'*, *'recognised'*, *'acknowledged'*.

Contact with reality
> *'Touch brings me into the present.'*

Touch is *'real'*, *'sincere'*, *'direct'*. *'You can't lie with it.'*

d) Spiritually/transcendence-based needs satisfied by touch

Some interviewees found that physical contact connected them with something bigger and deeper than everyday reality, a kind of ontological meta-level often labelled 'spiritual' or 'transcendent'.

Touch is *'about being whole; it's about we come from the same source and the same root, instead of living in the disconnected, isolated way we do in this society.'*

When I experience touch *'I feel part of the world and everything; part of the human race.'*

'Touch can remind me of a deeper, more meaningful reality — I feel part of humanity, nature, the cosmos, eternity, infinity.'

Two participants described a chain of experience leading from the physical to the transcendent: touch induced physical *'relaxation'*, which engendered a *'sense of peace'*, which in turn evoked the spiritual aspect of their personalities.

Growth, 'self-actualisation' (Goldstein, 1939:197; Maslow, 1968)

Physical contact increased *self-'awareness'*, *'self-acceptance'*. the feeling of being *'at one with myself'*, *'comfortable with'*, *'connected/ in touch with myself'*, *'whole'*, *'complete'*. It was *'human'*, *'natural'*, *'normal'*; and it nourished the *'sense of identity'*.

2) TOUCH PROMOTES POSITIVE RELATIONSHIPS

between toucher and touched. Both parties involved in the tactile interaction felt that it aroused *'loving'*, *'caring'*, *'giving'*, *'sharing'*, *'open[ness]'*, *'gratitude'* towards the other; they felt *'intimate with'*, *'comfortable'*, *'at ease with'* the other, *'included'*.

Sometimes these feelings spread beyond the touching pair in a domino effect. Fay, for example, found that the warm, spontaneous hugs of a new neighbour, in arousing warmth and energy in her, enabled her to give out the same feelings and *'touchy'* behaviour to others in her environment.

Sandra's ability to relate to others had been epiphanically altered by a chance meeting involving touch. She had tripped on a protruding paving stone and a passerby had caringly helped her up, sat her on a wall and gently held her hurt knee with one hand while resting the other hand reassuringly on her arm. Although it lasted only about five minutes, the experience had proved so powerful that it had infused Sandra's own behaviour ever since. Some time later she saw an upset teenaged girl sitting on a wall. She said that previously she would have felt inadequate, unable to contribute anything useful to the situation. However, having absorbed into her being the experience provided by her own good Samaritan, she spontaneously touched the child on the arm and murmured comforting words.

In some instances touch impacted on participants' thinking in that it fostered the *perception* of relationship, of togetherness:

> '*We're with each other*', '*there for each other*'.
> It's a '*mutual*', '*reciprocal*', '*two-way thing*'.
> Touch '*recognises/reinforces relationship*', also '*friendship*' '*closeness*', '*bonding*'. '*It breaks down barriers*'.
> '*It makes me more aware of*' and '*accepting of*' others.
> One participant used touch consciously in his work: '*I include people in a group by touching them.*'

Touch as communication

For some non-clients, physical contact broadened and deepened communication:

Touch '*says different things to words*', '*it says more*', '*it's stronger*', '*deeper*', '*more effective*', '*more powerful*'.

It also provided '*information*' about the other that was unavailable through verbal exchange — a clearer, fuller sense of the other's personality or being.

3) TOUCH EFFECTS POSITIVE CHANGE IN PEOPLE'S LIVES

Touch raised morale — it improved emotional state, mood, frame of mind; it increased self-esteem, and enhanced the ability to cope and succeed. Vivian found that a hearty hug in the morning gave her a boost of energy and happiness. As a result she felt able to meet work targets more quickly and easily. Lena found the same in her cleaning job. She had good and bad days. On a bad day she was tired, her muscles grumbled and her workload seemed insurmountable. A good day could be precipitated by a warm hug; it made her feel that life was worthwhile after all and she would bustle through her work humming favourite songs.

* * *

NON-CLIENTS WHOSE EXPERIENCES OF TOUCH HAD BEEN NEGATIVE (5.6%, *n* = 5)

The avoidance of hurtful or ill-intentioned touch, or touch from someone we have reason to dislike or distrust, is a rational response. However, habitual touch avoidance generally stems from irrational thoughts and feelings caused by negative past experience. This was the case with the five participants under this heading, all of whom experienced negative reactions to benignly intended touch because it stimulated memories of childhood abuse and/or neglect.

a) Negative physically-based responses to touch

'Tension'

Since relaxation was the most frequently mentioned consequence of welcome touch, it is perhaps not surprising that physical *'tension'* was the most commonly reported effect of unwanted touch. Not only actual touch but the *thought* of touch produced this effect and caused the participants in question to feel — aside from *'tense'* — *'contracted', 'strained', 'tight, my gut tightens', 'stiff, like an ironing board', 'wooden'.*

b) Negative emotionally-based responses to touch

The physical tension described by these interviewees was accompanied by negative feelings, commonly that of

'Fear'

When touched I feel *'fear, anxiety, panic', 'petrified, terror, shock', 'out of control, overwhelmed', 'untrusting, wary, on guard, vigilant', 'self-protective, self-defensive'.*

In addition to nervous and muscular tension, fear-emotions were sometimes accompanied by other physical sensations — *'stomach in a knot', 'sweaty', 'heart beating'* — the typical stress response symptoms described earlier (p.24).

Discomfort, 'shame, guilt, emabarrassment'...

I feel *'uncomfortable', 'awkward'* when people touch me.

This discomfort could be a general experience of physical and emotional discomfort, or a mixture of emotions that included a large discomfort component but also differentiated into other nameable feelings such as *'shy, embarrassment', 'shame', 'out of my depth', 'guilt — I shouldn't be doing this [i.e., touching]'* or *'I don't deserve this.'*

'Anger'

When touched I feel *'angry', 'rage', 'don't invade', 'get out of my space', 'get off', 'f*** off!'*

And — within the same emotional genre as anger but less intense — touch can be *'irritating'*.

Revulsion

Touch is *'disgusting', 'revolting, ugh, I can't BEAR it', 'I cringe','it makes the flesh crawl, yuck', 'I withdraw/draw back from it.'* from it.

A more muted form of this reaction was distaste or *'dislike'*, which in one instance included dislike towards the toucher.

c) NEGATIVE COGNITIVELY-BASED RESPONSES TO TOUCH

As may have been noticed, the emotional responses to touch described above were inseparable not only from physical sensations — the fight and flight ones — but also from thoughts, for example, the guilt that participants felt when touching was accompanied by the thought *'I shouldn't be doing this'*, or *'I don't deserve this.'*

* * *

PARTICIPANTS WITH MIXED TACTILE RESPONSES (n = 13, 14.44%)

For 13 participants childhood touch had been enjoyable on some occasions and unpleasant on others, therefore their responses to physical contact sometimes resembled those of the touch-acceptant and at other times those of the touch-aversive participants already mentioned. Each of these participants described the difference between touch-acceptant and -aversive states as 'relaxed' versus 'tense' respectively, and in all instances the relaxation was accompanied by positive and the tension by negative feelings. Now as adults if they received physical contact that was similar enough to past negative tactile events, it triggered unpleasant associations and was experienced as negative. The converse was true in the case of positively experienced physical contact.

Five men among these 13 interviewees felt *'nervous, scared, hesitant'* about touching others because they feared *'rejection'* or *'rebuff'* — women might reject their touch even if it was non-sexual, as might men because they feared it was unmanly or homosexual. These five participants were of non-tactile, Anglo cultures in which men generally did not touch each other except to shake hands sometimes in greeting and parting (although as stated earlier, Anglo tactile customs are changing and men in some social circles, particularly younger men, will now exchange greeting and parting hugs with friends.)

An unexpected cognitive response to touch expressed by two of the non-tactile English participants (and occasionally by other British individuals outside my sample) was the perception that tactile interaction, for example among Spaniards or Italians, was *'insincere'*. This suggests to me that a 'cycle of introjection' had taken place, that is, their childhood carers had rejected their authentic (sincere) touch needs and behaviours, they had introjected (internalised) their carers' anti-touch attitudes, in other words, had thoroughly absorbed them so that they had become part of their own personalities, and — coda to the cycle — were judging others according to these learned precepts (see Fromme et al., 1989:3).

Although not as vehemently so as participants who unequivocally rejected touch, the members of this mixed-response group were generally towards the less tactile end of the scale. They tended to be very selective in whom they touched, and to move cautiously into tactile communication with people who they felt sure were 'safe'. They were also less likely to initiate touch than more tactile individuals, with the exception of one participant who preferred to give rather than receive physical contact so that she could be *'in control'* of her personal interactions.

Summary

Participants whose previous tactile experience had been positive, or who had recovered sufficiently from a negative tactile past, responded positively to touch in the present — they felt

relaxed by it; warmed;
energised, invigorated;
strengthened, empowered;
nurtured, nourished, supported, comforted;
happy, optimistic, their pleasure in life heightened;
loved, lovable, valued, accepted;
loving, caring;
empathised with, understood;
safe, reassured;
whole, connected with themselves;
in touch with present reality, and in some cases with a deeper reality (humanity, nature, the cosmos ...);
their self-esteem, confidence, self-respect were affirmed;
and their relationships improved, were closer, more intimate.
If they were troubled by negative feelings such as anxiety, fear, worry, panic, depression or loneliness, physical contact allayed these feelings.

In contrast, participants with negative tactile-emotional histories generally felt tension, discomfort, anxiety, fear, panic, anger, irritation or revulsion in response to all, including well-intentioned, touch.

Those whose tactile histories had been a mixture of pleasure and displeasure tended to respond either positively or negatively to present-day physical contact depending on whether it was reminiscent of positive or negative past experience.

Note

1 '... warmth is a primary characteristic of touch...'
According to Major and Heslin (1982) touch communicates warmth when it occurs reciprocally within an equal relationship. However, when it occurs nonreciprocally and in an unequal relationship it can convey, and be interpreted as conveying, higher status, power and dominance in the toucher, and lower status and less power and assertiveness in the touch-recipient. The authors found that these two aspects of touch – warmth and status-difference – can be communicated either simultaneously or separately (see also Argyle, 1988:226; Fuller et al., 2011; Henley, 1977; Green, 2017:779–81).

Section II

Touch in psychotherapy

Chapter 7

Can touch help or hinder therapy? clients' experience

Bells of recognition may have pealed for therapists and clients looking at the summary of the last chapter, since the experiences reported by the beneficiaries of touch are goals of any therapy worthy of the name. As previously suggested, clients take their human condition — personalities, needs — with them into therapy. (To date I have found no evidence for the alien thesis mooted earlier, i.e., that clients transform into aliens as soon as they cross the therapy-room threshold and thus no longer need the same conditions to flourish as humans do.) Logically one might therefore assume that further research is superfluous — that at least some clients would enhance their happiness and health through touch from their therapists.

In order to test this assumption I interviewed 30 clients who had experienced touch in therapy, and spoke more informally with many others who had relevant experience.

The interviews with clients were conducted with a mind to my paramount research question, namely,

> '*Can touch help or hinder therapy?*'

As with the non-client participants, the words of client interviewees seemed to me a highly valuable contribution to psychological knowledge; I have therefore handed over to them and simply interpolated comments here and there in order to structure the material. The format used here is the same as that of the last chapter — **BOLD CAPITALS** for main headings; **bold** lower case for theme-words not actually mentioned by clients but which summarise what they expressed; '***bold italics and inverted commas***' for theme-words mentioned repeatedly by clients themselves; and '*italics and inverted commas*' for verbatim quotations from participants' interviews.

CLIENTS WHOSE EXPERIENCE OF TOUCH HAD BEEN POSITIVE

Twenty-seven of the 30 clients in my sample (90%) had found touch in therapy helpful. Since in my view the single valid test of successful therapy is whether the client experiences significant positive change as a result of it (Jacobson et al., 1984), I organised the material of these 27 interviewees in accordance with this criterion and emerged with the following change-related headings:

1) Touch produced positive change through its satisfaction of fundamental human needs.
2) Touch wrought positive change in
    a) the therapeutic relationship (the relationship between client and therapist);
    b) the accomplishment of therapeutic 'tasks' (the mechanisms of therapy — the processes and behaviours that need to occur in order for the client to achieve beneficial change); and
    c) the attainment of therapeutic goals.
    (It was Edward Bordin, 1979, who perceived therapeutic operations as comprising these three aspects.)

A single element of a client's tactile experience might produce change in one or more of these areas. For example, if through the therapist's touch the client feels safety and trust (fundamental human needs), that same safety and trust might enhance the client-therapist relationship and also facilitate the accomplishment of therapeutic tasks and goals:

Main Themes	(1) Touch wrought positive change through the satisfaction of fundamental human needs, e.g., for	(2) Touch produced positive change in		
		a) the therapeutic relationship	b) therapeutic tasks	c) therapeutic goals

Subthemes	safety and trust.	– by enhancing clients' sense of safety and trust in the therapist.	– because safety and trust increased self-disclosure and the willingness to risk new ways of thinking and behaving.	– because the self-disclosure and new ways of thinking and behaving increased psychological health and stability, awareness of self and others, and the ability to function successfully.

Example of the relationship between main themes and subthemes in client data.

1) TOUCH PRODUCED POSITIVE CHANGE THROUGH ITS SATISFACTION OF FUNDAMENTAL HUMAN NEEDS

Like non-clients, client participants needed touch both as an experience in its own right, and for the emotional and relational meanings it communicated, such as love and acceptance.

a) Physically-based needs satisfied by touch

'Relaxation'

Touch produced relaxation, a state much prized by participants. For Eva it was a 'corrective' experience and a source of relief:

> *'When I think about childhood memories there is a lot of physical tension in me. As a child I was left feeling hurt; I had to lie alone in bed after being abused and I had a lot of physical tension in my muscles and my mind. I feel the touch has helped with that — a lying-down hug being held close to [the therapist's] body melts away physical tension. If I feel somebody is physically containing me I can really relax and let go. I've had other kinds of therapy where there is no touch and it has always left me feeling rather tense.'*

Embodiment, 'real'

Physical contact can engender the experience of 'embodiment', that is, of being physically present, aware, alive — of *'being in'* our bodies. Sarah described herself as living in her head most of the time, a mode of being she found problematic. Touch in therapy had helped her

> *'hugely, because it draws you into your body. It brings your awareness back to your body if you live in your head. It's a much better feeling when you're in your body. And also then you're more aware of whether you're floating around, or grounded and solid.'*

If you were out of your body, said Werner,

> *'Touch brings you back into your body which is useful to keep things real.'*

b) Emotionally-based needs satisfied by touch

'Safety, trust', reassurance

Touch increased clients' sense of safety, security, and trust in the therapist and the therapy, qualities often cited as primary requisites for successful therapeutic outcomes (Benjamin, 1995a:26,28; Herman, 1992:168; Howe, 1993:16; Hunter & Struve, 1998:77,123).

Lynn had been sexually abused by her father. In many of her therapy sessions she was

> *'in that very young place, very vulnerable. I'd been abandoned — invaded, and also left — so when I was small I used to have dreams of my body not having boundaries, not being contained. Having someone holding me would make me feel safe because I could feel my boundary ... I felt more trusting of [the therapist] after she touched me.'*
>
> (By 'holding me' Lynn here means 'holding my hand'.)

The effects of safe touch in therapy often spread into extra-therapy life. Eva, for example, had *'become more trusting towards others'* so that she was able *'to hug and things like that more often, and to feel safe about it.'*

For Michaela touch was reassuring:

> 'It's showing me that it's really okay — I'm okay, what I'm going through is okay, it's going to be okay — and then I can be okay!'

Caring; 'holding, comfort, support, with me' feelings

— these were some of the words used to express the healing and strengthening effects of physical contact. Amy had internalised these qualities during the course of her therapy and so was better able to care for herself:

> 'Because of the holding from my therapist, I can hold myself better. I can comfort the frightened child inside me now.'

She was also more able to extend caring to others, for example,

> 'The touch has supported me a lot living on my own with a child. It has helped me to be more nurturing to my own daughter and give her more positive touch.'

A number of clients used the phrase 'with me' to express supportiveness:

> Touch said '*this person [the therapist] is with me.*'
> Susie

Sometimes just the availability of physical contact proved to be supportive whether or not the client actually opted to experience it (Hunter & Struve: 1998:27; Parkes et al., 1991):

> 'The therapist would say, "If you want me to hold your hand I will." It helped knowing it was there, and that I could.'
> Rosey

'Love'

Importantly, when touched by their therapists clients felt '*loved*'. This initiated an internal chain reaction; it enabled them to feel more self-love, and to reconceptualise themselves as loveable people:

> When my therapist touches me, '*I feel loved, unconditional love – and more and more unconditional self-love*'.
> Amy

End-of-session hugs *'helped me know that I was lovable'*.

Jason

'Even if I disclosed memories about negative actions I've done, if I afterwards had the touch and the holding, it showed me that now I don't have to feel guilty anymore, that I'm still a loveable person.'

Eva

When my therapist touches me *'I feel loved, which equals safety and trust.'*

Anastasia

'Acceptance'

Physical contact conveyed acceptance and dissipated self-shame:

'I felt I could go places with my psychotherapist that I felt ashamed about or felt really sticky or yucky or horrible – that she could then touch me. It would be like I'm not 'untouchable', so that would be a contrary message.'

Lynn

'... if you interact with a person and they're prepared to touch you physically it says that they find you acceptable in all sorts of ways that just talking doesn't confirm. It means they find you not repulsive and to them you're not smelly — your smell, and your general mien are acceptable, even likeable, because they wouldn't be able to touch you, to give you a full frontal hug if there was anything about you which they found repulsive. Non-verbal acceptance — it's another level of acceptance.'

Jane

For some clients a similar internal process occurred with acceptance as did with love, that is, tactually expressed acceptance from the therapist increased their *'self-acceptance'*.

'Happiness'

Sixteen of the 30 clients between them said that when touched in therapy their *'spirits lifted'* and they felt *'happy, wonderful, fantastic, great, good, lovely, well-being, yummy, enthusiastic about life'.*

Rob, for example, thought that when his therapist hugged him at the end of sessions it was

> *'a good signal that things have come to a conclusion. It's better than just "see you next week". I can feel the therapist's warmth, that she likes me and is wishing me well and it's a nice way of sending me off to face the week. If I was sad it might help me come out of that and make me better able to go out, and if I'm feeling in a better mood it might compound that — my spirits lift. It's a positive feeling.'*

Alleviation of unhappiness

In its capacity to raise people's happiness quotient, touch not only increased positive but alleviated negative feelings such as isolation, depression and anxiety:

> *'Without hugs you're isolated. Touch takes away isolation more than other things.'*
> Dave

> It gives *'the feeling that you're not alone — the antidote to the depressive world view that you* are *alone.'*
> Alice

Mia found that a single session with a body psychotherapist banished fear in an *'amazing'* way: *'Anxiety, worries about the future, fell away because you suddenly feel, Oh, that's part of me; it's there, in my body, you can touch it! It's not just a mysterious, horrible thing that's flying around in the air and taking you over — for me touch totally takes the fear out of things.'*

'Transformational' was Eva's description of therapeutic touch. *'I felt completely different after I had been held for a while. It was exactly what I needed. From feeling absolutely miserable and falling apart I woke up the next day and felt much stronger and that I could get things under control again ... The touch can change my mood from lonely and desperate to feeling more loved and contained and relaxed.'*

c) Cognitively- and emotionally-based needs satisfied by touch

'Self-esteem, confidence, valued, worthy'

> 'Touch makes me feel valued. I feel more worthy of love from other people now; I'm worth being loved, and being hugged.'
> Amy

> 'If someone feels able to touch me I have a sense that it's crossing barriers that I might have about my own self-confidence — barriers of "Am I okay?" ... Because I can get to a state where I feel untouchable — that sense of "Oh, God, will it ever happen again?" and in the meantime a frozen feeling. It becomes really special if other people can cross that feeling of being in a bubble — there's a sense of defrost, of warmth and contact — I'm just an ordinary person and people touch each other all the time and actually it's perfectly possible for that to happen to me!'
> Sarah

Chloe entered therapy because of a career crisis which caused her self-esteem to plummet. A hug from her therapist was an important part of a 12-session contract; it gave her the clarity and courage to enrol on a degree course about which she had fantasised for years:

> 'The hug was a vote of confidence; I felt really enabled.'

For Pippa the two-way nature of therapeutic embraces made her

> 'aware of how much I have to give as well as wanting and needing. It's like shifting from being a victim to having something to contribute.'

Rob expressed a similar idea. His (female) therapist's end-of-session hugs increased his self-esteem in two ways — not only by making him feel liked and valued, but also by allowing him to realise his own ability to give to others:

> 'If you're touching someone from whom you feel warmth, affection and positiveness, that makes you feel better about yourself. It brings out concern; it makes me realise that I can feel warmth, love, tenderness to other people. It makes you feel you can help

> *other people, and that makes you feel better about yourself rather than feeling I'm on my own and insignificant. You feel more important — you can affect other people and make their lives better; I'm better able to cope with life.'*

For Vicky, hugs and holding made her therapist's acceptance *'complete. It says that you and all the baggage that you bring with you is fine'.* This both bolstered her confidence and *'altered the way I was able to be with other people'*, which greatly improved her relationships.

Alice *'was feeling a failure. The touch was a salve to that feeling. It felt like being in safe hands, led out of a cul-de-sac.'*

> *Touch said, 'I'm happy to be with you. That makes me happy, and it's good for my self-esteem'.*
> Michaela

Growth; 'self-actualisation'

— in Maslow's (1968) meaning of the word, that is, becoming fully oneself, realising one's human potential:

'Human'

Steve found that end-of-session hugs over two years of therapy gradually *'reintroduced me to human contact ... I became a softer individual.'* It was a process of *'learning how to be a human being with an emotional life again'.*

Lynn was scathing about what she considered to be artificial boundaries between therapist and client:
Touching *'is a human reaching out. I've had therapy where that human reaching out feeling hasn't been present and it's felt very cold and clinical and like they're trying to protect themselves. It's so false. And what is there to be so scared of for God's sake? Just bloody drop all that I'm-so-perfect shit.'*

'Integration'

Several clients thought that physical contact had enabled them to integrate the therapeutic experience into their personalities and anchor it there. Eva, for instance:

> *'There's a very deep integration through touch; it helps me to integrate that I'm lovable.'*

Integration; reality orientation — *'present'*, *'real'*, grounding
Touch cohered people, gathered them up and delivered them into present reality.

> *'Touch makes you feel real.'* Vicky
> *'It brings me into the present.'* Werner
> *'Touch grounds me.'* Lisa
> My therapist's *'touching me connected me to myself because it kept me grounded.'* Amy

Integration as a result of 'embodiment'

> *'I'm more embodied; through the touch I was able to bring back the pieces I was scattering and losing in the world, and the energy... Lost parts of my selves return because I feel more whole again when I'm held, when I'm touched.'*
> Pierre

Some of the statements under the above 'self-actualisation' heading border on the 'spiritual'/transcendent in that they suggest the existence of a fundamental essence of humanness which underlies our shorter-term emotional experience and thoughts — a sense of something beyond, bigger and deeper, than the everyday. The clients in the section below fully embrace this metaphysical construction of human existence.

d) Transcendentally/spiritually-based needs satisfied by touch

> 'With touch *'you go beyond the mind. It's much more true — it's like a process of remembering who you are; you're in your essence'*.
> Naomi

'Whole'

> *'All the four parts of me — physical, emotional, mental, spiritual — touch brings them all together. It's very whole-making'.*
> Werner

'Connected'

A frequently expressed idea in this context was that of connection:

> *'Touch makes me feel connected – to myself, my body, to the therapist, to everything, to the source of who we are.'*
> Werner

2a) TOUCH WROUGHT POSITIVE CHANGE IN THE THERAPEUTIC RELATIONSHIP

A large body of research has found that a positive relationship between client and therapist is pivotal to effective therapy (e.g. Bachelor & Horvath, 1999; Hubble et al., 1999; Lambert & Barley, 2001; Norcross, 2001, 2002; Roth & Fonagy, 2005:461; Stiles, 2012). These findings apply across all therapeutic approaches in which this issue has been examined, including even those which in theory do not foreground the importance of the therapeutic relationship (e.g. behavioural therapy — Linehan, 1988; and cognitive behavioural therapy — Burns & Nolen-Hoeksema, 1992). It is therefore significant that (as in relationships outside therapy) the therapeutic relationship can be strengthened through physical contact.

'Warmth, acceptance; safety, trust'

Certain properties of touch that emerged earlier in this chapter enable it to effect this deepening of the client-therapist relationship, such as its capacity to convey '*warmth, acceptance*' and '*caring*', and to increase the client's feelings of '*safety*' and '*trust*'.

Containment

The quality of 'containment' is related to safety and trust (see Bion, 1962; Casement, 1985; Parry, 2011; Steckley, 2013; Winnicott, 1961:107, 1965). It could be described as the ability of the therapist to hold the client in a safe psychological embrace, no matter how distressing or chaotic the latter's experience. For some clients the embodiment of this holding in the form of an actual *physical* embrace added an extra measure of containment:

> *'It's very containing to be held [physically] in a session. It says, it's all right to be in the now with whatever is happening, there's*

> someone here who loves you and holds you with it. I think I could never have gone through this whole process of recovering from trauma through sexual and physical abuse and contain all these experiences in my mind with a therapist who was just talking to me — without having that physical holding. I would probably have gone mad. It makes a real difference from just verbal holding, or mental and emotional holding.'
> Eva

'Real, sincere'

Several clients thought that touch increased authenticity in the relationship:

> The touch said, "I'm not just saying it but I'll show it"; it's making it real, sincere.'
> Trish

'Real, help, security'

Alice had spent a few years with each of two therapists. The first (a psychoanalytic therapist) was somewhat cold and impersonal and did not use touch; the second (humanistic therapist) was warm, more human and natural in her behaviour towards clients, and did sometimes use touch. Alice preferred the latter because the therapeutic relationship felt more genuine with her, which gave her hope and security:

> '... two human beings in a room, rather than one human being and a cipher, someone that's trying to be a tabula rasa; it's more of a real relationship and the touch was another way of making it more real, which had a very good effect on my worldview because it made me feel that there was somewhere in the world that truth could be told: I could be myself, the therapist could be herself, and I could be helped — because if you're feeling depressed it feels like there is no place in the world where that can occur. And that was something I could really hold with me — I felt I really internalised it — the feeling that there was a port in the storm.'

'Real, connection'

The word *'connection'* cropped up here again:

> *The connection with the therapist and with myself's a lot deeper with touch. It's more direct, much more true. It's tangible — it's so real!'*
> Naomi

'Connected, closer'

> The touch *'made me feel connected with the therapist as a person, closer to her.'*
> Amy

'Relationship'

The first hug her therapist gave her was a landmark for Lisa:

> *'I felt valued by her in a way I hadn't before. It felt like a progression; we'd reached somewhere else in the relationship.'*

For Anastasia touch, love and relationship were bound together:

> *'Touch is the key. On a basic instinctive level, if someone wants to touch me they must love me; I must be lovely enough to be touched which is why you can short-cut the relationship, establish it faster... Holding hands you establish the connection immediately without saying anything.'*

Equalising

Several clients found that end-of-session hugs established a sense of equality within the therapeutic relationship — a

> *'sense that although we were therapist and client there was a human to human contact which was on a level. It makes it feel somehow related to the kind of interaction that I would have with a friend or family member. Usually in therapy I as client do a lot of talking and the therapist does a lot of listening — the*

uni-directional feeling of that is not really like a friend or family relation on the whole, whereas touch brings it into that more familiar territory'.
                                     Sarah

Because of his therapist's end-of-session hugs Bob thought that

'As well as him being a therapist and me being a client we were a couple of human beings and I like that very much!'

2b) TOUCH FACILITATED THE ACCOMPLISHMENT OF THERAPEUTIC TASKS

As observed earlier, specific therapeutic tasks need to be accomplished for positive change to occur in clients' lives. They do not all need to occur with every client, nor to the same depth, but it is very unlikely that none of these feature in a client's therapeutic experience. *Self-disclosure* is one of these tasks (Farber, 2006; Jourard, 1964,1974; Truax & Carkhuff, 1965), which generally leads to a second — that of *self-exploration.* Self-disclosure and -exploration within a safe space can in turn allow for *exposure* to memories and feelings normally avoided, and can facilitate *emotional release* (see Garfield, 1992). These processes — often considered essential mechanisms of therapeutic change — can be facilitated by touch between therapist and client (Jourard, 1963:341, 1964,1974; Jourard & Rubin, 1968:40; Pattison, 1973; Wilson, 1982:67).

Self-disclosure

'Safety, trust' leading to 'openness' and self-disclosure

Several aspects of touch encouraged self-disclosure and exploration, such as the *'deep level of trust and safety that comes with touch. It's like being held by the universe, and then you trust; then you're able to let go'.*
                                     Naomi

'If I know that me and this fella have an experience at the end of each session to give each other a hug, in the next session there's a greater spirit of trust and I'd be more likely to open up. The touch creates a greater state of openness, self-acceptance, giving me permission to say and do what I want in the session
                                     Bob

Lynn's was

> 'a very talking therapy. But there was a point when the therapist's words or her empathy would not be enough. I just needed her to hold me. That's when I would really drop down to my desperate places. When she first did that' [i.e., held one hand, about halfway through 12 years of therapy] 'it was such a relief. I felt so isolated and desperate; I was crying for help and she responded like you do — by reaching out. It made me feel safe. So I knew from then on I could really drop down and she would respond.'

A few months into therapy, when her therapist first hugged her at the end of a session, Trish felt that

> 'something really shifted in the relationship between us. I felt more safe with her because I trusted her more. I felt more warmth from her, and that she trusted me. There was something in the hug that changed that, that made the trust really real so that I could be more open, drop to more layers.'

'Warmth, acceptance, love/affection' and self-disclosure

Other facets of touch that eased self-disclosure were the warmth, acceptance and love/affection it communicated — although, as mentioned earlier, the therapist's emotional warmth often confounded attempts to determine the extent to which either touch or emotional warmth contributed individually to the desirable outcome.

Michaela thought that the warmth and acceptance transmitted *through* touch had provided an injection to her sense of well-being and her willingness to open up and *'spill the beans'*.

Eva found that

> 'If someone shows you love and affection one can be more open to them. It's as simple as that.
>
> People who disclose sexual abuse can feel very vulnerable. If my therapist is holding my hand it helps me to open up. It gives me permission now to talk about something which I had to keep secret for many years. There's of course verbal permission, but I think the actual physical touch gives me that feeling of support — that I don't need to be afraid to disclose things anymore.'

Eva had needed to relive and release past trauma during therapy sessions otherwise she became 'flooded' during the week and unable to cope. She found it easiest to engage in this process while lying down with her eyes closed. Her therapist, in 'person-centred' style, trusted her to know what she needed and followed her lead. For a good part of her sessions she therefore lay on a floor-duvet covered by a blanket. The therapist sat next to her on the floor and sometimes held her hand. In addition, towards the end of sessions after Eva had relived some harrowing memory of abuse, the therapist lay down next to her under the blanket, gathered her in her arms and held her, often keeping still, or sometimes gently stroking her hair or her back. After a period of silent holding, the therapist might summarise for Eva the story she had disclosed in the session, and perhaps speak affirming words to her, while continuing to hold her. Before Eva left, the therapist would hug her and kiss her goodbye. Each of these forms of touch had provided *'reassurance that it was okay to share what I had to say and that it will be safe for me to come again next time and open up more.'*

'Relaxation' promoted self-disclosure, and/or nurturance

A further stimulus to self-disclosure and -exploration was the relaxation induced by physical contact. A finding emerged in this connection which feeds into Tallman & Bohart's (1999:95) assertion that clients (rather than therapists) are the heroes of therapy, able to use what their therapists offer for their own self-healing: touch-induced relaxation was utilised by clients in two distinct ways — firstly, to *relax into calm*, that is, relax physically, rest, regenerate, feel nurtured, nourished; secondly, to *relax into arousal*, that is, into intense feelings that clients were otherwise unable to express fully, or at all, since they would normally have held these at bay by physically and psychologically tensing against them (Eiden, 1998:8; Goodman & Teicher, 1988:492; cf. Reich 1948:341).

Two clients commented on this dual function of touch-induced relaxation:

> 'Touch melts the armour. It relaxes... Or it can be very provoking; it can activate a very strong reaction and bring up a huge process.'
>
> Pierre

> Physical contact effected a *'letting go of all guard and defences and feeling safe enough to rest — or to discharge feelings'.*
> Anastasia

'Defences/resistance'

Pierre and Anastasia's statements indicate that touch can address the psychoanalytic concepts of 'defences' and 'resistance'. (These are the inbuilt self-protective mechanisms by means of which we shut away in the unconscious mind those of our experiences that contain more pain than we can consciously bear. We then sometimes resist the resurfacing to consciousness of these experiences in order to protect ('defend') ourselves from re-experiencing the pain (A. Freud, 1936).)

> With touch *'you lose your defences, you lose your armour — there are less layers, you can just go through to your core'.*
> Werner

> Touch *'eliminated my last doubts, my last resistance'.*
> Jason

Touch elicits feelings, sensations, thoughts and memories

> Physical contact *'helped me access my feelings and my body — it was an introduction to myself'.*
> Michaela

Touch communicates caring, and it is perhaps this as much as anything that heightens the desire and ability to self-disclose, as if the kindliness of a gentle touch conveys the message, 'This person is in sympathy with, reminds me of, the soft, emotional side of me so I no longer need to deny it or keep it under control; in this space and time I am free to express it.' It is a common experience that people who are upset can manage to 'hold it together' until empathically touched, say on the arm or shoulder, at which point they instantly burst into tears. Or else the upset or moved (touched) person says something like, 'Don't hug me, you'll start me off again and I've got to fetch the kids in a minute.'

For all of the above reasons — because it engenders safety, trust and relaxation; because it communicates acceptance, warmth and empathy — touch helps to elicit occluded or dormant aspects of clients' experience and to encourage their expression and release. There is evidence that some of the material involved in this process may not be accessible through verbal intervention but is only amenable through touch (Dunne et al., 1982:32; Ford, 1989; Hunter & Struve, 1998:128,134; Older, 1982:206; Smith, 1985:4647).

This was so in Rosey's case:

> '*I used to cry a lot with my therapist but it was restrained. Then after about six or seven months when I was crying she came and sat beside me and took me in her arms and hugged me — like a mummy. And that was very, very powerful because it enabled me to cry in an absolutely wracking, sobbing way which I couldn't have if I hadn't been contained in her arms — because I felt contained, safe, looked after ... and you can completely let go then and that was really wonderful — a very great release. It gave me a great sense of security.*'

For some clients the full, cathartic type of emotional release experienced by Rosey is essential to recovery (e.g. Powell, 2019).

Lynn's therapist, you may remember, held her hand six years into therapy (p.133). Shortly after this catalytic event, she visited a 'healer' whose use of touch evoked '*body memories of abuse — a sense that my body had memories, had feelings, that talking through words couldn't touch [sic].*' The two forms of therapy worked well in conjunction; she was able to take the memories recovered during healing sessions into her psychotherapy and process them there.

In Lynn's case the collaboration between psychotherapist and bodyworker occurred by chance. However, some authors advocate that non-tactile therapists embark on such collaboration deliberately because of the way in which touch can bring buried memories to consciousness and facilitate recovery (for suggestions on ways to achieve such collaboration see Benjamin, 1995a; Hunter & Struve, 1998:219).

This ability of touch to awaken dormant aspects of clients' histories is a phenomenon that earlier in life I would have dismissed as being on a par with fairies and other notions to which any properly brought-up (rational) present-day Westerner would be ashamed to give credence. However, having experienced it in my own therapy and then with my clients, and having encountered many therapists, clients and authors who have found similarly, I have no doubt whatever that physical contact has this capacity, and that touching a body-part involved in a past memory can sometimes draw that memory into awareness so that the conscious mind can process it (see Levine, 1997; Ogden & Minton, 2000; Rothschild, 2000).

Gilly, for example, complained of pain in her cheek during a therapy session. The therapist's gently holding her cheek evoked violent teeth-chattering and shivering, that is, manifestations of fear. These physical symptoms crystallised into a memory of being brutally punched on the cheek by her drunken father.

In Megan's case, memory release was precipitated by touch on a body-part less directly involved in the actual memory. Since her late teens — she was now 40 — she had experienced chronic pain and tension in her shoulders. Her therapist's gentle touch on the shoulders allowed her to relax them and relieved the pain and tension. However as soon as this occurred she felt a sharp, stabbing pain in her abdomen accompanied by a memory of being sexually abused; she had been unconsciously tensing her shoulders in order to keep at bay the more severe abdominal pain, and with it the horror of the associated memory.

Naomi found that touch elicited *'memories, feelings, sensations, or just awareness'*. It also intensified them:

> *'Sometimes it feels very painful because I start going down, sinking down into whatever's there. If you imagine normally you're on the surface, it's like diving to the bottom of the ocean. If I feel lots of fear or anger or frustration then I'll feel that pretty strongly. And other times the touch feels lovely — like light pouring into me.'*

Wendy's experience I found particularly remarkable. It concerned current events rather than her past history. Until her leg was injured in a car accident she had been very physically active and mobility had been a core facet of her identity. Having to hobble painfully rather than run and dance was thus deeply upsetting.

> *'After the accident I developed a regular throbbing, knocking pain where my heart is. It coincided with my heartbeat and was sometimes so bad that it woke me up at night.'*

Medical tests did not detect any heart problem.

Wendy was eventually so *'clogged up with feelings'* that she booked an appointment with a psychotherapist to whom she related the story of her accident.

> *'At some point in the story the therapist asked, 'Do you feel tension anywhere in your body?'*
>
> *I said, 'Yes, in my neck,' and touched the back of my neck to show her where the tension was.*
>
> *She came round behind me and very gently stroked that part of my neck – and it was is if she'd found a direct line to some place deep inside me which I didn't know was there. I started howling and sobbing uncontrollably; I could hear strange, wild animal sounds coming out of my throat as if they were separate from me. In the middle of the storm I shouted, "I don't want to live like this!", meaning life wasn't worth living with a damaged leg which stopped me expressing myself physically.*
>
> *The therapist let me get to the end of the outburst without interrupting; she didn't say a word — I probably wouldn't have heard her anyway; she simply used that gentle touch on my neck.*
>
> *Over a week later I realised that since the therapy session I hadn't once felt the throbbing pain in my heart, as if releasing those intense feelings and getting to the bottom of the* psychological *reason for the physical pain — finding out that I didn't want to live if I couldn't enjoy running and dancing — had somehow cured it.*
>
> *Being a sceptic I couldn't really believe the two events were connected. And maybe they weren't — maybe it was coincidence. But if I'm being honest I have to challenge my scepticism and say that I suspect the two events were very much connected — cause and effect, in fact — it seems just too much of a coincidence that I should have pain for weeks and then after a one-off event like that it should disappear immediately without trace.'*

Counteracting dissociation, reconnecting with reality, 'real, present'

The fact that physical contact can draw people into present reality was particularly important for clients who were dissociating, feeling fragmented/'all over the place', or who found it helpful to remain attached to a lifeline from the present while delving into painful memories from the past.

Lisa, for example, *'needed that [physical] contact to keep me in the present, in the moment — present with me and her in the room — when I was overwhelmed'.*

For Eva too touch imparted *'a sense of being present, in the now, so that I'm not in that traumatic situation anymore, even though I'm remembering it; I can feel there is another person here who is supporting me'.*

It is important to note, however, that **SOME CLIENTS FIND BEING TOUCHED DURING PAST MEMORY RECALL EXTREMELY JARRING — INTRUSIVE, AND DISTRACTING;** the therapist, after all, was not part of the client's past memory and any intervention during the reliving of it can distort, disrupt, even put a stop to his process. These clients may prefer being touched — hugged, held — when they have thoroughly finished reliving the past event, perhaps at the end of rather than during the session, as a way of being re-integrated and grounded before they rejoin the world.

For Sylvie the combination of sexual abuse and lack of caring touch during childhood had impaired her ability to be psychologically present. Thus far her therapy had not included touch and she was now keen to find a tactile therapist:

'I can hear and understand better if someone touches me when they speak to me,' she said, laying her hand on my knee to illustrate.

Wilhelm thought that

'The response to touch is something that you can't act; it comes from the core,' so working with touch was *'a lot more authentic, more real. It feels I am working on my whole self.'*

Touch and talk

A recurring theme, evident also in some of the above excerpts, was the comparison of touch and talk in relation to therapeutic efficacy. For Dan

'there's no greater therapy than physically felt warmth from another person — more so than just saying "I care." You get the intellectual message at the same time, but if someone has psychological problems there are so many barriers to believing words,

whereas with touch you can't not feel it, not be influenced by it, you can't block it out. It's so much more potent, more real. Primal. We're primed to respond to it from the minute we're born. Language comes later. It's extraordinary that it's not self-evident!'

Lynn found that sometimes only touch resonated with her state of being:

'If I'm in a body-emotional space a word coming over is on the mental plane and I just feel that's not doing anything for me; the therapist is going blah-blah — headspace talking to headspace — and I'm not in headspace at that moment. I'm in an emotion-body space. I need touch to communicate to where I am.'

For Dave there was *'something almost unreal about talking'* compared with the vivid impact of touch which *'reinforced the verbal work'*.

And Naomi found that physical contact *'cuts through, because words can affect your mind; they don't affect your body; they don't get in deep enough.'*

Rosey experienced the reparenting value of her therapist's touch (as had Sophie, p.142–143):

'Touch does something that words can't. For me it's very specifically about being a baby — feeling small and vulnerable and looked after in a way that is very therapeutic. It's a shorthand for lots of nice things — warmth, giving.'

Rob, discussing end-of-session hugs, thought that

'if you tried to express what you felt in the hug in words it wouldn't be the same — you could get the meaning across but you wouldn't be able to get the emotion. You could understand what the person was saying but you wouldn't get the feeling from the heart. It wouldn't work really — there has to be that physical, nonverbal thing.'

Pippa found that touch added depth to the therapeutic relationship — she felt *'a deeper empathy from the therapist with touch'* than with words.

'Touch,' concluded Susie, *'can say REAMS more than words.'*

2c) TOUCH FACILITATED THE ATTAINMENT OF THERAPEUTIC GOALS

Although the touch-induced satisfactions reported so far by clients clearly constitute therapeutic goals, I shall focus under this heading specifically on some of the most profound and permanent personality changes that occurred through touch — those that brought about a clear change of path in a positive direction, to the extent that clients sometimes perceived their lives in two halves — Before Therapy and After Therapy.

Clare felt rejected, *'untouchable'* and frustrated because her therapist refused to touch her. After eight years of this unsatisfactory experience she sought a new, tactile therapist. Clare considered the touch she received in this second therapeutic relationship to be the critical ingredient in her healing:

> *'The physical contact wakes up memories. It's a direct line to memory. You don't have to think because it's straight there in the body. The whole preverbal area that you can't access with words — the process of touch takes me to that place. Working through those early memories gave me a sense of peace for the first time in my life.'*

Pierre found that feeling his physical boundaries through caring touch had repercussions for his overall personality structure:

> *'I had very low self-esteem for a very long time. People could tell me that I was handsome, intelligent ... It didn't mean anything to me. I was not able to receive it. It went on the surface but it never penetrated in my body. The touch made me able to receive it, and it boosted my self-esteem. It made me more aware of who I am and respect who I am a lot more.*
>
> *When my body is touched [gesturing towards his chest],* 'I know my boundaries and I feel less invisible. I don't need to prove that I'm here. I don't need to make so much noise — to perform. I'm just here. And because I'm here, because I know myself and understand my senses and I've lived through my body [from] inside out, I'm also able to say "No"; if you have low self-esteem it's hard to say "No".'

Patrick had been sexually abused as a child and as a result was *'terrified'* of bodily contact when he first entered therapy. Over time, touch from his therapist taught him first to tolerate then to enjoy physical contact and was the major catalyst of recovery:

> '*Touch pushed me down a road to wholeness, connectedness, healing.*'

Naomi was another who felt that physical contact in therapy had swept her onto a different plane of being:

> '*Before I was pushing away a large part of myself and now I feel I'm really accepting all parts of myself — all the yucky, disgusting, horrible, shitty parts of myself — it's more and more unconditional self-love. If we hadn't had the touch, things wouldn't have changed so much — you can talk your arse off but it doesn't really change anything. It's helpful and it's releasing but all the shifts in consciousness happen in the moment through touch. That's where all the big changes happen. Then you actually experience exactly what you were talking about. You go into the direct experience of it; you're fully in it, you experience it in your body — and when you dive into an emotion and experience it fully in your body, then it starts to dissolve, and then it leaves you.*
>
> *I understand myself a lot better. Before I've known things, but now I've fully experienced them. I'm waking up, my health is improving dramatically*' [abdominal pain, exhaustion, and other medically unexplained symptoms], '*I'm much more in my body – more whole, lighter, and brighter.*'

Filling developmental gaps

Physical contact in therapy and the messages it transmitted sometimes filled the developmental gaps and healed the wounds caused by a lack of loving touch in childhood. Sophie had been held by her female therapist in approximately ten consecutive weekly sessions. Hers was one of the rare stories that offered a distinction between purely emotional love and tactile-emotional love:

> There was '*a lot of love in my family, and they expressed it. But although my mother was very loving, something was missing in the expression of the love. She found it difficult to be warmly maternal. There was something in her that couldn't give in that way — I remember not being held, so touch in therapy was the antithesis to that; I felt the therapist held me with a nestling, emotional, soft*

> *comfort. It felt wonderful, as if I was floating. It was comforting on a deep level. I felt more whole — much less of a void after being held — 'cause there was that sort of emptiness which I had a lot of my life. Touch makes you feel fuller, better in myself.'*

The healing-through-holding experienced by Sophie did not preclude her exploration of pain (a possibility sometimes cited as contraindicating touch-use). She recalled her therapist's support for her desperate sobbing as she relived being bundled into her pram during infancy and left alone in the garden to cry. The holding occurred *after* she had relived past distress and helped to heal it, 'made it better'.

> *'It's something that's stayed with me — it's a bit like, yeah, having reversed the hurt of something in the past, like being refound, not abandoned — found at the bottom of the garden and picked up. Made whole.'*

For Rosey too, therapeutic touch was reparative:

> *'My therapist used to kiss me goodbye on the cheeks. It was a kind of mummy kiss; I felt contained, safe, looked after. It gave me courage. It was very important because I never felt close to my mother. Something was missing; I was the middle of six siblings and for my first seven years there was always a baby around.'*

Rosey's before-therapy life was characterised by confusion, unhappiness, a feeling that something was wrong or incomplete. After therapy she felt more in touch with herself and others, had greater confidence, her outlook was far more optimistic, and she was able to fulfil deeply-held purposes — a stable relationship, a child, and a much-dreamt-of career.

Increased agency; the ability to function successfully

Eva found that physical holding became integrated into her being as psychological holding and improved her ability to function and succeed in life:

> *'To have the physical containment of my body has helped me to contain myself from session to session so that I could deal with*

what I had talked about, make changes I couldn't have made before — be more efficient, find a different flat, and take a training so that I can do some work.'

Modification of relationship patterns

As shown earlier, touch in therapy helped to rectify problematic relationship patterns. Through touch with a same-sex therapist Vicky found a more successful way of interacting with others (p.127), and Amy was able to nurture her daughter more effectively (p.123) ...

For several heterosexual participants, non-erotic touch in therapy also righted problems with opposite-sex relationships, both platonic and sexual. For example, hugs from an opposite-sex therapist made Dave more comfortable in the company of women generally:

> 'The embarrassment has gone. It's made me feel a lot easier in life.'

It also made him more able to express spontaneous warmth outside therapy through hugs, hand-holding, and conversational touch such as brief touches on arm or back when these were appropriate.

Lynn (who, concurrently with her usual psychotherapist, began seeing a healer who used touch — p.136, was still struggling with relationships at the end of 12 years of therapy:

> 'I knew I needed to work more with touch and my body and my emotions. I was so tense, and sometimes I couldn't feel my body. I'd worked through an awful lot of talking and feeling but I felt there was a deeper way of working — of talking, feeling and working with the body. I'd had lots of issues with lovers and partners and not being able to respond — to be in my body and be physical — so I knew past stuff was still locked in my body.'

In order to shift the final obstacles to her recovery, Lynn left both her original therapist and the healer and found a therapist who integrated touch into her work:

> 'I could allow my body and my feelings to come up; her holding me or touching me would communicate directly to that place — that

body part of me.' The process at last freed her *'to be physical and loving and expressive'* within a stable sexual relationship.

Ailene was 50 when she told me her story. She was born in Africa to mixed-race parents, and had been fostered from early childhood in the UK by a rigidly non-tactile, White Catholic family.

At the time of her interview, Ailene had never experienced a sexual relationship, a circumstance she traced back to childhood experiences. Her convent school had taught that touch and the body were sinful. Although her skin colour was light brown it was singular enough in a small, all-white town to make her so conspicuous that none of the boys would ask her out *'because it would have got back to the nuns at school by the next day'*.

The following is her remarkable account of how non-sexual touch from a male therapist resolved social-sexual problems (Hatfield, 1994; Montagu, 1986;204; Offit, 1977; see Harlow et al., 1963; Malmquist et al., 1966); it removed her fear of men, changed long-held self-negating patterns and awakened the desire for a sexual relationship for the first time since her teens:

> *'I came in for my first session feeling like ten tons because my body was so exhausted. The touch from the therapist was nourishing; my body felt loved and cared for. Different parts of my body were being heard. The first time you go into therapy the psyche says, "Someone is hearing me," and it was the same with my body. Because there was somebody there to listen, I could hear what my body was saying, and because I can hear what it is saying I am more caring of it.*
>
> *The part of my body that was holding its breath let go and the knowledge resonated through the whole of my body and the whole of my being — it was a holistic understanding that was very helpful. It's like the body secrets have been shared with all of me — like that moment when you tell somebody something you've held for years.'*

Touch elicited the pain she was storing, enabled her to release it and replaced it with increasing pleasure. As a result she could now allow her physical sensations into awareness rather than blocking them off as she had used to do in order to prevent the pain from surfacing.

> '*The touch made me aware that I had body armouring — and that's dropping. I think a lot of the energy now is reaching my body, which didn't before because it was armoured off. There's a different spring in my step. There's an aliveness to my body that wasn't there before and that helps all of me. It's a bit like Cinderella — let's go to the ball — the ball of life — my body can go to the ball. It might seem strange going to a ball and not having your body with you, but it can happen!*
>
> *I always thought this is a thick, dense body — that it didn't know anything, and I realised, that's where I hid my pain — in my body — so that I didn't have to feel anything. Now it's all right for my body to be sensitive; it doesn't have to find a way of desensitising itself because it's not frightened anymore, because a lot of the pain has gone. Now there's more pleasure in my body because it can be the instrument it is.*
>
> *Years ago I would be in a bad mood, I would have a headache and I didn't know it was because I was hungry — that's how not in touch I was with my ability to sense. That has improved in relation to a lot of things. My body was able to discover what it had been missing, also that it could respond in the way it did to touch. It feels much better!*'

Ailene had previously feared and shunned any kind of physical contact. However, within the safety of the therapeutic setting, exposure to touch dispelled the acute shame she had felt about her body and her sexual inexperience. In so doing it nourished her confidence as a woman, repaired her self-esteem:

> '*More and more my dresses are clingy; now I'll be out showing the shape of my breasts — that sense of wanting things to cling more to my body. It feels more sensuous. It's very freeing; I feel an inner freedom. My body can be part of that — it too is feeling freer and freer.*
>
> *With touch you get a whole experience — you get it directly — through your body and through your emotions, and that is very powerful. It's great that my body now feels it can be part of the whole. It feels more part of the team. It says, "I have a voice and I'm going to input information into this dynamic as a whole."*
>
> *The touch has given me understanding that I didn't have before on male-female relationships — that level of being comfortable. Now it's all right not to know certain things. Even if they're common to other women, it mightn't be for this body and that's*

all right. And that's been the most important thing — because there was always this feeling as a woman of lagging behind. I felt inadequate, but I don't anymore, and I feel that has come through touch. It's given me confidence. Before there was shame because I hadn't been in a relationship with a man. I would say, "At this age I ought to know." That was running through my head in my 20s and 30s, and now it doesn't matter. I used to sigh and think, "I'll never be there." There was this sense of a child with its nose up against a pane of glass looking at something you can't get at. I think there was that sense in my body of "I'm always outside, or I don't know the game and I don't know how to play it. I see it being played but I can't get in because I don't know the game."

I don't care now — it's all right if you don't know, and anyway, other people don't know either. And that brings a whole new train of events — or will do. My body is ready to play!'

* * *

CLIENTS WHOSE EXPERIENCE OF TOUCH HAD BEEN NEGATIVE

For three of the 30 clients in my sample (10%), touch in therapy had been a highly negative experience. Although the number of these participants is small, their experience is not unique (see Geib, 1982, 1998; Horton et al., 1995:452) and much may be gleaned from them about the misuse of touch in therapy. The following features were common to their narratives:

1) A history of negative tactile experience
All three had experienced negative touch in the form of childhood abuse. The physical contact from their therapists restimulated feelings associated with the abuse. (In no way does this imply that everyone who has been abused chooses not to be touched — readers will have noticed that this is patently not the case (and see Caldwell, 2002; Older, 1981) — nor that everyone who is uncomfortable with touch in therapy has been abused.)

2) The touch evoked fear
The most intense emotional response to touch for these clients was that of *'fear'* and allied feelings — *'panic, unsafe, out of control, overwhelmed, uncomfortable'*.

3) **The therapist's touch was perceived as caring.**
For one of the three this added to the discomfort caused by the touch itself in that it gave rise to conflicting feelings towards the therapist.

4) **The criteria for effective touch-use were disregarded**
There are established criteria for effective touch-use that need to be observed if the touch is to be therapeutic (see Chapter 11): briefly, therapists should ensure that clients have choice and control over every aspect of the touch; they should as a rule discuss the use of touch with their clients before using it, and they should not use it without the client's informed consent. With adherence to these stipulations any touch that occurs does so in a manner and at a pace that clients find acceptable and that enables them to process and heal painful touch-related issues.

In the case of the three interviewees under discussion, each of these criteria was infringed. For Mimi this resulted in her feeling *'really uncomfortable'* and *'imposed upon'*. Her mother was highly dysfunctional and had meted out unwanted, threatening touch that Mimi had found *'repugnant'*. Touch in therapy stirred unconscious memories of her mother's touch in a way that was too overwhelming for her to be able *'to think about'* them:

> *'I knew the therapist was doing it with good intention, good feeling. But it didn't respect my defences. It felt that the touch happened more quickly than I was able to let my defences down. I was struggling to stay in relation to the therapist and keep the contact going — that was difficult enough, never mind the physical dimension of it. It was overwhelming. I wasn't ready to let that kind of experience in. I felt backed up against a wall, cornered, as if you have no defence and something's coming at you — very threatening — panic!'*

Although this event was not discussed afterwards (let alone before), Mimi thought the therapist must have realised her discomfort because she never again used physical contact in their sessions. Fortunately the touch-intervention occurred after safety and trust were well established between therapist and client. Because her experience of therapy until that point had been positive, Mimi conceptualised the touch as a *'failed experiment'* and continued in therapy.

June and Emma, however, terminated their therapy specifically because of their therapists' touch. June had suffered consistent physical abuse at the hands of her mother and a terrifying experience of rape as an adult. Even talking about touch caused her to feel *'anxious inside me, a bit weepy. It's quite difficult for me [now in this interview] to carry on focusing on touch'.*

She described her only session with a male therapist:

'This guy' [the therapist] 'patted my knee to reassure me about something. It was horrid — stressful, scary, frightening. I immediately went into fight or flight mode.'

June chose flight, and later restarted therapy with a therapist who was more alert to her needs.

Emma had found her therapy *'really good'* — except that the therapist touched (held, hugged) her in every session without her permission. The touch was *'uncomfortable, unsafe'* and no opportunity was created for Emma to disclose this. She felt unable to broach the issue herself because she perceived the therapist to be acting out of caring and was afraid that to reject her touch would hurt or embarrass her. She was also reluctant to *'rock the boat'* and thereby *'spoil the nice feeling between me and her'.*

Eventually Emma's discomfort with the physical contact overshadowed the positive aspects of the therapy and she left to find a safe, non-tactile therapist (a psychoanalyst, whom she found very helpful).

Summary and conclusions

It is clear from comparing client and non-client material — this chapter and the previous one — that the same themes occur in both, indicating that the psychological factors determining the effects of touch in everyday life operate also within the therapeutic encounter.

When the criteria for effective touch-use were disregarded by the therapist and the touch inappropriately administered it was counter-therapeutic, even to the point of terminating therapy.

When appropriately applied, as in most cases (90%), touch greatly contributed to clients' well-being. It strengthened the therapeutic relationship; thawed 'resistance/defences'; and increased clients' acceptance of therapy and therapist. In so doing, it enabled and expedited the accomplishment of therapeutic tasks such as self-disclosure, self-exploration, exposure to painful feelings and memories, and emotional release; and it helped to stabilise overwhelmed or dissociating clients by grounding them in present reality.

By these means touch facilitated the achievement of therapeutic goals: it satisfied fundamental human needs both for physical contact in its own right and for the emotional qualities it conveyed (love, caring, acceptance, empathy, safety, trust...); it redressed developmental deficits in clients with negative tactile-emotional histories; it changed unsuccessful relationship patterns to successful ones; altered negative self-beliefs to positive; mended punctured self-esteem and self-confidence; promoted relaxation, well-being, pleasure and happiness; strengthened the psychological characteristics required to cope and succeed; and in a number of cases wrought profound, permanent personality change which enabled clients to adopt a significantly happier and more satisfying life-course. Moreover, there is indication that in certain circumstances, touch is the *only* therapeutic tool by means of which to achieve these outcomes.

Chapter 8

Wisdom from the literature

> Taboos imply the power of touch.
>
> Peloquin (1989:301)

One of the biggest surprises of this research for me was discovering the wealth of information on therapeutic touch that already existed. Having conducted my own research into the matter I then searched the literature for that of others. (The order of these two events was happenstance – of a fortunate kind, it turned out, since it prevented my being biased by published evidence and opinions.) Aside from many outstanding articles, there were whole books devoted to the topic, so well-argued and compelling that I would have expected them to set the world afire and change attitudes to touch forever. The fact that they did not and that I and mainstream teachers and colleagues were completely unaware of this impressive body of work is, I suspect, part and parcel of the touch taboo.

The literature is too abundant to report on in detail but too pertinent not to mention since it strongly supports the case for appropriately used touch in therapy. Besides, it may whet readers' appetites. I shall therefore present glimpses of it as a kind of minimally annotated list.

Since my research corroborates that of other authors I have arranged their findings under the same main headings as I did my own. In the first section of this chapter, as before, I have homed in on key words occurring in their work. These are presented in *'bold italics within inverted commas'*. Because of the similarity in findings across the board—because the concepts and actual words of both non-clients and clients in my samples recur repeatedly in the literature—readers may experience a sense of déjà vu, indeed, of ennui, in this chapter. It is to be hoped, though, that this repetition has the advantage of creating a tidal wave of evidence which roars so loudly that it can no longer be ignored.

POSITIVE TOUCH IN PSYCHOTHERAPY

When appropriately used
1) TOUCH IN THERAPY MEETS FUNDAMENTAL HUMAN NEEDS

Touch is the surest way to bring about *'embodiment'* — the enlivening experience of being 'in' our bodies (Jourard, 1966:230; 1968:148; Moran, 2010; Sartre, 1943) — and the sense of a *'body self'* which, according to some theorists, is the foundation of the psychological self (Fisher, 1986,1990; Freud, 1923:26;1927/1957:31; Schilder, 1935).

Physical contact can induce deep *'relaxation'* (e.g. Boyesen, 1970:32; Liss, 1976:244), with its attendant reparative effects (Fritz, 2016:228; Grandin, 1992; Nelson, 2006; Peloquin, 1989:310; Puszko, 2009; Siegal, 1989:34). It can transmit both physical and emotional *'warmth'* (Alagna et al., 1979:470; Boadella, 1976:316–317; Linden, 2015:9–11; see Howe, 1993:12,15), and is *'vitalising'* — or *'revitalising'* in the case of those who have become dispirited (Jourard, 1968:148; Keleman, 1981; Liss, 1976:242,248; Mahler & McDevitt, 1982:226).

Besides being **'an experience in its own right with considerable significance for personal development'**, touch transmits positive interpersonal messages and thus meets fundamental emotional needs (Woodmansey, 1988:58); it conveys the qualities of *'acceptance'* (Geib, 1982; Horton et al., 1995:451); *'empathy'* (Kupfermann & Smaldino, 1987:234; Peloquin, 1989; Wyschogrod, 1981:40); *'love'* (Boguslawski, 1979; Brown, 1973:113); *'affection'* (Joshi et al., 2010; Linden, 1968); *'understanding'* (Goodman & Teicher, 1988:493); *'concern'* (Older, 1977:198; Rogers, 1970); *'support'* (Holroyd & Brodsky, 1977; McCorkle, 1974; Smith, 1998a:11); *'caring'* (Berry, 1986; Heslin, 1974; Ingham, 1989; Purtilo, 1978); *'compassion'* (Thomas, 1994:42; Weber,1990:37); and *'comfort'* (Benjamin, 1995a; Dominian, 1971; Huss, 1977:15) — as Older observed (1982:201),

> touch is 'a source of comfort inherent in our mammalian heritage'.

Physical contact can therefore be *'affirming'* and *'validating'* (Peloquin, 1989:303); it can convey *'reliability'* (Kupfermann & Smaldino, 1985; Mahler & McDevitt, 1982); provide *'reassurance'*

(Bar-Levav, 1998:54; Majno, 1975:105; Spotnitz, 1972:457); and create or increase feelings of *'safety, security'* (Goodman & Teicher, 1988:492; Horton et al., 1995: 451; Hunter & Struve, 1998:129; Main, 1990) and *'trust'* (Clance & Petras, 1998:98; Benjamin, 1995a:28; Horton et al., 1995:443,451).

Touch can both evoke these positive feelings, and allay negative feelings such as *'anxiety'* (Hunter & Struve, 1998:109; Torraco, 1998:162); *'panic'* (Eiden, 1998); *'stress'* (Tobiason, 1981); *'depression'* (Hollender, 1970; Hollender & Mercer, 1976; Linden, 1968; Stein & Sanfilipo, 1985); *'acute distress'* (Holroyd & Brodsky, 1977,1980; O'Hearne, 1972:452); *'grief'* (Mintz, 1969a); *'self-hatred, shame'* (Benjamin, 1995a:26); *'isolation, loneliness'* (Mintz, 1969a; Robertiello, 1974a,b; Shepherd, 1979; Wilson, 1982); and the expectation or sense of *'rejection'* (Forer, 1969:230).

Physical contact can improve *'body image'* (Benjamin, 1995a:30) and increase *'self-acceptance'* (O'Hearne, 1972:453; Milakovich, 1998:88) and *'self-esteem'* (Andersen et al., 1987; Geib, 1982; Holroyd & Brodsky, 1980:443; Horton et al., 1995). Sometimes it lends an **unconditionality** to the communication of affirmative qualities, for example, it can express *'unconditional acceptance, unconditional love'* (Horton et al., 1995:451). And not only does it satisfy the need to receive these positive messages, but also to *'give, express, share'* them (Hunter & Struve, 1998:12,21), *'to give of the self'* (Goodykoontz, 1979:7).

Touch can be *'integrating'*, or *'reintegrating'* for those who feel as though they are falling apart (Kupfermann & Smaldino, 1987:234); it can strengthen the sense of identity, build a sturdier *'sense of self'* (Forer, 1969:230; Krueger, 1989,1990; Kupfermann & Smaldino, 1987; Mahler & McDevitt, 1982). In the words of Edith Wyschogrod (1981:37),

'Tactility is the sense which enables us to attain the feeling of a unified self.'

2a) TOUCH CAN STRENGTHEN THE THERAPEUTIC RELATIONSHIP[1] (Hunter & Struve, 1998:105; Kupfermann & Smaldino, 1987:234).

It is 'an action which bridges the gulf many people develop between themselves and others'.

Jourard (1968:136)

In the therapeutic as in any relationship, this 'bridging' function is achieved by the capacity of touch to facilitate interpersonal *'contact, connection'* (Gadow, 1984); *'closeness'* (Anderson, 1985); and *'intimacy'* (Burgoon et al., 1984; Thayer, 1986a, 1986b); and to convey the supportive *'I'm with you'* quality (Berger, 1977:46).

By engendering feelings of *'reciprocity'* (Frank, 1957:215,224; Merleau-Ponty, 1962:322; Older, 1982:240), *'mutuality'* and *'equality'* (Forer, 1969:231), touch offsets the potential power differential inherent in the therapist-client relationship (Benjamin, 1995b:26).

Physical contact is a primary means of *'communication'* (Geldard, 1960; Hall, 1959; Lomranz & Shapiro, 1974), which is fundamental to any relationship. It can also serve a secondary communicative function by reinforcing or modifying verbal messages (Hunter & Struve, 1998:17; Older, 1982:203; Thayer, 1982:264), and it can imbue communication with a sense of *'immediacy'* (Andersen et al., 1987:90; Mehrabian, 1971) (that is, alive, in-the-moment experience).

2b) TOUCH CAN FACILITATE THE ACCOMPLISHMENT OF THERAPEUTIC 'TASKS'[1] (Bordin, 1979)

It can *'lower resistance/defences'* (Timms & Connors, 1992; see Ferenczi, 1930); *'break through impasses'* in therapeutic progress (Milakovich, 1998:74); *'contain/hold'* clients who are experiencing pain and distress (Benjamin, 1995a:30; Eiden, 1998:7; Hunter & Struve, 1998:109; Steckley, 2013); assist in the *'endurance of pain'* (Bar-Levav, 1998:54); and *'access memories'* and *'emotions'*, some of which cannot be accessed through verbal interaction (Dunne et al., 1982:32; Ford, 1989; Hunter & Struve, 1998:128,134; Older, 1977:198,1982:206; Rosenthal, 1975; Smith, 1985:46–47).

> Touch facilitates the 'resolution of beliefs, behaviors, and/or emotions that have otherwise remained frozen in time'.
> Hunter and Struve (1998:134)

Because it increases *'trust'* (e.g. Benjamin, 1995a:28), *'safety'* (Hunter & Struve, 1998:129) and *'openness'* (Holroyd & Brodsky, 1980:443; Frank, 1957; Jourard, 1968; Schutz, 1967; for all three of these qualities, see Horton et al., 1995:443,451), physical contact can promote the *'self-disclosure'* and *'self-exploration'* (Derlega & Berg, 1987; Jourard & Rubin, 1968; Lomranz & Shapiro, 1974; Pattison, 1973; Pedersen, 1973) so necessary to both successful talking therapy and general psychological health (Jourard, 1968:47).

Touch is useful for *'establishing'* or *'re-establishing contact with reality'* in clients who are dissociating or acutely anxious (Geib, 1982; Little, 1981:117; Peloquin, 1989:303; Phelan, 2009:100; Spotnitz, 1972:457), and it can *'ground'* clients in the present even as they relive past incidents (Hunter & Struve, 1998:133).

That physical contact enhances the sense of self — increases *'ego strength'* (Forer, 1969:231; Hunter & Struve, 1998:130) — is particularly pertinent to therapists who consider positive ego strength important to successful therapeutic outcomes (Kernberg et al., 1972; Sohlberg & Norring, 1992).

As a result of the above properties
2c) **TOUCH CAN FACILITATE THE ACHIEVEMENT OF THERAPEUTIC GOALS**
— that is, produce positive change in clients' personalities and lives. It can provide *'corrective emotional experiences'* (Eiden, 1998:7; Goodman & Teicher, 1988:494) for those whose tactile-emotional histories have been wanting and can thus redress 'developmental deficits', a term proposed by Kohut (1977) to describe the psychological problems in adulthood caused by childhood emotional deprivation. In this role touch can serve an extremely important *'reparenting'* function (e.g. Fagan, 1998:147; Goodman & Teicher, 1988:494; Hunter & Struve, 1998:108,134; Mintz, 1973; Woodmansey, 1988:57); it can *change negative self-beliefs to positive*, such as 'I am unlovable' to 'I am lovable' (Horton et al., 1995:451); and *'provide a model'* of warm, respectful touch-use for those previously lacking in one (Gorlin, 1990; Older, 1982:209).

Physical contact can enhance *'self-awareness'* and *'insight'* (Timms & Connors, 1992:38), for example into emotions and sensations (Hunter & Struve, 1998:154); and it can foster *'development'* and *'maturation'* (Spotnitz, 1972:455,457) where this has been delayed or interrupted:

> Touch ... can contribute to growth, and it can contribute to healing where growth has been disrupted.
> Kertay and Reviere (1998:16)

Physical contact can reduce *'distress and trauma'*, *'posttraumatic stress disorder'* symptoms (Herman, 1992) and the impact of *sexual and physical abuse* (Field et al., 1997a; Lawry, 1998; Milakovich, 1998). This last it does partly by enabling abuse survivors to gain control over their bodies through learning to set personal boundaries in relation to touch (Benjamin, 1995a:28; Horton, 1998:132). They hereby reclaim a *'sense of ... power and agency'* (Horton et al., 1995:452). In addition, through safe physical contact survivors are able to explore, take pleasure in and benefit from non-sexual *'intimacy'* (Heslin & Alper, 1983); and to change their perception of touch, their bodies and themselves from one of pain, fear or disgust, to one of acceptance and pleasure (Benjamin, 1995a:28; Hunter & Struve, 1998:220; Imes, 1998:180).

For all of the above reasons, clients have experienced touch as a source of *'healing'* (Older, 1982; Peloquin, 1989:302,309; Thomas, 1994:42) and *'well-being'* (Eiden, 1998:6; Peloquin, 1989:302).

* * * *

Links between tactility and other aspects of personality

As maintained earlier, avoiding hurtful or ill-intentioned touch, or touch with someone we have reason to dislike or distrust, is a rational response. However, habitual touch avoidance is likely to indicate psychological problems such as low self-esteem (Andersen, 1999:48), 'communication apprehension' (Andersen et al., 1987) and difficulty in creating and sustaining relationships (Andersen & Leibowitz, 1978:90; Hatfield, 1994:4; Montagu, 1986:286).

Johansson (2013:51–52) found that, compared with touch accepters, touch avoiders were insecure and fearful of other people; they felt inadequate because of 'not knowing how to touch' others, and experienced anxiety about their own physical body and their appearance.

Forer's (1969:229) view of habitual touch-avoidance is sweeping:

> 'Psychoanalysis has shown that the taboo against touching..., the unconsciously-motivated renunciation of touching parts of bodies ... is predominant among conscience-dominated, obsessive-compulsive personalities who isolate their thought from their feelings, their minds from their bodies, their selves from others, emphasizing self-control, rationality, aloofness.'

Rolando Toro (1999, personal communication) considered that the non- or low-tactility characteristic of some societies, since it is incompatible with optimal health, amounts to 'cultural pathology'. And Larsen and LeRoux (1984) go so far as to maintain that same-sex touch avoidance reflects rigid, authoritarian — and Machiavellian! — attitudes.

Conversely, comfort with touch has been found to correlate with positive personality attributes such as self-confidence; assertiveness; active rather than passive modes of problem resolution; absence of negative affective states (shyness, loneliness, depression); openness to expressing intimacy; satisfactory social relationships; higher levels of social competence; and contentment with oneself, one's childhood, and with life in general (Fromme et al., 1989:3,5; see Jones & Russell, 1982; Johansson, 2013).

Fagan and Silverthorn (1998:72) conclude that

> 'people who are comfortable with their bodies, with touching, and with being touched have fewer emotional problems,' and that 'the ability to understand communication from others as communicated by touch is an important component of mental health ... Therapists may have more trouble accomplishing their therapeutic tasks if they cannot use touch to help people become more comfortable with and knowledgeable about this most basic area of emotional communication.'

NEGATIVE TOUCH IN THERAPY

Sexual interaction between therapist and client

The most harmful form of negative touch in therapy is generally that of sexual interaction between therapist and client[2] (Ben-Ari & Somer, 2004; Brown, 1988; Koocher & Keith-Spiegel, 2016; Pope, 1990a,1990b,2001; Russell, 1996; Sonne et al., 1985). According to a tally by Hunter and Struve (1998:101) at least 40 authors have likened the dynamics of therapist-client sexual interaction to those of incest (Freud among them (1915/1983), also Masters & Johnson (1976) who pioneered sex therapy).

Pope and Bouhoutsos (1986:5) found similarities between post-traumatic stress disorder (a common consequence of child sexual abuse – Trask et al., 2011) and the impacts on clients of sexual involvement with their therapists. They termed these phenomena the 'therapist-client sex syndrome' symptoms of which include an inability to trust others, labile mood, suppressed rage, guilt, a sense of isolation and emptiness, identity and boundary problems, cognitive impairment and increased risk of suicide.

Detrimental non-sexual touch in therapy

Not only is sexual contact within the therapeutic relationship generally harmful; *non*-sexual touch can be detrimental if used inappropriately, that is, without regard for clients' needs and wishes. It can evoke fear/panic (Forer, 1969:231) and anger (Geib, 1998:122), and in some instances cause premature termination of therapy (Horton et al., 1995:452). Clients who have been raised in tactually abusive and/or neglectful families in particular may experience touch as negative (see Fromme et al., 1989:12; Geib, 1982; Sorensen & Beatty, 1988), indeed, may be retraumatised by it (Benjamin, 1995a:30, 1995b:25). These deleterious consequences of non-erotic touch result from a failure to observe the established criteria for successful touch-use (see chapter 11).

LACK OF TOUCH IN PSYCHOTHERAPY

> If a therapist decides to touch a given patient, he or she must do so in a thoughtful manner and must be willing to accept responsibility for the patient's interpretation of the touch. Likewise, if the therapist decides not to touch, there must be a similar willingness to accept responsibility for the meanings that the patient will assign to the absence of a natural form of human contact.
>
> Kertay and Reviere (1998:16)

In some cases the lack of touch in therapy can harm clients by eroding their self-esteem; it can evoke feelings of being unlovable and untouchable (Horner, 1968; Imes, 1998:182) and a shaming sense that the natural wish for touch-comfort is somehow bad (Horner, 1968; Lewis and Streitfeld, 1972:210).

Summary and conclusion

> The therapist who chooses not to employ touch when such an intervention has the potential to facilitate therapeutic progress is just as accountable to claims of exercising poor clinical judgement as is the therapist whose touch interferes with therapeutic goals.
>
> Hunter and Struve (1998:151)

Touch 'interferes with therapeutic goals' when it is inappropriately used. As a rule, the form of touch that has the most negative impact on clients is that of therapist-client sexual interaction. However, non-erotic touch can also be counter-therapeutic if the therapist fails to observe the substantiated criteria for successful touch-use. In the large majority of cases touch *is* appropriately used and is significantly beneficial across a wide range of presenting problems. In view of this, some advocates of therapeutic touch conclude that to withhold physical contact when it would help diminishes the effectiveness of therapy. Moreover, since it is ethically incumbent upon therapists to do their best for their clients, depriving them of helpful touch could be considered unethical (Milakovich, 1998:80; Morgan, 1995:42), albeit unintentionally.

Notes

1 **'TOUCH CAN STRENGTHEN THE THERAPEUTIC RELATIONSHIP' and 'FACILITATE THE ACCOMPLISHMENT OF THERAPEUTIC "TASKS"'.**
    Several, though not all, studies have shown that touch in therapy increases the client's positive evaluation of the therapist (Alagna et al., 1979; Boderman et al., 1972), and the therapy (Heslin & Alper, 1983; Pattison, 1973). In one study, for example, clients who were touched by therapists on the shoulder or back perceived them as more attractive, more trustworthy and as possessing superior expertise compared with non-touching therapists (Hubble et al., 1981; Zur, 2007a). This is interesting in view of research showing that the more expert and plausible a therapist is perceived to be, the more likely it is that healing will occur (Frank, 1961,1973; La Crosse, 1980:325; Snyder et al., 1999; Strong, 1978; Strupp et al., 1969:77).
    In contrast, a study by Stockwell and Dye (1980) revealed no significant difference between touched and untouched clients' perceptions of their therapists. The researchers suggested that this might be because their client-participants were touched according to the dictates of a prearranged experimental plan rather than in response to their own needs and internal processes (see Horton, 1998:127). (This seems likely, given how important it is that any touch which occurs does so in answer to clients' needs!)

2 **'The most harmful form of negative touch in therapy is generally that of sexual interaction between therapist and client....'**
    Such interaction is prohibited in the ethical codes of all major psychotherapy organisations, such as the British Association for Counselling and Psychotherapy (BACP) (2010) and the American Psychological Association (APA) (2010).

Chapter 9

Origins of the touch taboo in psychotherapy

> Taboo implies a prohibition which is maintained on the basis of tradition rather than rationality.
>
> Mintz (1969a:234)

Taboo in this context can be defined as a practice, or the discussion of it, that is avoided for sociocultural reasons.

The previous chapters have shown that touch provides enormous benefits in both everyday life and in therapy. Why then is it avoided in so many talking therapies? How is it possible that these therapies are prepared to reduce their overall efficacy by forgoing the powerful asset of physical contact?

The answers to this question lie in a confluence of historical factors that have prevented sections of the psychology establishment either from being aware of the evidence concerning touch, or from appraising it realistically.

Freud and psychoanalysis

The taboo against touch in psychotherapy originated with the very first talking therapy in the Western world, namely *psychoanalysis,* or *psychodynamic therapy.* (These two terms are often used interchangeably. For readers new to them, psychoanalysis/psychodynamic therapy was founded by Sigmund Freud (1856–1939) who posited that part of the human mind is unconscious, and that a major source of adult personality lies in childhood experience. He believed that repressed memories and feelings from early childhood are stored in the unconscious mind and can be the cause of psychological problems; if this repressed material were brought to consciousness and expressed, the patient was likely to be cured (Breuer & Freud, 1895; Jones, 1961:223; Yakeley, 2012:268). These principles, or variants of them, are widely accepted today, although other Freudian theories have been discarded in most modern psychology.)

Ironically, it was Freud who initiated the use of therapeutic touch (Breuer & Freud, 1895). He would place his hands on a recumbent patient's forehead with a view to eliciting repressed memories, or would massage a patient's neck and head to encourage emotional expression.

It was Freud also who first provided a theoretical rationale for the use of touch in psychotherapy:

> The ego is first and foremost a bodily ego ... [it] is ultimately derived from bodily sensations, chiefly from those springing from the surface of the body. It may thus be regarded as a mental projection of the surface of the body ...
> Freud (first sentence, 1923:26; rest of quotation, 1927/1957:31)

From this premise one might assume that a deficit of needed bodily sensations would beleaguer ego development (McNeely, 1987:70; Smith, 1985:3–4).

However, like Victorian England with which it was roughly contemporaneous, Freud's Vienna was beset by several touch-negating precepts. One was the 'mind-body duality' inherent in Western thought — the separation of body from mind — an idea that can be traced back to the Greek philosopher Plato (427?–347 BC; see Plato's 'Phaedo') and is particularly associated with the French philosopher René Descartes (1596–1650) (Descartes, 1642; McNeely, 1987:12; Smith, 1998a:4).

This mind-body dichotomy paved the way for the development of related cultural memes, among them the evaluation of intellect as superior to body and emotion — what Don Tucker calls 'intellectual chauvinism' (2007:40); and 'scientism', that is, 'excessive belief in the power of scientific knowledge and techniques' (Oxford English Dictionary) or, as Doron Swade has put it, 'the deification of science as the superordinate discourse in Western culture' (personal communication, 2005).

Christian doctrine was a major contributor to these aspects of 19th-century thought. It too separated the body from the human entity as a whole, and it was permeated by the puritanical denigration of bodily pleasures. Over the centuries it acquired formidable power to dictate behaviour even in the most personal areas of life.

The Christian Church was focused on gaining influence and consolidating power during the Middle Ages. In this regard, Christian leaders discouraged people from engaging in physical contact outside the sanction of official Church policies. Nonsanctioned touch was viewed with intense suspicion and was portrayed to represent witchcraft or curses of the devil or was simply judged as nonsensical. Through time, Church policies became increasingly restrictive and punitive against those who violated the established Christian norms about physical contact.

Hunter and Struve (1998:46)

Sexual pleasure in particular was deemed impure, sinful; and sexual thoughts and deeds were ringed around with guilt and shame. There are still individuals today who carry deep scars as a result of this aspect of Christian dogma, such as the men I have counselled whose guilt with regard to sex has rendered them sexually impotent (and see Ailene, p.145–147).

In this ideological milieu, affectionate non-erotic touch came a cropper on several counts — not only because it was considered unscientific and non-intellectual but because it belongs to the soft, nourishing genre of experience to which the puritan responds with self-denial. Moreover, it can at times resemble, and contains the possibility of crossing over into, sexual touch. This was an added reason for its being regarded with suspicion, to the extent that much of Christian society became vigilantes on the look-out for physical contact just in case it should harbour hidden sexual motives. (There still remains a strong tendency in current Anglo-Christian societies to construe most forms of touch as sexual, nudge-nudge-wink-wink.)

Freud was embedded in the intellectual life of his place and time, was a scientist (a doctor and neurologist) by training, and the touch-discrediting concepts mentioned above had been part of his world since earliest childhood. Unsurprisingly, these concepts wove themselves into the very core of psychoanalysis. Physical contact at the time lacked intellectual cachet and — probably because he was keen for his newly formulated theories of the human mind to achieve scientific respectability (Smith, 1998a:7) — Freud abandoned his earlier use of touch when presenting *psychoanalyse* (psychoanalysis) to his contemporaries (Freud, 1912–1913; Mintz, 1969b; Older, 1977:198). ('Psycho*analysis*' is a left-brain, scientific-sounding sort of word.) The puritanism of Freud's Vienna, and the sensual and sexual repression that were part of it, are reflected in the *rule of abstinence*, an underlying tenet of psychoanalysis which embodies the denial of needs. Traditional psychoanalysts did indeed deny their clients' basic relational needs for empathy, support and warmth: they were cold and impersonal. The need for touch was especially strenuously denied; it was not only subject to the rule of abstinence but was in addition fraught with difficult, conflicting emotions.

In all, therefore, rather in the way that arctic conditions favour the existence of polar bears, 19th- and early 20th-century Austria produced perfect evolutionary conditions for the creation and proliferation of a therapy, such as psychoanalysis, with an inbuilt touch taboo.

The influence of national cultures on touch in therapy

Following its beginnings in Austria, psychoanalysis was adopted and influenced by English and American converts to the approach. As Jules Older pointed out (1977:198), the leading psychoanalytical theorists are thus from three cultures — Teutonic, English and American — which share a strong anti-touch tradition. And, as discussed earlier, tactility is determined largely by culture.

Moreover, cultural influences are so woven into our psyches that we are often notoriously blind to their presence and therefore do not query them. Therapists and theorists share this human characteristic: they emerge from the societies in which they practise and are likely to approach their work with the conditioning prevalent in their cultures of origin. This is due partly to the *'mere exposure'* effect (Zajonc, 1968; Panksepp, 1998:38,259), that is, simply being exposed to something, whether it be home cooking or religious beliefs, generally predisposes us towards it. However (as is flagrantly clear from practices such as female genital mutilation (FGM) and child marriage) what we unthinkingly accept because it is the cultural norm is not necessarily what is best for us, our children, our clients or our societies. It is therefore of benefit to question and, if necessary, to repudiate traditional mores. Since research findings show unequivocally that touch is a fundamental human need, I suggest that, in the same way as with any negative cultural practice, the taboo against touch warrants questioning — and repudiation.

I have not done a formal study of whether or how therapists from tactile and non-tactile societies differ in their attitudes to physical contact in therapy but my impression is that those from tactile cultures are more likely to touch their clients.[1] A South American therapist I interviewed who had lived in England from the age of nine carried her bicultural upbringing into her work in that she treated her Latin and English clients differently. I requested a demonstration of this while I role-played the client. When I was the Latin client she sat immediately next to me and touched me. *'Let the feeling come out of your belly,'* she said gently in Spanish, touching my middle, her head bent towards me. The enormous warmth and caring she communicated was — touching! It contrasted with her behaviour towards me as I role-played the English client, when she sat a few feet away and was less warm and intimate.

Whereas Anglo therapists largely accept the no-touch-in-therapy rule, psychoanalysts and non-psychoanalysts alike, therapists I have encountered from tactile cultures have regarded the rule with bewilderment. A Dutchman I met while writing this book was astonished to learn that in some therapies touch is prohibited and that I felt it necessary to write a book about its therapeutic value. 'But that's known!' he exclaimed. At the time he was working in a Dutch elderly people's home where many of the residents had dementia or Alzheimer's. Whereas talking to them sometimes failed to arrest their attention, touching them (for example, on knee or arm) was often the only way to call them out of their own worlds into reality so that for a while they could experience the enlivening warmth of human interaction. With patients who were particularly unreachable, tickling them briefly and lightly on the nose sometimes did the trick.

He related a moving story about an elderly man in the home who hit a woman resident over the head with a stick. The rest of the staff understandably wanted to separate the aggressor from the other residents. However Johan, my Dutch friend, was disinclined to do so. 'Leave him with me for five minutes and he'll be happy again,' he suggested. He then took off his coat and wrapped it round the old man. From his illustrative gesture I could see that the wrapping motion was a caring, 'tucking in' one. 'Congratulations,' he said thereafter, heartily shaking the old man's hand, 'you have a new coat!' At this the man looked ecstatic and exclaimed emotionally, 'All I've wanted all day is a hug!' Johan then gave him a hug.

The coat was a sensitive and generous means to get beyond the prevailing male culture in which 'men don't hug', particularly elderly men brought up in a past generation; to express warmth and connection they playfully 'poke or punch' each other, said Johan. He pointed out that it was different with women and men; with women he as a heterosexual man needed to be sure that the touch was not sexual, and was not perceived as sexual by the recipient.

In the case of the elderly resident described by Johan, touch was the needed restorative. Coming from a tactile culture, Johan could see the need and respond to it without having to contend with an internal barrier of anti-touch prejudice. It seems probable that it would be more difficult for therapists from non-tactile cultures to do this, or even to be aware that they may perhaps entertain such prejudice.

Subcultural influence on touch in therapy

As stated earlier, national cultures are not the only determinants of tactility. Minority subcultures too can influence how and to what extent we touch others, and some of these subcultures are created by activities and trainings which foster tactile behaviours that differ from the mainstream; for example, arts trainings such as drama and dance give rise to communities in which touch is far more liberally exchanged than is the norm in non-tactile Britain (see p.102).

Importantly in this context, psychoanalytic training also engenders communities of like-minded members. As with any training, it generally biases its trainees towards the particular viewpoints it teaches. In all 25 therapists I interviewed officially and many others with whom I spoke unofficially, attitudes to therapeutic touch corresponded with those of their trainings, even though these were sometimes at variance with their extra-therapy attitudes and behaviours.

A study by Milakovich (1998:89) found that therapists are significantly more likely to touch their clients if they are given explicit permission to do so by their tutors and supervisors. And like Milakovich and others (e.g. Pope et al., 1987), I found that exponents of therapies other than psychoanalysis sometimes touched their clients, whereas psychoanalytic therapists on the whole did not. Thus none of the six psychoanalysts in my sample of therapists used touch; their trainings had strictly prohibited it. Three of the six reported feeling obliged to respond in kind if a new client held out a hand to shake before the latter had learned that hand-shakes between client and therapist are not customary in the traditional psychoanalytic setting.

The remaining 19 therapists in the sample practised non-psychoanalytic therapies and used touch to different extents with their clients.[2] Their trainings had either not forbidden it or had actively encouraged it. A male practitioner among them used touch with clients in group but not in individual therapy because he feared being misunderstood or sued.

Two therapist interviewees exemplified the powerful influence of trainings particularly clearly. The first had been psychoanalytically trained and therefore started out non-tactile. Excited by a chance discovery of massage and body psychotherapy, she completed further study in these approaches and now combined verbal and tactile therapy. The second therapist was initially non-psychoanalytic in orientation and was happy to offer the occasional hug or reassuring hand on a client's arm. However, after retraining in psychoanalysis she became strictly non-tactile.

The subcultural factor is especially influential in communities created by psychoanalytic trainings, since historically these communities have been closed. This has encouraged their 'cultural encapsulation' (Wren, 1985); in a closed environment tradition is more likely to be insulated against outside change and to continue unchallenged.

The fortunes of psychoanalysis

Psychoanalysis spread. Freud was a gifted thinker, speaker and writer who attracted others to his ideas. He was also part of the altruistic post-World War I zeitgeist in Europe which aspired to social justice and equality; through psychoanalysis Freud envisaged creating a healthier society that would never again stray into the horror of war. To further this end he opened free therapy clinics for the poor, as did others whom he inspired (Danto, 2005). Psychoanalysts and their protagonists founded formidable numbers of training institutions and consolidated ties with other establishment bodies such as the medical profession, universities, and publishers who promulgated psychoanalytic thought.

Initially the only Western talking therapy on offer and thus free of opposition from alternative approaches, psychoanalysis eventually established itself so securely as the sole respectable method of examining the human mind that by the time other therapies came along they went more or less unnoticed by psychoanalysts and often by the general public. The psychoanalytic hegemony thus remained intact, and with it the touch taboo. Furthermore, psychoanalysis was by then so powerful within the therapeutic canon that aspects of it — including attitudes to touch — became integrated into many non-psychoanalytic therapies.

Since Freud's era the touch taboo in everyday life and in therapy has loosened its hold. Non-psychoanalytic therapies have come to the fore and psychoanalytic influence has declined somewhat. However, despite these changes, Anglo society has not moved on quite enough to challenge the status quo with regard to therapeutic touch; the above-mentioned habits of mind — mind-body dualism, scientism and remnants of the repressive aspects of Christian ideology — are still sufficiently present in Anglo-Western discourse to leave the touch taboo intact.

* * *

It is important to note, firstly, that although some psychoanalytic trainings unfortunately still follow the cold, unempathic tradition, many others have embraced positive approaches and release graduates who are wonderfully warm, empathic and supportive; secondly, that the qualities of empathy and warmth are invaluable in their own right and there is no automatic conflation between these qualities and touch. Indeed, for some clients touch is wholly inappropriate (see chapter 11), whereas empathy is appropriate for all clients.

* * *

Summary

The national cultures that have influenced psychoanalysis are those of Austria/Germany, North America and England, all of which have non-tactile traditions. The attitudes inherent in Anglo tactile norms are thus both reflected in and perpetuated by the touch taboo in Anglo therapy. In addition, psychoanalytic trainings form a subculture that has strictly maintained non-tactility. The touch taboo in psychoanalysis is held in place by these dual national and subcultural forces.

For a considerable time the psychoanalytic approach within therapy discourse was so powerful that some of its tenets — including those respecting touch — spread beyond its own confines and became integrated into many non-psychoanalytic talking therapies.

This state of affairs still persists since the cultural forces that gave rise to the touch taboo, although diminished, are nevertheless still sufficiently in place in Anglo society to buttress the touch taboo in therapy.

Notes

1 **'I have not done a formal study of whether or how therapists from tactile and non-tactile societies differ in their attitudes to physical contact in therapy but my impression is that those from tactile cultures are more likely to touch their clients.'**

   If this hypothesis is valid it would be interesting to know whether it extends to psychoanalytic therapists (perhaps someone would be interested in taking up the issue). Would a fully tactile South American psychoanalyst be as anti-touch as a British one? That is, would the dictates of the traditional psychoanalytic canon be more influential than those of national culture even in a fully tactile society?

2 **'The remaining 19 therapists in the sample practised non-psychoanalytic therapies and used touch to different extents with their clients.'**

   Psychoanalysis dominated psychotherapy discourse until a fundamentally different approach – the *humanistic* approach – was created by Carl Rogers (1902–1987). Rogers initially trained in psychoanalysis but subsequently rejected it and evolved a system that redressed what he considered were its deficiencies. His groundbreaking article of 1957, 'The necessary and sufficient conditions of therapeutic personality change', became the bedrock of humanistic therapies. According to Rogers, the most important of these necessary conditions are 'unconditional positive regard', empathy, and congruence (that is, being real, genuine, rather than a blank screen). These qualities are communicated by therapist to client. They contrast sharply with the impersonal behaviour of traditional psychoanalysts. Watching footage of Rogers at work one sees his tremendous warmth, acceptance – love – for his clients. (Rogers would have cited 'love' as one of his necessary conditions, but would not have been published had he done so. He therefore coined the term 'unconditional positive regard' (Merry, personal communication, 2000). Later, though, he refers to 'nonpossessive love' (e.g. in Shostrum's film, 1965).)

Because humanistic therapists generally behave warmly, supportively and genuinely towards their clients, and because touch is a natural way to communicate these qualities, it is not surprising that humanistic therapists will sometimes touch their clients.

The 19 non-psychoanalytic therapists mentioned above were all of the Rogerian, humanistic mould. The specific forms of therapy they practised were person-centred, integrative, gestalt, body psychotherapy (see p.80,207–208), life coaching and massage therapy.

Chapter 10
Counterarguments to the touch taboo

> We live in a culture in which touch is easily sexualised and has sexual connotations and is therefore avoided. Do we, as therapists, contribute and collude with the client's apprehension about touch? Do we fear that touch invites sexual contact? Do we refrain from it out of fear, and not because we believe that it is bad for the client?
>
> Eiden (2002:1)

It is understandable that therapists in non-tactile cultures, psychoanalysts especially, are wary about incorporating touch into their work. Bernd Eiden outlines several reasons for such wariness. His first is *'fear of the therapeutic relationship being sexualised ...'* (Eiden, 2002:1).

Although the word 'taboo' implies that the embargo on non-erotic touch in therapy is irrational, in this regard the taboo has logic to it: it is indisputably the case that any — even non-erotic — touch, is more likely to lead to therapist-client sexual interaction than no touch.

However, as the wise educationalist Peter Abs advised (1974:23),

'One must again and again return to the person before us'.

— in this context, one must discover whether the fear of sexualisation is valid in terms of how people *actually* feel when experiencing non-erotic touch. Do they become sexually aroused? Do they receive non-erotic touch as it is intended or are they instead unable to distinguish between sexual and non-sexual contact?

On both these counts the answer is clearly 'no' in the case of children who thrive on abundant non-sexual touch, are traumatised by sexual touch and, according to the reports of abuse survivors, are generally able to distinguish between the two.

Perhaps, then, the belief holds true for adults; perhaps individuals who have developed sexually are unable to distinguish non-erotic from erotic contact, so that all touch for them is actually or potentially sexually arousing. Certainly in Anglo cultures this would appear to be true of some adults because of the tendency in these cultures to perceive most touch as sexual.

However, these are precisely some of the individuals whom therapeutic touch has helped. It has enabled them to experience the difference between sexual and non-sexual physical contact, and to accept tactile nurturance — to sink into a hitherto unknown realm of relaxation and well-being. Their experience and personalities have thus been deepened and their relational opportunities multiplied and enriched.

My own, small client sample of 30, the majority from *non*-tactile cultures ($n = 22$, 73%), showed that at least some non-tactile individuals are able to discriminate between erotic and non-erotic physical contact: none of the 30 was either sexually aroused by their therapist's touch or misattributed sexual intent to it, and 27 of the 30 (90%) found it significantly helpful. Within tactile cultures the ability to distinguish between sexual and non-sexual touch is even more likely. Indeed, studies suggest that it is the norm in many such cultures to do so, and to experience non-sexual touch as nurturing (see Rosa in this text, p.94; Jung & Fouts, 2011; Konner, 1976; Marshall, 1976:315–318; Prescott, 1975; Tronick, 1995, 2007).

In the opinion of Reuven Bar-Levav (1998:55),

> Forbidding touch on the basis of the possibility of stimulating an erotic transference [see p.177] essentially reflects the fears in the therapist. ... such an assumption is also theoretically incorrect. The yearning of a patient for the therapist's love is not sexual [but the] yearnings of the panicky infant to be mothered safely and perfectly.

Attachment theory (Bowlby, 1969,1973,1980) adds weight to this view; in emphasising the supreme importance of a close, intimate bond between child and primary carer, attachment theory

> logically implies (and experience confirms) that patients who lacked adequate mothering in early life require — like children — actual physical care-giving.
>
> Woodmansey (1988:57)

Whether or not individuals have received adequate parental care in childhood, security and emotional warmth are required for optimal well-being throughout life (Bowlby, 1988:46; Clarkin & Levy, 2004:209; Howe, 1993:59; Montagu, 1986; Rutter, 1980:275). This is even more the case when people are distressed, frightened or ill (Bowlby, 1979:129; Stein & Sanfilipo, 1985; Woodmansey, 1988:59) which is often when they attend therapy. In these negative feeling states there is a tendency for adults to revisit earlier, more dependent stages of development and to benefit from the forms of nurturance by which children are comforted (Bowlby, 1988:140; Dominian, 1971:897; Howe, 1993:12,59) — which may well include touch (Hunter & Struve, 1998; Morris, 1971; Smith et al., 1985; Stein & Sanfilipo, 1985; see Hollender & Mercer, 1976; Montagu, 1986:28).

In this connection we see one of the bizarre illogicalities that come with taboo territory: responding to a baby's need for being held in everyday life is known to be essential for the baby's healthy development. However, holding a client who has regressed to childhood and powerfully experiences the same need is considered inadmissible (Smith, 1998a:7).

Such is the power of the taboo that the staunchest advocates of touch sometimes appear to succumb to its pressure. Spotnitz (1972:458), for example, maintained that gratifying infantile needs 'smothers the incentive for change and fixates the patient at his current level of development'. Very occasionally even Hunter and Struve, within their outstanding contribution to touch literature, appear to fall prey to taboo-think. In no way does this diminish my enormous admiration for these authors, as is evident from the scores of times I cite them. Their book, *The Ethical Use of Touch in Psychotherapy* (1998), is essential reading for any therapist interested in touch-use. I refer to them here merely to illustrate the power of taboo — if they are perhaps swayed by it then surely anyone could be.

Hunter and Struve (1998:106) echo Spotnitz's sentiments regarding fixation: 'Touch ... can have the effect of assisting a client in fixating on gratifying her emotional needs within the therapeutic relationship because it is safer to do so.'

The notion of 'fixation' calls for scrutiny lest it be one of those that has been around for so long in psychoanalytic parlance that we accept it without checking its validity. It implies obsession, or being stuck. It would be inappropriate — would pathologise a healthy state of affairs — to describe a baby as fixated on the one-to-one love from his primary carer even though it is the lynchpin of his life. Care should be taken not to pathologise an adult who has been inadequately nurtured in the past and who as a client relishes the tactile nurturance that is his birthright. It is a sign of health that the desire to meet his needs is still alive in him and presents itself for fulfilment when the opportunity arises (— it is what I call 'theratropic', that is, involving the natural pull towards health, the innate capacity to heal).

I have found no actual evidence of 'fixation' in the above sense (and indeed, wonder whether any exists?); children mature and change, and in general so do adults. Just as total relaxation and trust characterises the healthy dependency of early childhood, so an unhurried period of the same gives badly-parented clients the nourishment and strength they need to thrust themselves into genuine independence; and at both periods of life the individual herself will indicate when the dependent stage is completed. To follow this development through to its natural end requires trust also from the therapist — trust in the client and in her therapeutic process — and perhaps patience, since clients who have not received sufficient tactile care in childhood will require different, sometimes copious, amounts of it before they are sufficiently filled up with nurturance to move on from this phase.

I am aware though that simply because I personally have not encountered this kind of fixation doesn't mean it does not exist! If it does, however, the risk of incurring it might be worth taking at least in some instances, since individuals whose touch-needs have been denied have a hole in their make-up that requires filling if they are to normalise and reclaim their wholeness.

Hunter and Struve themselves (1998:108,134) present compelling examples of the healing value of 'reparenting' touch and cite the satisfaction of 'nurturance' needs as a major touch-benefit (1998:107). They nevertheless assert, contradictorily I think, that 'it is generally inappropriate to use touch in a situation in which the client is *merely* attempting to use that physical contact to gratify infantile needs' (Hunter & Struve, 1998:149, my italics). For the client, however, 'providing nurturance' in the manner of a temporary parent figure is no different experientially from 'gratifying infantile needs'. Also, I wonder why the authors refer to the '*mere*' gratification of needs when their own excellent examples show that for some clients such gratification is central to healing.

Hunter and Struve again (1998:106): 'The assumption that when a client has reached her fill of this type of embryonic bliss, she will get on with her development may not happen'. This is true. However, presumably the development has not yet happened in the *absence* of 'embryonic bliss'. Furthermore, if we extrapolate from research evidence, such bliss is a healthy experience in its own right, whatever happens after it (see, e.g. p.30–31). Indeed, in the natural order of human development *an individual's confident independence and positive sense of identity is only possible if her or his needs for complete dependence as a baby have been satisfied*. Therefore, if the touch-deprived client receives sufficient tactile nurturance in therapy she is then perhaps *more* likely to 'get on with her development'.

'Touch, just like any other therapeutic intervention, needs to propel a client forward along the developmental path,' Hunter and Struve continue (1998:106). A most important and valid assertion; if inexpertly handled, touch (like any intervention) can impede therapeutic progress, for instance, collude with clients' patterns in avoiding the pain that may accompany such progress. It is worth noting therefore that for some clients, such as Sophie (p.142–143), it was specifically the 'embryonic bliss' experienced through the 'gratification of infantile needs' that in large part 'propelled her' on her journey to wholeness. The touch she received was appropriate, well timed and in no way interfered with her feeling and expressing the pain she was carrying. Similarly, for others in this study (for example, Rosey, p.136,140,143), reparenting touch was instrumental to healing.

Nevertheless, let us don psychoanalytic spectacles for a moment and assume that the touch taboo is a rational strategy for preventing both therapist-client sexual interaction, and also non-erotic touch since this might lead to sexual interaction. Even accepting the epistemological framework of psychoanalysis, we are obliged to admit that the taboo fails as a strategy in both supposed purposes.

With respect to sexual interaction between therapist and client, research has shown that it occurs (Pope et al., 1994), and that it is liable to cause serious harm to the client (e.g. Pope & Bouhoutsos, 1986). On this basis a *prohibition* against sexual touch in therapy is right and proper. Prohibition or limit-setting, however, is not taboo. A sensible prohibition is instituted on rational grounds for people's benefit. Taboos, as has been pointed out, are generally irrational and can be of questionable benefit.

Given that the taboo fails to prevent sexual interaction it would seem professionally responsible to try a more workable strategy. We are not in a position to discover through controlled experiments whether or not *more* therapist-client sexual interaction would occur in Anglo-cultural therapy if the taboo did not exist, since it does. However, that such harmful interaction occurs at all is reason enough to do our utmost to prevent it. I suggest that dismantling the taboo — clearing away the irrationality and emotional charge that attaches to taboos — might be more effective than the present status quo. It would entail changes in current therapy practice, such as the open discussion of tactility; examining the available evidence with left brain logic and realism; instituting prohibitions on rational grounds where appropriate; and educating therapists in tactile matters.[1] The teaching of touch awareness and related issues might make it easier for therapists to recognise signs of sexual attraction in themselves (Gutheil & Gabbard, 1993) and, before erotic desire became overwhelming, to deal with it in the supportive environment of supervision (Hunter & Struve, 1998:254).

To any who fear that thinking or talking about sexual interaction would increase its prevalence, research offers comfort. In a study by Pope and colleagues (1986), 95% of male and 76% of female psychologists in private practice reported experiencing sexual attraction to at least one client. However, 90.6% of males and 97.5% of females did not act on the attraction and engage in erotic contact with their clients. It appears therefore that the thought of sexual interaction is different from the deed and as a rule can be entertained with impunity (Hall, 1987; Hunter & Struve, 1998:253). In fact, disclosure of sexual desire on the part of therapists might well decrease the prevalence of sexual interaction since talking openly about feelings often diffuses their intensity (Baruch, 1949; Evison & Horobin, 1985,1999; Heron, 1979; Hunter & Struve, 1998:254; Jackins, 1982).

While every breach of ethical touch-use, without exception, is extremely serious, it is well to bear in mind that relatively few clinicians do misuse touch (Pope et al., 1986) and that the *fear* of sexual involvement, although for the most part unfounded, means that a large number of clients are denied a powerful form of healing.

Moreover, just as any psychological technique, touch included, can be used mistakenly, so any technique can be used unethically and this is ever a

> cause for an indictment not of the technique but rather of the clinician who misused it. Touch is too valuable a tool in the service of human healing to deny its use to the psychotherapist.
> Hunter and Struve (1998:xiv)

It might be worth taking into account also that the dark, steamy secrecy of taboo is notoriously friendly to those who find forbidden fruit, in this case of a sexual flavour, more alluring than that freely available for picking in the light of day.

The taboo fails equally with respect to its second presumed purpose — that of preventing non-erotic touch. Research shows that, like sexual touch, it occurs — and notably more so than is overtly allowed (Hunter & Struve, 1998:54, 68; Older, 1977:199; Woodmansey, 1988:57). This is because one of the taboo's effects is to make therapists chary of admitting to touch-use for fear of censure (Wilson, 1982:66; Toronto, 2001:38). In studies where respondents have remained anonymous, over 50% of therapists admitted to using non-erotic touch with clients (Forer, 1969:230; Holroyd & Brodsky, 1977; Tirnauer et al., 1996:92).

These therapists are therefore touching 'outside the checks and balances of ... supervision' (Hunter & Struve, 1998:138). They hereby forfeit the support and relatively objective stance of a supervisor who might be able to spot pitfalls and potential improvements in their touch practice (Hunter & Struve, 1998:145).

The problem is compounded by the fact that supervisors are no less subject to the effects of the taboo than their supervisees; they too may be uncomfortable with touch and unschooled in its use. Since in the therapist-supervisor relationship it is the latter who has the greater authority and power, it is not surprising that

> the assumptions and theories of the supervisor affect the way the supervisee presents.
>
> Inskipp (1996:275)

At least two of the tactile therapists I interviewed concealed their use of touch from their (psychoanalytic) supervisors, even though they felt they would have been mistaken not to touch. One was an English practitioner whose clients included several fully tactile individuals from South American cultures. Embraces or kisses at the beginning and end of sessions were natural to them and the lack of these interpretable as cold and uncaring. The second therapist was herself South American and used touch with Latin (though not with English) clients for similar reasons — because in Latin cultures *'touch is a natural part of language'*; not to use it would thus impoverish communication and be perceived as unempathic.

It appears, therefore, that the use of non-erotic touch takes place willy-nilly, perhaps because, in the words of Spotnitz (a psychoanalyst) (1972:457), it 'is essential as a natural human contact'. Here again it would seem more effective to deconstruct the taboo so that honest discussion can be had and guidelines on touch be disseminated. A greater level of reflection and skill-sharing might then inform a practice that to a considerable extent is already occurring.

As Hunter and Struve (1998:70) point out, clients are routinely treated for the effects of damaging, shaming *verbal* abuse by means of *verbal* intervention. By the same token, the most direct means of repairing *tactile* abuse can be through *tactile* intervention that contradicts the earlier abusive experience — for just as words have power both to harm and heal, as stated earlier, *there is harmful and there is healing touch. These are distinct entities with opposite motives, and with opposite effects.* If clients have been damaged through harmful touch, is it not adding insult to injury to deprive them of healing touch? Is it not also illogical? — like refusing a starving child wholesome fare because he has eaten only contaminated food to date. For Lynn (p.122,124,136,144), Eva (p.121,129–130,133–134,219–220), Patrick (p.141–142) and many others (Benjamin, 1995a:25–30), healing touch was the major factor in their recovery from abusive touch in childhood.

The second of Eiden's reasons for the touch taboo in psychoanalysis is the fear that touch will disrupt or contaminate transference by undermining the 'neutral' relationship (Eiden, 2002:2).

(For readers unfamiliar with the term 'transference', it is used in psychoanalysis to describe the human tendency to 'transfer' (or some would say 'project') feelings and thoughts we have experienced in the past onto people in the present. For example, if the client as a child was angry with her mother she is likely at some point to vent this anger on the therapist. Somewhere in her mind she is equating the therapist with her mother and replaying her past daughter-mother relationship, that is, transferring her attitudes from her mother to the therapist. In psychoanalysis this transference or projection mechanism is considered a useful way of bringing to light the nature of the patient's neuroses and problems.

The 'neutral relationship' is the type of relationship between therapist and client advocated in traditional psychoanalysis; the therapist in this model is detached, objective, a sort of sentient blank screen. By means of such neutrality, the theory goes, the client can get on with projecting his story onto the blank screen without the personality of the analyst intruding and muddying things. This is assumed to limit the extent to which the therapist interferes with (or 'contaminates') the client's material, in particular the 'transference'.)

There are three main issues here. Firstly, the nature of any transference is determined by the client's past experience which is often hidden from both client and therapist consciousness. Anything the therapist does or does not do may therefore affect transference without the therapist's being aware of it and, as Willison and Masson (1986:498) observe, '*Absence* of any physical contact is likely to cause transference distortions (that is, the client may view the therapist as a cold, withholding parent figure)' (my italics). Since the source of problems for a good number of clients lies in the lack of emotional-tactile warmth from their primary carers, it does indeed seem likely that, for some clients, rigid touch avoidance and the coldness it signifies are more liable to contaminate transference than the warmth and caring communicated by touch-use (Kupfermann & Smaldino, 1987; Mintz, 1973:185).

Secondly, not all therapists agree that disrupting transference is detrimental. On the contrary, highly effective therapy has been performed by practitioners who deliberately do so (for example, Evison & Horobin, 1985,1999). When transference is disrupted, the client's feelings and thoughts are deflected away from the therapist to where they actually belong (very often the client's mother, father or another important figure) so that the client can deal directly with the primary source of the problem.

Thirdly, some clients experience the 'neutrality' of the psychoanalytic relationship as uncaring and inimical to therapeutic progress. For these clients at least, the sooner and more thoroughly it is undermined the better.

A further reason for the touch taboo identified by Eiden has more to do with the current sociopolitical climate than with that of 19th- and 20th-century Vienna which generated the above factors. It is the two-fold fear (a) of transgressing professional boundaries, and (b) of litigation (Eiden, 2002:2).

The fear of transgressing professional boundaries, I think, centres around the definition of 'professional'. I suggest that 'to the best standards possible in terms of client well-being' is more valid a definition than 'according to established codes of conduct within the profession', which it is often taken to mean. It is important that such established codes are viewed critically and, if not in the best interests of the client, are opposed. If a substantial body of research such as that concerning touch is ignored or misconstrued, then I think it behoves therapists to challenge 'professional' boundaries in the interests of integrity. In this case, genuinely professional standards might contravene sanctioned protocols.

Fear of litigation compounds the difficulties of breaking the touch taboo. This is a 'catch-22' since it is the taboo itself that helps to make non-erotic touch a target for litigation. Arnold Lazarus addresses this fear:

> Those anxious conformists who go entirely by the book and live in constant fear of malpractice suits are unlikely to prove significantly helpful to a broad array of clients ... **one of the worst professional/ethical violations is to permit current risk-management principles to take precedence over human interventions**.
> Lazarus (1994:255, my emphasis)

Fortunately for some clients, ethical and effective therapists who use touch have shown that it is possible, even in the current fear-ridden climate, to put humanity before expediency.

Summary and conclusion

A major reason for the taboo against touch in therapy is the fear of sexual interaction between therapist and client. The fear is valid in that such interaction is generally harmful to the client.

However, clinicians rarely interact sexually with their clients — and the touch taboo does not stop the few who do. It *does* stop therapists from openly discussing and reflecting upon their tactile attitudes and behaviours, and from acquiring nuanced awareness and training in tactile issues. This includes the small number of therapists who are at risk of sexual transgression; because touch is a taboo topic, the latter are unlikely to examine and check their erotic impulses towards clients in the steadying environment of supervision.

The taboo fails also to prevent non-erotic touch between therapist and client. This is largely to be expected since touch is a natural means by which humans communicate qualities that are vital to successful therapy, such as empathy and caring. Unlike sexual touch, non-erotic touch occurs fairly widely in therapy. Here again, the effect of the taboo is to discourage therapists from admitting to their use of touch and, as a result, they are employing it without the salutary scrutiny of supervision.

Most unfortunate among the taboo's consequences is that the highly valuable benefits of physical contact are denied the many clients who could gain by it. Therefore, rather than touch-use in mainstream talking therapy being the sole preserve of relatively few exceptional therapists, it would be to clients' advantage if the profession as a whole were to discard the taboo and eagerly, wholeheartedly, embrace the asset of physical contact, rather than avoid it or employ it under cover.

Aside from those above, other anti-touch arguments have been propounded. Sometimes these have been co-opted by taboo-supporters, but often they comprise legitimate contra-indications and risks of touch-use and as such they belong in the next chapter.

Note

1 '... dismantling [the taboo] ... would entail ... open discussion ... and educating therapists in tactile matters ....'
    It might also encourage further research into the factors contributing to therapist-client sexual involvement, although some research on the issue does already exist. Gutheil and Gabbard (1993:188), for example, identified signs of increasing sexual interest which they believe constitute a 'slippery slope' to actual sexual contact, and Holroyd and Brodsky (1980:25) found that the variable predicting therapist-client sexual interaction was not non-erotic touch per se but the practice among some therapists of touching clients of one gender only, as in male therapists who touch only attractive female clients.

Chapter 11

Criteria for the successful use of touch in therapy

There are a number of criteria for the successful use of touch in therapy that are widely agreed in the literature:

1) *Choice, consent, control*
    The client has the *choice* in all tactile issues including, importantly, over whether to be touched at all. Many potential errors in the use of touch are avoided if therapists bear in mind the simple maxim, 'Never touch a client who does not wish to be touched for whatever reason' (although even in this seemingly straightforward stipulation there may be the occasional exception, as in the case of a violent client who needs to be physically restrained (Phelan, 2009:100–101).
    This fundamental rule applies as much to clients who are generally tactile but to whose issues, mood or frame of mind touch is irrelevant at the time of the session (Clance & Petras, 1998:98, 103; Imes, 1998:170).
    If client and therapist do decide that physical contact would be helpful it is then essential that the touch occurs with the client's informed *consent* (see Phelan, 2009:100), and that the client exercises complete *control* over all aspects of it — over where, when, how and for how long she is touched. This might involve her saying, 'NO. I don't want to be touched,' or 'Stop touching'; 'Touch this part of my body and not that'; 'Just hold my arm without stroking it'; or 'I liked that touch but now I want it to stop,' and so on.
    It may be useful for therapist and client to pre-arrange a signal — 'a previously established feedback loop' (Hunter & Struve, 1998:127) — that clients use if they want the touch to stop, are at all unsure about it, or need pause to process what

they are experiencing before it continues. For example, the client could perform a distinctive hand gesture, or hold up a hand and say 'Stop!' or 'Stop touching!' In co-counselling (Heron, 1979; Jackins, 1982) a client in comparable situations says, 'Stop, I mean it!' (The 'I mean it' is presumably added in case the client needs to shout 'Stop!' as part of role-play.) Particularly for clients whose boundaries have been violated by abuse, the empowerment they experience through controlling what happens to their bodies in this way negates previous messages of powerlessness.

Hunter and Struve (1998:143) advocate that clients demonstrate understanding of their right to 'define and enforce' their touch-boundaries and their ability to say 'No' before touch is considered (see these authors' excellent sections on client empowerment (Hunter & Struve, 1998:75–95,141–142)).

An exercise that encourages clients to say 'No' — and one that can be joyfully liberating — is for the therapist to move her arm as if about to touch the client and for the client to say 'No' in response. The therapist then refrains from touching and withdraws her arm. The sequence is repeated until the client wishes to stop (— part of an exercise devised by Anna Fortes Mayer, 2010).

2) This second criterion arises out of the first:
Touch is **dictated by the client's need** and perceived as such by the client; it is never a personal demand or need of the therapist.

> Touch must serve the conscious, agreed-upon goals and direction of the therapy as both explicitly contracted and implicitly communicated.
> Kertay and Reviere (1998:27)

A mistake sometimes made by therapists who are tactile in everyday life, particularly those at the beginning of their careers, is to be unaware or lose sight of the fact that not everyone expresses themselves tactually. I was guilty of this; early in my career for example I worked with Marie, a delightful person in her early 30s. I suspected that she'd had experiences which caused her to be wary of touch but that it was irrelevant to her to work on them at the time because other issues were far more pressing. However, there was such warmth and ease between us that when we came to the end of our final session it didn't occur to me that she wouldn't naturally express her warmth in a goodbye hug since it was so natural to me to do so. I realised my mistake when I hugged her and her body instantly stiffened in my arms. It took a few other similar incidents and feedback on the subject from three clients for me properly to realise the wide range of tactile differences among humans.

3) Open and detailed *communication/discussion between therapist and client about the touch* on offer and associated issues, such as relationship boundaries. Such discussion is encouraged if the therapist expressly invites clients to verbalise their responses both to the therapist's touch proposals before any touch takes place, and to actual touch 'events' after they have occurred (Hunter & Struve, 1998:137, 139).

Particularly with clients who have been sexually abused, the therapist needs to make it absolutely clear that any touch which takes place between him and the client is non-sexual. This message might need to be repeated frequently for abuse survivors. It may be relevant also to members of non-tactile cultures who tend to construe most touch as sexual. Unless the therapist states explicitly and clearly that any touch he administers is non-sexual in nature, such clients are perhaps more likely to be sexually aroused by non-erotic touch or to develop a longing for a sexual/romantic relationship with the therapist (see 'sexual feelings', p.185).

4) *Congruence between touch-use and the level of client-therapist intimacy.* Because touch creates and affirms intimacy, there is a danger that it might outstrip the level of intimacy between protagonists, particularly at the beginning of the therapeutic relationship (although there are exceptions to this — see p.192–193). Later in the relationship when intimacy has deepened, touch is more likely to be helpful.

The fifth criterion comes in two parts:

5a *Therapists who use touch should be comfortable with it* (Hunter & Struve, 1998:151; Lawry, 1998:202). As Edward Smith puts it, touch should be 'ego-syntonic' with the therapist's personality — should flow out of it naturally, organically (Smith, 1985:148, 1992). Lack of ease with touch on the part of a practitioner who uses it is likely to communicate itself to the client and be counter-therapeutic. Touch must be genuine (Kertay & Reviere, 1998:25; Mintz, 1969a).

5b) *Therapists who use touch should be competent at using it* (Fagan, 1998:150; Hunter & Struve, 1998:142; Sanderson, 1995:256). The various competencies required are outlined below.

THE RISKS AND CONTRAINDICATIONS OF TOUCH-USE

As noted earlier, the risks of touch-use arise when the above criteria are disregarded. To investigate this general premise in more detail:

- Touch is strongly contraindicated if it would impede the attainment of therapeutic goals, for example by allowing clients to avoid their feelings. This includes any feelings of discomfort and tension that might underlie interpersonal encounters for the client and that may therefore be triggered by the therapeutic relationship (Hunter & Struve, 1998:150; Kupfermann & Smaldino, 1987:225). As Kertay and Reviere observe (1998:29),

   > Ill-timed touch can 'soothe ... when in fact the patient needs to tolerate and explore the pain being experienced.'

   Early on in therapy, physical contact should generally be avoided with clients whose tactile-emotional experience has been negative since it may arouse intense fear, 'freezing', disorganisation, or dissociation (Hunter & Struve, 1998:84,216,225). In these states clients may be unable to set their own touch boundaries (Hunter & Struve, 1998:225). This is especially true of survivors of sexual and physical abuse (Benjamin, 1995a, 1995b; Herman, 1992; Hunter & Struve, 1998:215). In short-term therapy, therefore, it is likely that touch-use would be inappropriate with these clients, however helpful they might find it in longer-term therapy (but see p.192–193).

- Touch carries risks to both therapist and client if the latter has a history of violence, poor impulse control, socio-/psychopathy, or paranoia, or if she is undergoing a psychotic episode, is enraged (Hunter & Struve, 1998:147,148,150; Older, 1982:201), or is acutely hostile (O'Hearne, 1972:453). Clients in these conditions are more likely to misinterpret the intention of nurturing, non-erotic touch (O'Hearne, 1972:453; see Lynch, 1978). Survivors of abuse whom experience has aught to perceive all touch as hurtful or as sexual may also be at risk of such misinterpretation (Fox & Pritchard, 2001:231).

- As noted earlier, touch should not be used with clients who are unable or unwilling to tolerate the deeper intimacy it expresses (Hunter & Struve, 1998:132).
- Physical contact should not be employed to alleviate *therapists'* discomfort with clients' distress, since this is very likely to interrupt the natural unfolding of the client's therapeutic process and impede his progress (Bacorn & Dixon, 1984). (As Hunter and Struve (1998:147) point out, this caution is applicable to all therapeutic interventions, verbal and physical.)
- Touch should not occur if the *therapist* has feelings that would devalue its purpose, such as hostility, dislike, resentment, anger, or sexual attraction towards the client (O'Hearne, 1972:453).
- As already stated, touch should be avoided if the therapist is uncomfortable with it (Hunter & Struve, 1998:151; Lawry, 1998:202; Smith, 1985:148,1992) or unfamiliar with the issues pertaining to its use (Sanderson, 1995).
- *Sexual feelings.* Hunter and Struve advise avoiding touch during or after the client has explored sexual topics, or after either therapist or client has experienced sexual arousal, lest these factors increase the danger of either participant sexualising subsequent touch. Importantly, these authors remind us that

> it is always 'the *therapist's responsibility* to interrupt and process any touch that leads to sexual arousal'.
> Hunter and Struve (1998:147, my italics)

If the client does develop sexual feelings for the therapist, it is important he knows that *there is no shame in this whatsoever.* The same applies to the therapist. As with any human feelings, sexual feelings are best noticed and fully accepted. However, it is equally important that both client and therapist know that in the therapeutic setting such feelings are not acted upon. The therapist should process her feelings in supervision, and hopefully the client will feel able to process them in his therapy session although this will depend, among other factors, on whether or not he has built up sufficient trust in the therapist.

If the client 'sits with' his sexual feelings — consciously feels them — the chances are that they will 'pass through' him and transform into something else. If not, or if he finds it too painful to bear the frustration of thwarted sexual/romantic impulses, it might be preferable for him to transfer to another therapist.

* * *

A study by Pamela Geib (1982,1998:122) highlighted the unsatisfactory results of flouting the above criteria for successful touch-use. Four of the ten women clients in her study had found non-erotic touch unhelpful for similar reasons to Emma and June (p.148–149):

- The therapist failed to discuss the touch with them before it occurred. This meant that they had not given it informed consent and were denied the powerful 'corrective' experience of being in control of their bodies (Hunter & Struve, 1998:75–95,141–143).
- The therapeutic relationship therefore replayed clients' damaging childhood relationships rather than facilitated their resolution.
- The clients felt loved and worthwhile when their therapists touched them. However, they were not able to express their negative emotions and thoughts for fear of forfeiting these positive feelings. In this sense they felt trapped by the closeness of the therapeutic relationship.
- As a result they felt angry towards the therapist, and guilty about their anger because they understood the therapist to be loving and caring.
- They perceived their therapists as 'needy and vulnerable', and therefore 'in need of protection' from their negative feelings (Geib, 1998:122) (which means that in this respect the caring role was reversed).

* * *

Many other aspects of touch have been researched by therapist-theorists, including analysis of its properties, its meanings, and the awareness, knowledge and attitudes needed by therapists who use touch. To dwell briefly on each of these:

Properties of touch

- The different properties of touch (for example, its duration) vary its meaning for the recipient (Weiss, 1966,1984,1986).

The *duration* of a unit of touch can be brief, lengthy or anything in between. A goodbye hug with Rob might last a few seconds and convey a bracing, 'you-can-do-it!' optimism. In contrast, the full-body holding that Eva received at the end of sessions as she lay in her therapist's arms could last for half an hour or more (p.134) — long enough to convey a sense of timelessness so that she could sink into the experience, relax fully and recuperate, without feeling hurried or nervous that it would be abruptly curtailed before her need for it had come to a natural end.

Location — the body-part or -parts involved in the touch (Bacorn & Dixon, 1984; Hunter & Struve, 1998:18,112; Jourard, 1966). In general I find clients most comfortable, at least initially, with touch on hands, arms and shoulders (Wheaton & Borgen, 1981; see also Bacorn & Dixon, 1984; Suiter & Goodyear, 1985). As Hunter and Struve (1998:112) warn, however, 'Even those areas of the body ... may be unsafe to touch for a client who was the recipient of abuse that was targeted on any of those body regions.'

Pressure — from firm to light. Firm touch can be containing, supportive, safe; sometimes encouraging, invigorating, vitalising; and occasionally challenging (as in wrestling or pushing against a cushion held by the therapist). Lighter pressure can express tender caring.

Stillness or mobility, that is, whether the toucher's hand or hands rest immobile upon the recipient or perform some kind of movement (Heslin & Alper, 1983). I have found still touch to be more in tune with the client when she is in a deep, inward-looking state, for instance after a cathartic experience. A still embrace, for instance, can express an oceanic or cosmic quality. It can also say, I am stopping my normal flow of activities to focus on YOU in a fully intentional, conscious way; I am thoroughly relaxed and comfortable being with YOU and not tempted by embarrassment or superficiality to distract either of us through movement or speech.

Characteristics of mobile touch

Type of action. Mobile touch involves different types of action (Weiss, 1986), for example, stroking or patting (see Nguyen et al., 1975). Stroking is usually experienced as calming and nurturing. Patting also can be intended as calming, or as cheering. However, I do not myself remember ever patting a therapy client because I find that people who seem uncomfortable with touch or with themselves sometimes resort to patting, for example, patting someone on the back while hugging them because they feel too awkward to remain still and thoroughly relax into the hug, be fully present in it.

On the other hand, a touch-shy man may perhaps be warmed and welcomed by a friendly hug-cum-pat on the back whereas he might initially be uncomfortable with a still, intentional hug.

Speed of action. Slow touch can be relaxing, calming; quick touch can be energising and also agitating or irritating.

The type, pressure and speed of touch in particular alter the impact of mobile touch: stroking that combines slow speed with gentle pressure conveys love, tenderness, cherishing; a handshake that is both firm in pressure and brisk in speed can be heartening and vitalising.

Very fast, light, short strokes can signal discomfort with touch or with intimacy, or fear that one's touch will prove unwelcome — as in the following exchange between friends Melanie and Alison. The latter had confided an unhappy experience and Melanie's face was full of genuine empathy and caring. She took Alison's hand and stroked it with very light, hurried movements while talking continuously at great speed. Her touch seemed to say, 'I am touching you in order to express my caring, but I am doing so with nervous, fast, feathery, fidgety strokes because I'm unsure of how you will receive my tactile expression and I am myself uncomfortable with it — it's not an easy, natural form of expression for me. I'm talking quickly at the same time so that if you withdraw your hand in discomfort I can pretend that my touching it was an absent-minded action which occurred by chance because all my concentration was absorbed by what I'm saying; and so that we can both pretend the touch hasn't happened. I am too afraid or embarrassed to express fully and openly that I am touching you meaningfully, in order to convey my love and caring.'

It takes a strengthening of identity, centredness, confidence, a deepening of feelings, to move from this type of touch to being able to be present in a full, still hug, or to give or receive a slow stroking movement which is clearly intended to transmit loving care.

Sequence of action in mobile touch (Hunter & Struve, 1998:115). A sequence of action might be created by the therapist's following the progression of a client's pain with her hand — for example when the therapist followed Donna's pain as it gradually moved down her body from her head to her pelvis (p.196). Or perhaps, in order to express tender caring, the therapist might gently stroke the client's hair from below the hairline on her forehead, over the top of her head, and down the back of the head in line with the flow of the hair ...

Degree of *agency* — whether the touch is passive, active (Rose, 1984) or reciprocal (Frank, 1957:215, 224; Merleau-Ponty, 1962:322; Older, 1982:240). In therapy the client is quite often a passive recipient of touch and the therapist the active toucher. On the other hand, if a client is pushing against the therapist's hands or body, for example, in order to reverse feelings of powerlessness at the hands of an abuser, the touch is reciprocal. Agency can change over time; a goodbye hug earlier in therapy might be more passive on the client's part and active on the therapist's, whereas it might later become reciprocal.

Energy. Touch can transmit energy (Kunz & Peper, 1982) which perhaps is in part why clients find it vitalising and 'remoralising' (in the sense of morale rather than morals). The idea of working with energy — unblocking it, restoring its flow, moving, strengthening, transmitting it — is found particularly in body therapies, and in 'body psychotherapies' (psychotherapies that incorporate bodywork).

Modes of touch. Different modes of positive touch are formed by various combinations of the above properties. As mentioned previously, they include brief 'conversational' touch, for example on arm or shoulder, to more prolonged contact with a body-part, such as hand-holding, a hand resting on someone's arm, or an arm round shoulders; and more or less full body contact as in hugging, holding, rocking, cradling ... (Hunter & Struve, 1998:169–174; Smith, 1998b).

Meanings of touch. David Edwards (1981:29) distinguished several meanings of interpersonal touch: nurturant; cathartic (in the therapy setting this can help clients to release feelings); information gathering (as in doctors palpating patients or feeling pulses); celebratory (footballer hugs and slaps on backs; in therapy, hugs that celebrate clients' achievements or good news); prompting (for example, physically guiding a client's movement in order to illustrate it); ludic (playful, such as ice-breaker games in group therapy); aggressive (as in wrestling to express anger); and sexual. Except for the last, Edwards considers all of these forms of touch useful in therapy provided they are used with 'judgement, sensitivity, and skill' (see also Hunter & Struve, 1998:115; Jones & Yarbrough, 1985; Zur & Nordmarken, 2016).

Relationship of touch to verbal statements. Physical contact can reinforce or modify the effect of words (Thayer, 1982:264). A warm squeeze of the hand can emphasise the words 'Lovely to see you!'; holding a hand, or placing a hand on someone's shoulder, can magnify the empathy conveyed through voice-tone and words in such comments as, 'You look worried about that'; and a slightly challenging remark, for example 'Just a minute; let's give Joey a turn', can be softened by a touch on the arm.

Personal variables, such as previous tactile and relational experience (Hunter & Struve, 1998:99). Because clients' histories are so varied, responses to touch can be highly idiosyncratic (Hunter & Struve, 1998:112,127,138; Peloquin, 1989:305,306). A touch on the arm that one client would find supportive might produce panic in another (see Seagull, 1968); a client who was abused may respond differently to physical contact from a male or female therapist depending on the gender of his abuser; or he may be more comfortable with touch from a female or a male depending on whether he felt more physically comfortable with his mother or father.

Personality is another variable that may dictate the appropriateness of touch (Willison & Masson, 1986); an outgoing and/or naturally kinaesthetic personality might be more ready to fling her arms exuberantly around another than one more reserved or less confident.

Sociocultural factors. Therapists need to be aware that clients may be of sociocultural groups whose tactile norms differ from their own. Ethnicity in particular stands out in this context[1] (Willison & Masson, 1986). Physical contact from an opposite-sex therapist would be inappropriate for clients whose culture prohibits opposite-sex touch in all circumstances apart from marriage, whereas for these clients a friendly hug from a same-sex therapist might be acceptable. In other cultures the opposite may apply — an Anglo-Western man might feel awkward if hugged by another male, perhaps because he fears homosexual implications; he might more readily accept a hug from a female therapist.

Physical environment. Sofas where people can sit next to each other lend themselves more to some kinds of touch than chairs (for instance, sitting side by side, the therapist holding a client's hand, or with an arm around the client's shoulder). Less formal settings in general — for example, those provided with floormats or beanbags — can be more conducive to certain types of touch such as full body holding, than more formal settings.

AWARENESS, SKILLS, KNOWLEDGE, ATTITUDES NEEDED BY THERAPISTS WHO USE TOUCH

Self-awareness and self-reflectiveness

It is most important that therapists are conscious of their own issues, motivations, assumptions and biases in relation to physical contact and of how these might influence their use or non-use of touch in therapy (Benjamin, 1995b:23; Thomas, 1994). Does my impulse to touch this client arise from my own need for tactile comfort or closeness rather than his? Even if it springs from a surge of compassion that I would naturally express through touch, am I at the same time keeping in mind *his* needs and assessing whether the touch is appropriate for him at this moment?

How do I feel if the client declines my touch? Is my ego invested in my touch-offering? (Thomas, 1994;42); do I feel rejected, hurt, humiliated, or disappointed, even if just a little (Hunter & Struve, 1998:141), or do I instead maintain unwavering empathy and understanding?

And is my sexual appetite satisfied outside therapy, or is the desire to touch this attractive client tangled up with sexual need? (see Holroyd & Brodsky, 1980; Lawry, 1998:204; Pope et al., 1994; Smith, 1998b:46; Woodmansey, 1988:63).

Therapists should be able to process such issues with supervisors — preferably those who are sufficiently versed in tactile matters.

Skill at reading non-verbal cues

Non-verbal communication is particularly important for therapists to monitor if touch is used. Even if therapist and client have carefully paved the way for touch, when it actually occurs clients might not be experienced, confident or articulate enough to verbalise any misgivings that may arise unexpectedly. This is especially so at the outset of touch-use. Therapists need be alert and respond to a subtle stiffening of bodily or facial muscles, or a slight alteration in facial colour (that is, increased pallor or flushing through changes in blood flow). Muscle stiffening, or increased pallor, are often signs of negative feelings such as uncertainty, fear or distaste; flushing may be positive (for example, a sign of pleasure), or negative (as in nervousness, fear or embarrassment). The swift, unconscious touching of a body-part, often the nose, is another common sign of discomfort and unspoken thoughts (both in and outside therapy). At the first appearance of any such uneasiness or hesitancy in the client, touch or the intention to touch should be abandoned, at least for the time being, and the client's feelings discussed and processed (Hunter & Struve, 1998:138).

In the case of individuals who commonly dissociate, such as abuse survivors (Benjamin, 1995a:25; Hunter & Struve, 1998:6,216), the therapist needs to recognise signs of dissociation, for example, physical tension, freezing, shallow breathing, holding of breath, staring into space and unresponsiveness (Steele & Colrain, 1990).

Touch in relation to different stages of the therapeutic relationship

The therapeutic relationship has been conceptualised as a three-part beginning-middle-and-end process (Horton, 1996), a view shared by several pro-touch authors (Benjamin, 1995a:25; Herman, 1992:168, 195, 207; Hunter & Struve, 1998:220; Wilson, 1982:69; Willison & Masson, 1986).

The beginning stage

Touch is inadvisable before safety and trust have been fully established within the therapeutic relationship (Benjamin, 1995a) which means that it is usually best avoided during the beginning stage of therapy. Premature touch-use can evoke fear and dissociation in the client (Hunter & Struve, 1998:84) and, as we have seen, cause premature termination of therapy (p.146–147 above; Horton et al., 1995:452).

There are exceptions to this: some clients at the beginning of the therapeutic relationship benefit from touch because of its capacity to *enhance* feelings of safety and trust (e.g. Clance & Petras, 1998:98; Hunter & Struve, 1998:220). Woodmansey (1988:57), for instance, found that whereas some clients 'are at first afraid to be touched', with others 'it may be necessary to communicate ... by touch before treatment can start'.

A second exception is that of crisis intervention in which immediate gentle touch can produce a feeling of safety, expedite establishment of the therapeutic relationship, and inspire hope (Wilson, 1982).

Third, touch from the outset of therapy is generally appropriate with clients from tactile cultures (for example, South America, Spain) for whom physical contact is an integral part of communication and who are likely to feel offended or rejected if embraces and kisses are not exchanged at the beginning and end of sessions. (This is not often mentioned in Anglo touch literature; Clance and Petras (1998:101) point it out, and it emerges clearly from my own study.)

The middle stage

During the middle stage of therapy, touch can fulfil any of the purposes already discussed — it can engender safety and trust; convey nurturing and warmth; assist in problem-processing, for example, encourage the surfacing and release of emotions and memories; modify self-defeating relationship patterns, particularly those of which problematic responses to touch are a component (Benjamin, 1995a; Wilson, 1982:70); and increase self-esteem, body-acceptance and happiness.

The end stage

Here touch can be used to consolidate the gains of the middle stage — to ingrain securely clients' feelings and thoughts of being lovable and worthy of tactile care; to accustom clients to self-acceptance and self-esteem as an enduring state; to cement closeness and ease within the therapeutic relationship; if necessary, to reinforce the experience of touch as nurturing and pleasurable rather than distressing (Benjamin, 1995a:28; Hunter & Struve, 1998:220; Imes, 1998:180); to confirm physical contact 'as a significant and healthy dimension of relationship' (Hunter & Struve, 1998:109); and to anchor an outlook of life-satisfaction and happiness firmly within the personality.

Timing

> Meaningful touch is a matter of appropriate timing.
> Schmahl (1964:74)

Timing is of critical importance in touch-use not only in the broader sense of its position within the therapeutic relationship but also in a micro-sense. As shown earlier, clients' needs are multi-faceted. They may sometimes require the satisfaction of unmet childhood needs for loving touch without which therapeutic progress will be impeded; on other occasions they may need to experience the pain of adverse experience, including the anguish and longing caused by emotional and/or tactile deprivation. Even the briefest ill-timed touch can shut down this latter experiential process and *hinder* therapeutic progress. With sensitive timing, however, both needs can be satisfied — if necessary within a single session, as occurred in Sophie's and Eva's therapy (pp.142–143,134).

The next two points emerged in the preceding material, namely:

Insight into each client's individual perception of touch
(see p.190) gained through discussion with the client and observation of her body language; and,

Awareness and knowledge of clients' cultural touch-norms
(see p.190) Sue & Sue, 1990; Smith, 1998b:41) — whether or not these norms differ from mine, the therapist's (Benjamin, 1995b:23; Hunter & Struve, 1998:89), for example with respect to same and opposite-sex touch, or to touch between individuals of different age and status (Hunter & Struve, 1998:89; Jourard, 1966; Jourard & Rubin: 1968; Holroyd & Brodsky, 1980).

A 'consistent theoretical rationale' (Eiden, 1998:6) for the use and non-use of touch, including the ability to justify instances of physical contact in terms of therapeutic goals and the practitioner's overall philosophy of therapy (Benjamin, 1995b:25; Hunter & Struve, 1998:150; Eiden, 1998:6; Keith-Spiegel & Koocher, 1985:146; Thomas, 1994).

Regular supervision (Benjamin, 1995b:23; Hunter & Struve, 1998:138; Kertay & Reviere, 1998:28; Lawry, 1998:202; Sanderson, 1995:256; Woodmansey, 1988:57), preferably with a supervisor who has understanding and experience of touch-use (Kertay & Reviere, 1998:32), or at the very least accepts it as a valid form of intervention (Older, 1977:199). Peer supervision can also be very helpful (Benjamin, 1995b:23; Lawry, 1998:202).

Fulfilling personal lives

In general it is advantageous for therapists to enjoy satisfying emotional and sexual relationships outside therapy to minimise the risk of their attempting to meet the need for these through their clients (Benjamin, 1995b:24; Butler & Zelen, 1977; Fagan, 1998:150; Lawry, 1998:204; Shepherd, 1979:11).

Training in touch-use

In addition to standard forms of psychotherapy training, a number of authors stress the need for theoretical and practical education specifically in touch and related issues so that therapists who use physical contact are working within their level of competency (Fagan, 1998:150; Hunter & Struve, 1998:142; Sanderson, 1995:256).

The study of structured touch techniques (as in massage for example) is not necessary in order for therapists to be able to respond to clients with compassionate 'human' touch. However, such study can enrich the therapist's experiential and 'theoretical sensitivity' (Glaser, 1978; Strauss & Corbin, 1990:41) with respect to tactility. A good basic training in traditional Swedish massage is useful in this respect.

It *is* necessary that trainees' theoretical curricula should include the study of existing touch research such as that concerning the issues raised in this chapter, including the important matter of our —

Motives for touching (Krieger, 1975; Thomas, 1994)

— the wholehearted, passionate and unswerving intention to give love, care, empathy, support..., to leave no stone unturned in the service of this intention. Dolores Krieger (1975) spoke of 'the *intent* to...heal' (my emphasis).

As suggested earlier, even the most thoughtful advocates of touch seem occasionally to slip into taboo-speak under the pressure of anti-touch prejudice. Thus Hunter and Struve, normally scrupulous in their respect for clients' needs, nevertheless enjoin therapists '*never* — under *any* circumstances — [to] touch the breast, buttock or genital areas of a client' (Hunter & Struve, 1998:112), or 'between belt and knee' (ibid., p.143), and that end-of-session hugs should always be '*brief*'(ibid., p.119) (their emphases). This is an excellent injunction for any therapist who entertains even the merest possibility of using touch with selfish/sexual motives, and it is applicable to very nearly all situations in which touch is used — but not quite all, which means that as a global, black-and-white restriction it could occasionally detract from therapeutic outcomes: it could prevent the therapist from responding flexibly to each unique circumstance (Glickauf-Hughes & Chance, 1998:167); it could shift the criterion for touch-use from the needs of the client to what is perhaps a (wholly understandable) fear of opprobrium from a touch-aversive psychological community and a litigious wider culture; it could entail the inappropriate attribution of sexual intent to non-sexual touch — a feature of Anglo culture which the authors themselves regret (Hunter & Struve, 1998:85,94); and it does not allow for differences of gender and sexual orientation which affect the interpretation of touch (as the authors themselves point out — Hunter and Struve, 1998:80,89,221). A female client for example might receive touch on her breast or pelvis differently from a female than from a male therapist.

A case in point is a client with whom I worked, Donna, who found that she could more easily bear the physical and emotional pain accompanying memories of sexual abuse if I placed a hand on the body areas that hurt while she relived these memories. Sometimes the pain moved downwards from her head to her shoulder, then to the heart area which incorporated part of her breast, and down via her belly to her lower pelvis. I followed it with my hand. To treat her breast and pelvis differently to other body-parts is likely to have denied her need for support; interrupted her process, in this case a deep absorption in the experience she was reliving; and misinterpreted her psychological state by implying a sexual attitude towards her breast and pelvis on my part which was absent in her mind. It would therefore have entailed a breach in my empathy and understanding. Also, at the end of a gruelling session, hugs with Donna were of varying lengths depending on her need in that moment.

An addition to the existing touch literature which might lessen the attraction of occasionally-limiting blanket rules such as the above is an explicit emphasis on therapists' *motives* for employing touch (see Thomas, 1994:61–73). Responsibility for the lacuna in this area perhaps lies to some degree with our scientific culture, in which the mention of 'love, care' and 'compassion' is unfashionable and rarely features in mainstream academic journals (see Forer, 1969:229; Naisbitt, 1982:39).

Although as humans we sometimes fall short of our ideals, we are less liable to do so if our trainings and literature encourage them — in this context, less likely to fall prey to the misuses of touch if trainee and practising therapists are encouraged to think in terms of these qualities of love, caring and the like.

In the ideal psychotherapy model there is no room in the therapist's psyche for self-seeking motives that might hinder the attainment of therapeutic goals, since his helping-motives are unshakeably in place, and his entire being filled with the desire to assist clients' progress towards full health.[2]

Summary

There are established criteria for effective touch-use, the most critical of which is that the client should be in control of any touch that occurs. When these criteria are observed, touch can be a highly effective therapeutic tool which enhances clients' achievements; when these criteria are disregarded, touch can be ineffective and can impede therapeutic progress.

It is therefore important that therapists who use touch are familiar with research into this fundamental aspect of communication.

Notes

1 'Therapists need to be aware that clients may be of sociocultural groups whose tactile norms differ from their own. Ethnicity in particular stands out in this context.'
Aside from ethnicity, Willison and Masson (1986) mention socioeconomic status, educational level and age as possibly affecting clients' tactual attitudes and behaviours, and Hunter and Struve (1998:xvi,89) mention sexual orientation in this connection.

2 'In the ideal psychotherapy model ... the therapist's ... helping-motives are unshakeably in place and his entire being filled with the desire to assist clients' progress towards full health.'
This statement is based partly on personal experiences which have led me to believe that such models can and should be taught. For example, I was fortunate in witnessing the exceptional co-counselling teacher, Peter Clark, train scores of counsellors of widely differing personalities to attain this ideal with remarkable consistency. Reasons for this achievement were, I think, his emphasis on therapists' helping-motives, and an ability to inspire students with the idealism inherent in the humanistic world view.

Chapter 12

Dismantling the touch taboo

Some readers persuaded by the evidence in favour of touch may wish to explore the possibility of relaxing the touch taboo in their lives and, in the case of therapists, in their practice. For non-therapists, and for therapists who are non- or less tactile, this may be challenging since it can mean altering deeply entrenched behaviours and beliefs; for therapists who are tactile in everyday life it will be easier to bring tactility into their work. Whatever one's tactile starting point the process can be a rewarding and exciting adventure.

Here are some suggestions for dismantling the taboo:

RAISE YOUR AWARENESS OF YOUR OWN TACTILE BELIEFS, PREFERENCES AND HABITS

Work out where you are on the tactility scale (see Chapter 4):

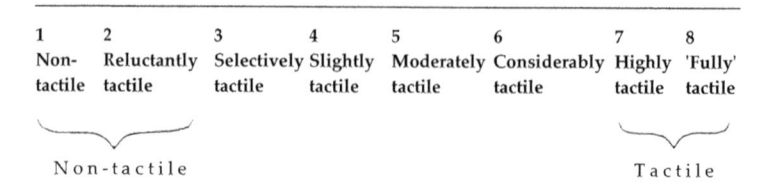

1	2	3	4	5	6	7	8
Non-tactile	Reluctantly tactile	Selectively tactile	Slightly tactile	Moderately tactile	Considerably tactile	Highly tactile	'Fully' tactile

Non-tactile ⟵⟶ Tactile

Keep a touch diary

Focus on your sensations, feelings and thoughts in your entries, for example:

'When A touched me on the arm I felt ... [sensations and feelings]'.
   Or:
'When B hugged me I felt ... [sensations and feelings], and I thought...'

Dismantling the touch taboo 199

This was Tessa's diary:

Thurs, 12th Nov
Exchanged hug with Isobel. Enjoyed the warm impulse to hug her but felt slightly uncomfortable in the actual hug – physical tension down my front especially in my stomach – so I made it a quick hug and wittered on while it was happening because I was a bit embarrassed, uncomfortable.

Hug with Jim. Both knackered when we got to bed. Told him about horrible Mary at work. He gave me one of his gorgeous comforting hugs and nasty Mary just dissolved away – she didn't matter at all any more. I completely relaxed with my head on his chest and floated off to sleep in a minute. Had my usual thought – how LUCKY I am to have Jim.

Fri, 13th Nov
Oh no. Kissed Bella goodbye. She was aiming for my left cheek, I was aiming for her left cheek and we met in the middle and kissed on our lips by mistake. Uncomfortable, embarrassing! Pretended to laugh it off. I'm giggling now thinking about it — with embarrassment, and because actually it's quite funny! (after the event).

Sun, 15th Nov
Walked arm in arm down the pavement with Aunty Nel. Felt very relaxed and warm towards her. Happy. I love Aunty Nel.

Mon, 16th Nov
Harry passed me in the street on his bike and jumped off it to give me a hug. He was all sweaty. Yuck. I quite like Harry. I don't like his sweat. It's put me off him a bit.

Tessa's diary is written in the usual, anecdotal way. You might want to use a more formalised method of recording touch-events instead (or as well), for example, by drawing and filling in the following columns.

Situation	Sensations	Feelings	Thoughts	Images	Behaviour

This method, drawn from cognitive behavioural therapy, has the advantage of ensuring that all aspects of an event are explored.

With regard to 'Images' — the fifth column above—note that some people think in pictures and some don't. Either is fine. If you don't (or even if you do but no image comes up in relation to a particular event), leave this column blank.

Here are three examples:

1)

Situation	Sensations	Feelings	Thoughts	Images	Behaviour	Reminds me of...
Talking to Annie. Told her I hadn't got the part in the play. She touched me sympathetically on the arm just below my elbow.	My body relaxed a bit, especially the knot of tension in my stomach and the tightness in my throat.	Moved (by her caring and empathy). Warm. Happier. Grateful (to have her as a friend).	Glad I've got a good friend. It's more important than the part in the play; there'll be other parts.	Two quick flash-pictures, one of my agent telling me about another part to go for, the other of my Mum looking pleased for a change because I'd got it.	Smiled and laughed for the first time in 2 days. Went to café and had tea with Annie.	N/A. Or perhaps: Dad putting his arm on my shoulder and then giving me a hug when I didn't get into the netball team.

2)

Situation	Sensations	Feelings	Thoughts	Images	Behaviour	Reminds me of...
With Kerry. Longing for a hug but Kerry not a huggy person.	Cold and tired, physically (and emotionally →)	Dispirited, disconnected. Longing (for physical/emotional comfort). Afraid (to ask for it). Disgruntled (because I can't have what I want).	If I say I feel like a hug she might snub me with one of her humorous quips out of embarrassment. I don't like Kerry that much. She's not such a good friend. Better to be on my own.	Picture of me lying in warm bed with my book and a bar of nuts and raisins chocolate.	Cut short the afternoon. Told Kerry I felt a bit rough and wanted an early night. I smiled and agreed when she said we must meet soon even though I didn't feel like seeing her soon, i.e., I lied because I was afraid to hurt her feelings.	My best friend going away to Italy in year 2. Tried to make friends with Tina but it wasn't the same — not on the same wavelength. I pretended to like Tina more than I did (not only to her, also to myself) because I was so lonely and yearning for a best friend.

Dismantling the touch taboo 201

3)

Situation	Sensations	Feelings	Thoughts	Images	Behaviour	Reminds me of...
Getting quite friendly with Jack because we go home the same way. Today he tried to hug me goodbye when we got off the train.	Tension. I froze. My whole body became stiff with tension especially stomach, pelvis, throat, mouth.	Fear Revulsion Shame	I hope he's not going to get soppy and physical — it'll spoil everything. I don't want him to see how I feel — he might think I'm weird and not want to be friends anymore. Don't want to tell him why I feel like this because I'm ashamed of the feelings and of what happened to me that caused them.	N/A. Or perhaps: Uncle T's fat, greasy face.	Tried to cover up my feelings by saying a bright, chirpy goodbye but I could feel my smile was stiff and my voice was tense and higher than usual.	N/A. Or perhaps: Abuse. Uncle T. He always started with a hug, pretending to be nice. He was never nice, he was DIS-GUSTING.

If you'd like to investigate further you could add an extra column, namely:

Does the situation remind me of anything? (Schiffman, 1971).

Any of the activities below may provide further entries for your touch diary.

Explore your tactile history

If you've delved into the optional, *'Does this remind me of anything?'* question, you have already begun exploring your tactile history. Another way of doing this is to answer the following questions:

Did these people touch you in a way you liked?	How did you feel when they touched you; what were your sensations, feelings, thoughts?
Your mother/female primary carer e.g. Yes/often/sometimes/rarely/no/ never... If you like, rate the person's touch on a scale of 0–10, 10 being perfect, and 0 totally unsatisfactory.	e.g. I felt warm, easy, relaxed, loved/I felt slightly edgy, tense, uncomfortable because I could feel *she* was stiff, awkward, uncomfortable. This created conflict in me — I longed to relax into her hugs but because of her tension I couldn't. I feel sad, frustrated, angry about it. I have this thought at the back somewhere that no-one is comfortable touching me because there's something off-putting, yucky about me.
Your father/main male carer	....
Your siblings (you may have had different tactile relationships with different siblings)	....
Extended family members — grannies, grandads, aunts, uncles, cousins...	....
Family friends and associates, your friends and associates	....
People other than the above — acquaintances, strangers	....

Look for patterns in your tactile responses

If you've experimented with the above suggestions you will probably already have spotted some patterns. A way of delving further is to ask, *'Does the way I respond to touch now remind me of anything in the past?'* Answers to this question can enable us to link our present-day tactile responses to patterns set by early touch experience. Here are two of Kay's answers:

> I love it when Mrs Hartley hugs me, folds me into her warm, soft body when I take her shopping over. It reminds me of how my Mum hugged me when I was little.
>
> I stiffen when Joe hugs me in the same way I did when Mr Stone from next door used to grab me. Something about Joe reminds me of ghastly Mr Stone. He has the same colouring and size. Or perhaps I have a tendency to stiffen with any man just in case he's going to treat me the way Mr Stone did.

Co-counselling (Heron, 1979; Jackins, 1982) offers an excellent procedure called the *identity check* for when we have an irrational dislike of someone because they remind us of someone else:

- Ask yourself, or even better, have somebody else ask you:
  How does Joe remind you of Mr Stone?
  (e.g. same colouring — dark hair, green eyes.)
  How else does Joe remind you of Mr Stone?
  (About the same height. And they're both thin.)
  How else does Joe remind you of Mr Stone? ...etc.
  Keep asking or being asked the *'How else?'* question until you can no longer think of any other way in which Joe resembles Mr Stone.
- Then ask or be asked:
  How is Joe different from Mr Stone?
  (e.g. his ears stick out more.)
  How else is Joe different from Mr Stone?
  (His nose is smaller.)
  How else is Joe different from Mr Stone?
  (He smiles quite a lot and I never saw Mr Stone smile.)
  Keep being asked or asking yourself *'How else is Joe different?'* until you've thought of all the answers you can. If there isn't a rational reason to dislike the person the questionee often ends up laughing and saying something like, 'Actually he's not really like him at all!'

Draw/paint/cut and paste...

Some people find it rewarding to explore issues visually, for example through drawing/painting/collage-making...

N.B. You don't have to be an artist to do this! In fact it can be better if you aren't because artists are sometimes too self-conscious to gain from the exercise. If you like, draw stick figures with pencil or ballpoint that are intelligible only to you.

Create a picture of yourself as a child being touched, or lacking touch. Then answer the questions:

How does that child in the picture feel?
What does she need/want?
What would she say if he could?

(This exercise is based on one from Viola Brody's Developmental Play Therapy workshops.)

Invent your own picture titles, for example, *How I feel now as an adult when I'm touched/How I feel when X touches me…*

Explore your touch experiences with others:

Therapy

If items in your touch diary bring up difficult feelings, or if you simply want to explore tactile issues with someone else, it may be rewarding to find a therapist to talk to.

Peer discussion

Or you may want to explore your experiences of touch with a like-minded person or persons (in addition to or instead of a therapist). This has the advantage of costing nothing. You and the other group members could take your touch diaries along with you when you meet and share as much or as little of them as you like.

Groups

If there is a group of you, the usual considerations with regard to groups apply, such as taking care that the ethos of the group is accepting/non-judgmental, caring, supportive, emotionally generous, inclusive. Sharing 'air-time' is another important factor affecting the success of groups, that is, taking roughly equal amounts of time to share the verbal parts of any exercises you do (see below), and to share talking time in general. (There may be occasional exceptions to this if someone is very upset and needs more time.).

SEEK OUT WAYS OF EXPERIENCING MORE TOUCH

Create a more tactile environment for yourself

Find out by observing or asking people with whom you associate whether they like hugs and exchange them with those who do.

Hugging circles

Form hugging circles with others in your neighbourhood or work/leisure place who'd like more touch in their lives. Agree with willing candidates to hug as a matter of course when you meet, particularly when greeting and parting (unless for some reason you don't feel like it that day, in which case say so). Making hugs an open, explicit objective allows members of the circle clear permission to give and receive hugs and to enjoy them. They needn't take long. A cheering, heartening hug can last a few seconds and lift your mood for far longer.

If you meet together in a group, you could try group hugs in a huddle or circle. These can be very warming and relaxing.

A hugging circle could become a hugging community. Perhaps think about including in your circle or community some elderly people who may be missing touch.

'Hug trails'

— great fun. Drop in to a trail of fellow huggers (one or more) on the way to work or leisure and share a quick hug. Your trail could include converging at a street corner and exchanging hugs in passing.

Rate your happiness levels before and after hug events, and/or in the longer term, before and after being involved in the hugging circle/hug trail. You could use a scale of 0–10 to do this, with 10 meaning totally happy and 0 meaning totally unhappy. If you don't like scales and numbers you could use adjectives — 'totally happy, quite happy, not at all happy,' etc.

Create a space for non-sexual, 'human' touch

When exploring touch with others you might wish to adopt features of the 'cuddle workshops' originated in 2010 by Anna Fortes Mayer. Part of Fortes Mayer's purpose in creating these workshops was to counteract attitudes to touch in non-tactile Britain where nurturing 'human' touch is relatively scarce and the touch that does occur is often sexualised.

Participants in cuddle workshops make an agreement that any touch they exchange during the workshop is non-sexual. In this way a space is created in which human warmth and tenderness can flower — can be openly, and safely, expressed and received — without fear of their being misunderstood as sexual. Kissing is also vetoed in cuddle workshops because it is so readily linked with sexual interaction in non-tactile cultures.

The question might arise, 'But what if I happen to get turned on?' If you do, fine; as stated earlier, there is no shame in this whatsoever. Notice the sexual feelings, accept them fully (the chances are they will 'pass through' you and change into something else), remind yourself that you are in a space in which you have agreed that sexual feelings are never acted upon, and return your mind to giving and receiving 'TLC' (tender loving care), to honouring and cherishing each other for our humanness.

A second important agreement is to respect your own touch boundaries. Sit out of an exercise if you do not wish to participate in it — if it feels too risky or you're just not in the mood for tactile connection; or simply sit silently with your partner and, if you like, exchange eye contact. If someone is touching you in a way you don't like, place your hand on his hand to stop him and ask explicitly for — describe and demonstrate — the kind of touch you do want (Fortes Mayer, 2010; Virginia Thorne, personal communication, 2016).

Engage in activities that involve touch

Join a massage course, a 'cuddle workshop' (www.cuddleworkshop.co.uk/about-us), or certain forms of dance/movement to which touch is integral, for example, Biodanza (www.biodanzaassociation.uk); Vital Development (vitaldanza.com); or Contact Improvisation (www.contactimprovisation.co.uk/london.html).

(The first two of these dance forms require no movement experience at all; the third can be more physically demanding.) If you like World Music and want a gentle introduction to physical contact in the form of hand-holding in a circle, you might enjoy Circle Dance.
Arrange one-to-one massage.

Attend therapy with a therapist who uses touch

There are four kinds of therapists who use touch:

1 Those who include natural, human touch in their therapy, such as hand-holding and hugs, when this is helpful to the client.
2 Those trained in bodywork/physical therapy, but not in psychological therapy (although bodywork of course affects other aspects of the self aside from the bodily).

Examples of physical therapies you might want to explore are:
    Massage (of which there are many types — traditional/Swedish massage, deep tissue massage, reflexology, sports massage, Indian head massage, Korean hand massage, Thai massage ...);
    Acupressure;
    Aromatherapy;
    Bowen;
    Craniosacral therapy;
    Healing touch (Mentgen);
    Osteopathy;
    Reflexology;
    Rolfing/structural integration;
    Rosen Method Bodywork;
    Shiatsu (sometimes classified as one of the many forms of massage);
    Therapeutic touch (Krieger & Kunz) ...

3 Those who are trained in body *psycho*therapy, that is, in both bodywork *and* psychological therapy, and who use both as needed. This means they should be able to respond appropriately if the touch evokes strong feelings.

Examples of body psychotherapies are:
Biodynamic Massage (Boyesen);
Bioenergetics (Lowen);
Core energetics (Pierrakos);
Biosynthesis (Boadella);
Emotional Anatomy (Keleman);
Hakomi (Kurtz);
Integrative Body Psychotherapy (Rosenberg);
Radix (Kelley)...

Co-counselling (Jackins, 1962,1982 ; Heron, 1979) is a psychological therapy that involves much touch — hugs, holding, wrestling — any non-sexual tactile experience which the client needs at the time.

A quick internet search for the physical therapies and body psychotherapies mentioned above will yield further details.

4   Those who use a mixture of any of the above.

Attend workshops that explore touch

Or organise your own

Find one or more others with whom to explore responses to touch. Devise your own touch exercises, or try the following examples. They are adapted from Jon Kabat-Zinn's 'Mindfulness-Based Stress Reduction' (MBSR) courses (e.g. Kabat-Zinn et al., 1986, 1998) and draw also upon Anna Fortes Mayer's 'cuddle workshops' (www.cuddleworkshop.co.uk/about-us). You may need a timer or stopwatch of some kind — if there are more than two people present, one could verbally guide the exercises and time them.

The passages below in *'italics and inverted commas'* are suggestions of what the guide might say, if there is one. It's important that she or he speak calmly, slowly, gently, and with pauses in order to give listeners time for their experiences. Dots represent suggested pauses. Except for the words of the possible guide, ALL THE EXERCISES ARE PERFORMED IN SILENCE. The suggested duration of each exercise is a rough guide to be changed as needed.

EXERCISE 1, Version 1

Duration: About 2 minutes.
In pairs, sitting side by side.
1a) *'Take your partner's hand... Close your eyes if you find it comfortable to do so. If that's not comfortable, look down or ahead of you, so that you're not exchanging eye contact...*

'THROUGHOUT THE EXERCISE <u>ACCEPT</u> EVERYTHING YOU EXPERIENCE WITHOUT JUDGMENT, AND WITHOUT TRYING TO CHANGE IT.

[THIS REQUIREMENT APPLIES TO ALL OF THE FOLLOWING EXERCISES.]

'Focus on the sensations you're experiencing as you hold your partner's hand... Be aware of her or his skin touching yours... Be aware of its texture... of its temperature... Notice the weight of the hand you're holding... You might feel sensations in your hand, or you might not [for example, you may feel warm, hot, cool, cold, no sensation, tingly, heavy, light, rough, smooth, relaxed, tense, stiff...]. *Whatever you experience is completely fine. Just notice it... and accept it..............*

At the end of the 2 minutes:

'If you've closed your eyes, open them, and gently let go of each other's hand.'

1b) *'Face your partner, and each take a turn for about a minute to share your experience of the exercise with her or him — if you want to, or as much or little of it as you want to.'*

[The guide tells participants when to swap speaker and listener roles, either in words or by making an agreed-upon sound such as ringing a bell. If you do not wish to share verbally, you could use the time to sit with your partner silently and, if you like, exchange eye contact.]

If you are comfortable 'being with' your sensations or no-sensations as above you could extend the exercise further by placing your attention on your feelings (as in emotions rather than physical sensations):

Exercise 1, Version 2

Duration: about $2^{1}/_{2}$ minutes.

Version 2a) Start as above (i.e. with Version 1a, that is, focusing on the sensations in your hand), then add:

'...*Now be aware of any* emotions *you have as you hold this person's hand......* [e.g. comfortable, happy, uncomfortable, sad, safe, unsafe, not feeling anything, numb, contented, glowing, warm, loving, peaceful, nervous, agitated, irritated, angry...] *Just notice and accept everything you're feeling, without trying to change it....................*

'Gently let go of your partner's hand.'

Version 2b) Share your experience verbally with your partner (i.e. repeat Ex. 1, Version 1b).

Exercise 1, Version 3

Duration: About 4 minutes.

Version 3a) Start as above (Versions 1a and 2a, i.e. focusing first on sensations, second on emotions), then add:

'...*Notice any* thoughts *that occur along with the emotions you're feeling............*'

[Here are a few examples of thoughts that people have uncovered under or alongside their feelings:

'I'm uncomfortable with silence; I don't think my touch is enough to stop this person getting bored with me; I need to talk to keep him/her interested';

'I like having permission to be silent while in physical contact with someone';

'This is more intimate than I feel comfortable with'.

If this last thought occurs to you remember that you have the choice and the right to stop touching immediately, unless you choose to continue exploring the uncomfortable feelings and thoughts.]

'*Let go of your partner's hand.*'

Version 3b) Share verbally (i.e., repeat Ex. 1, Version 1b).

The next four points apply to all of the material that follows:
* Each of the exercises can be done in the above versions — first focusing on sensations, then on emotions, and then on thoughts (i.e., the guide would be speaking Ex. 1, Versions 1a, 2a and 3a, adjusting them as appropriate, for example, changing 'hand' to 'hands' in Ex. 2, or omitting mention of hands altogether in the hugging exercises below).
* If it seems appropriate for the group, when participants are focusing inwards on their sensations/emotions/thoughts, the guide could expand the experience of the exercises by encouraging participants to pay attention to their breathing: '*Be aware of your breathing ... Notice the rise and fall of your breath......*'
* In any of the exercises, either perform the different versions separately, or run some or all of them together depending on what you think will best suit participants. Adjust the duration of the exercises accordingly.
* All exercises end with an opportunity for participants to share verbally (that is, with Ex. 1, Version 1b).

EXERCISE 2

Duration: About 2 minutes.

In pairs, with partners facing each other and seated closely enough to hold both of each other's hands comfortably. (It may be easier if partners arrange their feet so that they are 'offset' or 'zigzagged'. If this sounds confusing, find the position by sitting with your feet about a foot apart, opposite your partner's feet, and with your toes not quite touching your partner's toes. One of you then move your feet about six inches to one side.)

Version 2a) Exactly the same as 1a) except that the guide speaks of '*your partner's hands*' *instead of 'hand'.*

Version 2b) Share verbally (i.e., repeat Ex. 1, Version 1b).

EXERCISE 3

Duration: About 3 minutes.

In pairs, with partners facing each other and seated closely enough to hold both of each other's hands comfortably.

3a) For $1^1/_2$ minutes carry out the first paragraph of Ex. 2a above. Then for another $1^1/_2$ minutes:

'Now keep hold of each other's hands as you open your eyes and look into your partner's eyes... Continue looking into each other's eyes.............

'Gently let go of your partner's hands.'

3b) Share verbally (i.e., repeat Ex. 1, Version 1b).

In the third version of this exercise (the one that focuses on thoughts), these are some of the thoughts that people have experienced:
'There are no boundaries between us; I am you; you are me... We are one';
'Tears are welling up because this is reminding me of the love I didn't get.'
'I am one with you, with all of humanity, with all of creation';
'I can't stand this; it's excruciating';
'I'm sinking into a warm lake of joy';
'Permission to simply be with someone and look into their eyes in a relaxed way — the essence of bliss';
'It's unbearable to look into someone's eyes. I feel exposed, naked, raw';
'This is timeless, infinite, eternal';
'I'm *painfully* tense and uncomfortable';
'My heart is breaking';
'The glory, the sacred privilege, of looking into another soul'...

EXERCISE 4

Duration: about 30 seconds to a minute.

In pairs, standing facing each other. It may be more comfortable to arrange your feet so that they are 'offset' or 'zigzagged' (see Exercise 2, p.211

4a) *Give each other a hug. Be aware of the sensations of the other person's body touching yours* [warm, hot, cool, cold, tingly, relaxed, tense, etc.]....

Let go of your partner.

4b) Share verbally (i.e., repeat Ex. 1, Version 1b).

Where there is a group of you, you could swap partners and have several hugs before taking turns to share verbally with your final partner, or with a small group of participants, or with the whole group in a circle taking turns to speak. Whatever the sharing arrangement, say 'pass' if you do not wish to share your experience. (If someone says 'pass' avoid questioning her, pressing her or commenting in any way on her decision not to share; just pass on to the next person.) If the group is large and time-limited the sharing could be done more randomly, for example, sit in a circle and only those who are keen to express something raise hands and take turns to share.

It may sometimes be a good idea to swap partners between the experiential and verbal parts of the exercise in case one of the pair has not enjoyed the experience — it might then be easier to express displeasure openly without worrying about whether the original partner will be hurt or offended.

EXERCISE 5

This exercise has a different element to it:

5a) Perform any of the above exercises as suggested, accepting your sensations, then your emotions, and finally your thoughts.

Once you have done that, experiment with changing your thoughts as you hold hands or hug. It can be like inserting a different coloured filter into a spotlight. With the new thought in your mind, once again accept all sensations, emotions, and any other thoughts that arise.

For example, the guide might choose from the following thoughts, giving time - from one to two minutes - for people to experience the thought fully. (A few of the thoughts mentioned on p.212 would also be appropriate here):

'Now notice how you feel if you think the following about your partner:

'We are two fellow human beings; we have the same needs, the same feelings...

'I honour the life and the love within you' (this is one of several translations of the Hindu greeting, 'Namaste')...

'Everything heals in the presence of love...'

'If you have done any less-than-loving deed, it was done out of hurt; with my touch I help you to heal your hurt... /With your touch you help me to heal my hurt...'

'With my love, with my caring, I support you; with your love and caring you support me...' / 'With our love and caring we support each other...'

'I celebrate you as a miracle of creation...'

'Through my touch I am pouring love into your being...'

'I receive the gift of your love into my being...'

5b) 'Share with your partner what you experienced with each thought. Did your feelings and attitudes change? If so, how did they change?

EXERCISE 6

Duration: about 2 minutes. Sit opposite each other in pairs; one partner is 'A', the other 'B'.

6a) For a minute:

'Partner A place your hands on your knees with palms facing upwards. Close your eyes if that's comfortable for you. Partner B stroke partner A's hands with your own hands gently, tenderly, slowly, with a smooth, continuous movement. Both partners notice any sensations you feel.........

[For a few seconds:] *Partner B simply hold partner A's hands... And now let go of partner A's hands.*

[For another minute:]

'Swap roles [— repeat 6a with partner A stroking partner B's hands]'.

6b) Share verbally (i.e., repeat Ex. 1, Version 1b).

This exercise could also be performed 'changing the spotlight filter' (as in exercise 5a, p.213–214.

EXERCISE 7

Duration: about 4 minutes.

In pairs, sitting opposite each other. One partner is 'A', the other 'B'. I suggest doing this only when you're comfortable with the exercises above — touching a face is generally experienced as more intimate than touching hands.

7a) *'Partner B close your eyes if that's comfortable for you. Partner A, with both hands, gently, tenderly, stroke your partner's face in a smooth/continuous, slow movement. Avoid your partner's eyes and mouth... Be aware of the sensations in your hands, and partner B, be aware of sensations in your face as you receive your partner's touch............*

'Swap roles [that is, repeat 7a changing 'partner A' to 'partner B' and vice versa]'.

7b) Share verbally (i.e., repeat Ex. 1, Version 1b).

EXERCISE 8

The same as Exercise 7 but with partners looking into each other's eyes.

Exercises 7 and 8 can also be performed 'changing the spotlight filter' (as in Ex. 5a, p.213–214).

* * *

'Pro-touch' supervision

If you are a therapist who uses or wishes to use physical contact with clients it is helpful to find a pro-touch supervisor — one who has an understanding of touch, is comfortable with it, and preferably who uses it in his work. If he himself does not use touch, he should at least support your use of it and be able to think about it with you.

Summary

Some readers persuaded by the evidence in favour of touch may wish to relax the touch taboo in their lives and, in the case of therapists, in their practice. There are various ways to do this. Raising awareness of one's own tactile beliefs, preferences and habits is a helpful starting point. It is also fruitful to create a more tactile environment for oneself by seeking out activities that involve touch.

Chapter 13

Overall summary, conclusions and final thoughts

> ... to a very significant extent, a measure of the individual's development as a healthy human being is the extent to which he or she is freely able to embrace another and enjoy the embraces of others ... to get, in a very real sense, into touch with others.[1]
> Montagu (1986:286)

> If touching helps patients it should be provided; if it harms them it must be avoided. It cannot be regarded as an optional extra or something to be tolerated but not really approved of. And whatever we do we must do openly and also encourage and support our students in doing.
> Woodmansey (1988:57)

I began this investigation in 2004 because I was puzzled about certain issues relating to touch. Sixteen years later, my research has led me to the following conclusions:

- Touch is a primary colour in the palette of human need; it cannot be substituted for anything else. Receptors and neurological pathways for the various sensory inputs differ (Gray et al., 1995; see Linden, 2015). Although I might be able to imagine it, I cannot experience actual touch other than through bodily contact (Forer, 1969:230; Jourard & Rubin, 1968:39) any more than I can know actual colour with my eyes shut or sound with my ears blocked. 'Metaphorical' touch (Peloquin, 1989:308) — through eyes, voice, and empathy — while essential, does not fulfil the same function.

Therefore, if touch was missing in the individual's history and personality formation, it seems likely that only the provision of touch will redress the deficit and repair its negative impacts on psychophysiological health, just as rickets sufferers will only be cured by adequate doses of vitamin D.

Of the 42 participants in my study who were non-tactile in early adulthood, 40 (95.2%) progressed towards greater tactility. This perhaps suggests that tactility is part of the healthful state towards which 'self-righting' (Werner & Smith, 1992) organisms gravitate once they are freer from the constraints of their childhood environments.

- In therapy, touch can both help and hinder therapeutic progress. If used unskilfully, in common with any intervention, it can negatively affect outcome. If used sensitively, as in most cases, it can be a powerful tool for positive change, and for certain clients the single most potent catalyst of such change.

- *The taboo against touch in psychotherapy is based on cultural conditioning rather than on theoretical and clinical evidence.*

And, as Older observed (1977:198),

> only by recognizing that our behavior as therapists is linked to cultural prohibitions, can we choose to act differently when this is appropriate.

Evidence for the apposite use of physical contact in psychotherapy is significant and compelling. Cultural prohibitions with regard to tactility run counter to this evidence and obstruct the absorption of touch-use into mainstream talking therapy. For certain clients this can severely limit its effectiveness.

I therefore think it logical, and ethical
— that psychotherapy trainings at very least initiate open discussion on touch, include touch research in their reading lists and, at best, offer touch training in their curricula;
— that touch is incorporated into the repertoire of helping tools by therapists who feel able to use it;
— that such therapists are supported by supervisors who preferably are themselves trained in touch issues;

— and that the editors/gatekeepers of influential journals welcome touch research into the mainstream arena (as some have).

Articles on the use of physical contact in therapy have been published by touch-friendly areas of healthcare such as nursing, bodywork and body psychotherapy. However, in the main, these flourish in paradigmatic ghettos whence assimilation into general psychotherapy discourse is barred by anti-touch traditions. As a result, the rich world of tactual wisdom still awaits integration into verbal therapies. While aiding therapists in the work of relieving distress, such integration would require some among us to question and alter our culturally derived non-tactile positions — a challenging journey perhaps, but one with far-reaching benefits for ourselves, our clients and perhaps even for members of non-tactile societies beyond the world of therapy.

Although I have adduced my own and others' evidence for the advantages of touch, I do not wish the allure of research to obscure my initial response to the notion of touch research, namely, that it is an indictment of Anglo-Western values; that in a society which had kept more in contact with its humanity, the value of caring touch would be a phenomenon too obvious to need 'proving', in the same way that a scientist does not need to cut off the legs of a cat to prove it can't walk without them.

Finally, it is in clients' testimonies that incontrovertible arguments for therapeutic touch are to be found. I would therefore like to leave the last word to my client participants and designate brave and beautiful Eva as their spokesperson. In charting recovery from sadistic childhood abuse, her narrative encapsulated most of the themes discussed in this book and movingly conveys the healing properties of touch:

> 'The touch has helped me to change a lot, to integrate, to change some patterns in my mind. Loving touch tells me I am a good person, that I was a lovable child. If someone physically touches me and holds me, that message goes into my body and into my subconscious. It gives a message to the body that I can't get just on a verbal level — it gets into my bones and into my cells.

The compassion of having received holding even if I talked about negative things I have done — that love and compassion and nurturing can help to heal on a very deep level. It has helped me transform something in myself, to have more love and compassion for myself — and for others — and to forgive myself; to make a new imprint. To rewrite my history.'

Note

1 '... **to a very significant extent, a measure of the individual's development as a healthy human being is the extent to which he or she is freely able to embrace another and enjoy the embraces of others ... to get, in a very real sense, into touch with others'** Montagu (1986:286).

In this light, degree of comfort or discomfort with touch could be considered an index of psychological health. Where assessment of personality or psychological health is deemed necessary, assessors might find it interesting and useful to ask assessees about their attitudes to touch. Such enquiry can lead to salient information about their personal histories and might provide indications of mental-emotional health status.

'... **if touch was missing in the individual's history and personality formation, it seems likely that only the provision of touch will redress the deficit and repair its negative impacts on psychophysiological health...**'

Perhaps relevant here are those depressed clients who improve with therapy but who still do not reach the 'standard deviation' (the health norm) for the general population (Roth & Fonagy, 1996:78,80). Extrapolating from clinical reports I wonder whether in some instances their residual distress might be due to the failure of therapists to provide touch. The psychiatrist Bar-Levav (1998), for example, has used touch to reverse life-long depression (see also experiment involving touch by Gursimran et al., 2015).

Bibliography

Abramovich, E. (2005). Childhood sexual abuse as a risk factor for subsequent involvement in sex work: a review of empirical findings. *Journal of Psychology & Human Sexuality, 17(1–2)*:131–146.

Abs, P. (1974). *Autobiography in Education*. London: Heineman Educational.

Ader, R. & Conklin, P.M. (1963). Handling of pregnant rats: effects on emotionality of their offspring. *Science, 142(3590)*:411–412.

Afifi, T.O., Brownridge, D.A., Cox, B.J. & Sareen, J. (2006). Physical punishment, childhood abuse and psychiatric disorders. *Child Abuse & Neglect, 30(10)*:1093–1103.

Afifi, T.O., Fortier, J., Sareen, J. & Taillieu, T. (2019). Associations of harsh physical punishment and child maltreatment in childhood with antisocial behaviors in adulthood. *JAMA Network Open, 2(1)*:e187374.

Afifi, T.O., Mota, N.P., Dasiewicz, P., MacMillan, H.L. & Sareen, J. (2012). Physical punishment and mental disorders: results from a nationally representative US sample. *Pediatrics, 130(2)*:184–192.

Aguilera, D. (1967). Relationships between physical contact and verbal interactions between nurses and patients. *Journal of Psychiatric Nursing Mental Health Services, 5(1)*:5–21.

Aha! Parenting (2019). How to set effective limits with your child. www.ahaparenting.com/parenting-tools/positive-discipline/effective-limits

Ainsworth, M.D.S., Blehar, M.C., Waters, E. & Wall, S. (1978). *Patterns of Attachment: A Psychological Study of the Strange Situation*. Hillside, NJ: Erlbaum.

Aisa, B., Tordera, R., Lasheras, B., Del Rio, J. & Ramirez, M.J. (2007). Cognitive impairment associated to HPA axis hyperactivity after maternal separation in rats. *Psychoneuroendocrinology, 32(3)*:256–266.

Alagna, F.J., Witcher, S.J., Fisher, J.D. & Wicas, E.A. (1979). Evaluative reaction to interpersonal touch in a counseling interview. *Journal of Counseling Psychology, 26(6)*:465–472.

Aldwin, C.M., Molitor, N.T., Avron, S., Levenson, M.R., Molitor, J. & Igarashi, H. (2011). Do stress trajectories predict mortality in older men?

Longitudinal findings from the VA normative aging study. *Journal of Aging Research.* doi: 10.4061/2011/896109.

Alkadhi, K. (2013). Brain physiology and pathophysiology in mental stress. *International Scholarly Research Notices (ISRN). Physiology 2013, Article 1D 806104*:1–23.

Allen, D.M. & Tarnowski, K.J. (1989). Depressive characteristics of physically abused children. *Journal of Abnormal Child Psychology, 17(1)*:1–11.

Altindag, O., Altindag, A., Asoglu, M., Gunes, M., Soran, N. & Deveci, Z. (2007). Relation of cortisol levels and bone mineral density among premenopausal women with major depression. *International Journal of Clinical Practice, 61(3)*:416–420.

Aly, H., Moustafa, M.F., Hassanein, S.M., Massaro, A.N., Amer, H.A. & Patel, K. (2004). Physical activity combined with massage improves bone mineralization in premature infants: a randomized trial. *Journal of Perinatology, 24(5)*:305–309.

Alyahri, A. & Goodman, R. (2008). Harsh corporal punishment of Yemeni children: occurrence, type and associations. *Child Abuse & Neglect, 32(8)*:766–773.

Amacher, N.J. (1973). Touch is a way of caring. *American Journal of Nursing, 73(5)*:852.

American College of Obstetricians and Gynecologists (2011). Adult manifestations of childhood sexual abuse. Committee Opinion No. 498. *Obstetrics & Gynecology, 118(2, pt 1)*:392–395.

American Psychological Association (APA) (2010). *Ethical Principles of Psychologists and Code of Conduct.* www.apa.org/ethics/code/

Anda, R.F., Brown, D.W., Dube, S.R., Bremner, J.D., Felitti, V.J. & Giles, W.H. (2008). Adverse childhood experiences and chronic obstructive pulmonary disease in adults. *American Journal of Preventive Medicine, 34(5)*:396–403.

Anda, R.F., Chapman, D.P., Felitti, V.J., Edwards, V., Williamson, D.F., Croft, J.B. & Giles, W.H. (2002). Adverse childhood experiences and risk of paternity in teen pregnancy. *American College of Obstetricians and Gynecologists, 10(1)*:37–45.

Anda, R.F., Felitti, V.I., Bremner, J.D., Walker, J.D., Whitfield, C., Perry, B.D., Dube, S.R. & Giles, W.H. (2006). The enduring effects of abuse and related adverse experiences in childhood: a convergence of evidence from neurobiology and epidemiology. *European Archives of Psychiatry and Clinical Neuroscience, 256(3)*:174–186.

Andersen, J.F., Andersen, P.A. & Lustig, M.W. (1987). Opposite sex touch avoidance: a national replication and extension. *Journal of Nonverbal Behavior, 11(2)*:89–109.

Andersen, P.A. (1985). Nonverbal immediacy in interpersonal communication. In A.W. Siegman & S. Feldstein (Eds). *Multichannel Integrations of Nonverbal Behavior*: 1–36. Hillsdale, NJ: Lawrence Erlbaum.

Andersen, P.A. (1999). *Nonverbal Communication; Forms and Functions*. Mountain View, CA: Mayfield.

Andersen, P.A. & Leibowitz, K. (1978). The development and nature of the construct touch avoidance. *Environmental Psychology and Nonverbal Behavior, 3(2)*:89–106.

Andersen, P.A., Lustig, M.W. & Andersen, J.F. (1986). *Communication patterns among cultural regions of the United States: a theoretical perspective*. Paper presented at the annual convention of the International Communication Association, Chicago, IL.

Andersen, S.L. & Teicher, M.H. (2004). Delayed effects of early stress on hippocampal development. *Neuropsychopharmacology, 29(11)*:1988–1993.

Andersen, S.L., Tomada, A., Vincow, E.S., Valente, E., Polcari, A. & Teicher, M.H. (2008). Preliminary evidence for sensitive periods in the effect of childhood sexual abuse on regional brain development. *Journal of Neuropsychiatry and the Clinical Neurosciences, 20(3)*:292–301.

Anderson, D.W. (1985). *Positive Physical Interaction with Students* (AAHE Monograph Series). Washington, DC: American Academy of Higher Education.

Anderson, D.W. (1986). *On the Importance of Touching*. ERIC document Reproduction Service No. ED 270 232.

Anderson, G.C., Marks, E.A. & Wahlberg, V. (1986). Kangaroo care for premature infants. *American Journal of Nursing, 86(7)*:807–809.

Angelakis, I., Gillespie, E.L. & Panagioti, M. (2019). Childhood maltreatment and adult suicidality: a comprehensive systematic review with meta-analysis. *Psychological Medicine*. doi: 10.1017/S0033291718003823

Arata, C.M. (2002). Child sexual abuse and sexual revictimization. *Clinical Psychology: Science and Practice, 9(2)*:135–164.

Argyle, M. (1988). *Bodily Communication* (2nd ed.). New York: Methuen.

Arnsten, A.F.T. (2009). Stress signalling pathways that impair prefrontal cortex structure and function. *Nature Reviews Neuroscience, 10(6)*:410–422.

Arriola, K.R.J., Louden, T., Doldren, M.A. & Fortenberry, R.M. (2005). A meta-analysis of the relationship of child sexual abuse to HIV risk behaviour among women. *Child Abuse & Neglect, 29(6)*:725–746.

Arseneault, L. (2017). *Addressing the Mental Health Consequences of Bullying*. London: Economic and Social Research Council (ESRC).

Azuma, K., Adachi, Y., Hayashi, H. & Kubo, K.Y. (2015). Chronic psychological stress as a risk factor of osteoporosis. *Journal of University of Occupational & Environmental Health, 37(4)*:245–253.

Bachelor, A. & Horvath, A.O. (1999). The therapeutic relationship. In M.A. Hubble, B.L. Duncan & S.D. Miller (Eds). *The Heart and Soul of Change*: 133–178. Washington: American Psychological Association.

Bacorn, C. & Dixon, D. (1984). The effects of touch on depressed and vocationally undecided clients. *Journal of Counseling Psychology, 31(4)*:488–496.

Badley, E.M., Shields, M., O'Donnell, S., Hovdestad, W.E. & Tonmyr, L. (2018). Childhood maltreatment as a risk factor for arthritis: findings from a population-based survey of Canadian adults. *Arthritis Care & Research*. doi: 10.1002/acr.23776.
Bailey, S. (2012). Kangaroo mother care. *British Journal of Hospital Medicine, 73(5)*:278–281.
Bakwin, H. (1942). Loneliness in infants. *American Journal of Diseases of Children, 63(1)*:30–40.
Bakwin, H. (1949). Emotional deprivation in infants. *Journal of Pediatrics, 35(4)*:512–521.
Bandura, A. Ross, D. & Ross, S.A. (1961). Transmission of aggression through the imitation of aggressive models. *Journal of Abnormal and Social Psychology, 63(3)*:575–582.
Banyard, V.L., Williams, L.M. & Siegel, J.A (2001). The long-term health consequences of child sexual abuse: an exploratory study of the impact of multiple traumas in a sample of women. *Journal of Traumatic Stress, 14(4)*:697–715.
Bardeen, J.P. (1971). *Interpersonal perception through the tactile, verbal, and visual modes*. Paper presented at the Meeting of the International Communication Association, Phoenix, Arizona.
Bar-Levav, R. (1998). A rationale for physical touching in psychotherapy. In E.W.L. Smith, R.C. Clance & S. Imes (Eds). *Touch in Psychotherapy: Theory, Research and Practice*: 52–55. New York: Guilford Press.
Barnard, K.E. & Brazelton, T.B. (Eds). (1990). *Clinical Infant Reports. Touch: The Foundation of Experience.* Full revised and expanded proceedings of Johnson & Johnson Pediatric Round Table X. Madison, Connecticut: International Universities Press.
Barnett, K. (1972). A theoretical construct of the concepts of touch as they relate to nursing. *Nursing Research, 21(2)*:102–110.
Barnett, O.W., Miller-Perrin, C.L. & Perrin, R.D. (2011). *Family Violence across the Lifespan: An Introduction* (3rd ed.). London: SAGE.
Barron, D.H. (1955). Mother-Newborn relationships in goats. In B. Schaffner (Ed.). *Group Processes*: 225–226. New York: Josiah Macey, Jr., Foundation.
Baruch, D.W. (1949). *New Ways in Discipline*. New York: McGraw-Hill.
Bauer, B.A., Cutshall, S.M., Wentworth, L.J., Engen, D., Messner, P.K., Wood, C.M., Brekke, K.M., Kelly, R.F. & Sundt, T.M. (2010). Effects of massage therapy on pain, anxiety, and tension after cardiac surgery: a randomized study. *Complementary Therapies in Clinical Practice, 16(12)*:70–75.
Baumeister, D., Akhtar, R., Ciufolini, S., Pariente, C.M. & Mondelli, V. (2016). Childhood trauma and adulthood inflammation: a meta-analysis of peripheral C-reactive protein, interleukin-6 and tumour necrosis factor-α. *Molecular Psychiatry, 21(5)*:642–649.

Bellis, M.A., Hughes, K., Leckenby, N., Jones, L., Baban, A., Kachaeva, M., Povilaitis, R., Qirijako, G., Ulukol, B., Raleva, M. & Terzic, N. (2014). Adverse childhood experiences and associations with health-harming behaviours in young adults: surveys in eight eastern European countries. *Bulletin of the World Health Organisation, 92(9)*:641–655.

Belsky, J., Conger, R. & Capaldi, D. (2009). The intergenerational transmission of parenting: introduction to the special section. *The British Journal of Developmental Psychology, 45(5)*:1201–1204.

Ben-Ari, A. & Somer, E. (2004). The aftermath of therapist-client sex: exploited women struggle with the consequences. *Clinical Psychology and Psychotherapy, 11(2)*:126–136.

Bendall, S., Jackson, H.J., Hulbert, C.A. & McGorry, P.D. (2008). Childhood trauma and psychotic disorders: a systematic, critical review of the evidence. *Schizophrenia Bulletin, 34(3)*:568–579.

Bender, L. & Yarnell, H. (1941). An observation nursery; A study of 250 children on the psychiatric division of bellevue hospital. *American Journal of Psychiatry, 97(5)*:1158–1174.

Benjamin, B.E. (1995a). Massage and bodywork with survivors of abuse. Part 1. *Massage Therapy Journal, 34(3)*: 23–32.

Benjamin, B.E. (1995b, Fall). Massage and bodywork with survivors of abuse, Part II. *Massage Therapy Journal, 34(4)*: 23–30.

Bennett, R.H., Bolling, D.Z., Anderson, L.C., Pelphrey, K.A. & Kaiser, M.D. (2014). FNIRS detects temporal lobe response to affective touch. *Social Cognitive Affective Neuroscience, 9(4)*:470–476.

Berger, M.M. (1977). *Working with People Called Patients*. New York: Brunner/Mazel.

Bernard-Bonnin, A.-C. (2004). Maternal depression and child development. *Pediatrics & Child Health, 9(8)*:575–583.

Bernstein, L. (1957). The effects of handling upon learning and retention. *Journal of Comparative and Physiological Psychology, 50(2)*:162–167.

Berry, A. (1986). Knowledge at one's fingertips. *Nursing Times, 82(49)*:56–57.

Berson, N. & Herman-Giddens, M. (1994). Recognizing invasive genital care practices: a form of sexual abuse. *American Professional Society on the Abuse of Children Advisor, 7(1)*:13–14.

Bhan, N., Glymour, M.M., Kawachi, I. & Subramanian, S.V. (2014). Childhood adversity and asthma prevalence: evidence from 10 US states (2009–2011). *BMJ Open Respiratory Research, 1(1)*:e000016. doi: 10.1136/bmjresp-2013-000016

Biggar, M.L. (1984). Maternal aversion to mother-infant contact. In C.C. Brown (Ed.). *The many Facets of Touch*: 66–72. Skillman, NJ: Johnson & Johnson Baby Products.

Bijleveld, C.C.J.H., Hill, J. & Hendriks, J. (2016). Sexual abuse within the family: intergenerational transmission of victimhood and offending. In H. Kury, S. Redo & E. Shea (Eds). *Women and Children as Victims and*

Offenders: Background, Prevention, Reintegration: 905–921. Switzerland: Springer/Verlag.

Billhult, A., Lindholm, C., Gunnarsson, R. & Stener-Victorin, E. (2009). The effect of massage on immune function and stress in women with breast cancer – a randomized controlled trial. *Autonomic Neuroscience, 150(1–2)*:111–115.

Bion, W.R. (1962). *Learning from Experience.* London: Heinemann.

Black, S., Jacques, K., Webber, A., Spurr, K., Carey, E., Hebb, A. & Gilbert, R. (2010). Chair massage for treating anxiety in patients withdrawing from psychoactive drugs. *Journal of Alternative Complementary Medicine, 16(9)*:979–987.

Blanchard, R. (2001). Fraternal birth order and the maternal immune hypothesis in male homosexuality. *Hormones and Behavior, 40(2)*:105–114.

Blauvelt, H. (1956). Neonate-mother relationship in goat and man. In B. Schaffner (Ed.). *Group Processes*: 94–140. New York: Josiah Macy, Jr., Foundation.

Blinder, M.G. (1966). Differential diagnosis and treatment of depressive disorders. *Journal of the American Medical Association, 195(1)*:8–12.

Blizzard, R.M. & Bulatovic, A. (1996). Syndromes of psychosocial short stature. In F. Lifshitz (Ed.). *Pediatric Endocrinology* (3rd ed.): 83–93. New York: Marcel Dekker.

Boadella, D. (1976). *In the Wake of Reich.* London: Coventure.

Boderman, A., Freed, D.W. & Kinnucan, M.T. (1972). "Touch Me, Like Me": testing an encounter group assumption. *Journal of Applied Behavioral Science, 8(5)*:527–533.

Bogaert, A.F., Skorska, M.N., Wang, C., Gabrie, J., MacNeil, A.J., Hoffarth, M.R., VanderLaan, D.P., Zucker, K.J. & Blanchard, R. (2018). Male homosexuality and maternal immune responsivity to the Y-linked protein NLGN4Y. *Proceedings of the National Academy of Sciences (PNAS), 115(2)*:302–306.

Boguslawski, M. (1979). The use of therapeutic touch in nursing. *Journal of Continuing Education in Nursing, 10(4)*:9–15.

Bohart, A.C. & Greenberg, L.S. (1997). *Empathy Reconsidered: New Directions in Psychotherapy.* Washington, DC: American Psychological Association.

Boisset-Pioro, M.H., Esdaile, J.M. & Fitzcharles, M.A. (1995). Sexual and physical abuse in women with fibromyalgia syndrome. *Arthritis & Rheumatism, 38(2)*:235–241.

Bolbol-Haghighi, N., Masoumi, S.Z. & Kazemi, F. (2016). Effect of massage therapy on duration of labour: a randomized controlled trial. *Journal of Clinical and Diagnostic Research, 10(4)*:QC12–QC15.

Boone, T., Tanner, M. & Radosevich, A. (2001). Effects of a 10-minute back rub on cardiovascular responses in healthy subjects. *American Journal of Chinese Medicine, 29(1)*:47–52.

Bordin, E.S. (1979). The generalizability of the psychoanalytic concept of the working alliance. *Psychotherapy: Theory, Research and Practice, 16(3)*:252-260.
Borysenko, J.Z. (1985). Healing motives: an interview with David C. McClelland. *Advances: Journal of the Institute for the Advancement of Health, 2(2)*:29-41.
Bowlby, J. (1953). Some pathological processes set in train by early mother-child separation, *Journal of Mental Science, 99*:265-272.
Bowlby, J. (1958). The nature of the child's tie to his mother. *International Journal of Psychoanalysis, 39(5)*:350-373.
Bowlby, J. (1969, 1973, 1980). *Attachment and Loss, Vols 1-3*. London: Hogarth Press & The Institute of Psychoanalysis.
Bowlby, J. (1979). *The Making and Breaking of Affectional Bonds*. London: Tavistock.
Bowlby, J. (1988). *A Secure Base: Clinical Applications of Attachment Theory*. London: Routledge.
Boyesen, G. (1970). Experiences with dynamic relaxation. *Energy and Character, 1(1-2)*:21-30.
Boynton-Jarrett, R., Rosenberg, L., Palmer, J.R., Boggs, D.A. & Wise, L.A. (2012). Child and adolescent abuse in relation to obesity in adulthood: the black women's health study. *Pediatrics, 130(2)*:245-253.
Brazelton, T.B. & Cramer, B.G. (1991). *The Earliest Relationship: Parents, Infants and the Drama of Early Attachment*. Cambridge, MA: Perseus Books.
Bremner, J.D. (2003). Long-term effects of childhood abuse on brain and neurobiology. *Child and Adolescent Psychiatric Clinics of North America, 12(2)*:271-292.
Bremner, J.D. (2006). Traumatic stress: effects on the brain. *Dialogues in Clinical Neuroscience, 8(4)*:445-461.
Breuer, J. & Freud, S. (1895). *Studien über Hysterie, Deuticke, Leipzig & Vienna*. Translated and edited by J. Strachey (1955) as *Studies on Hysteria*. In The Standard Edition of the Complete Works of Sigmund Freud, Vol, 2. London: Hogarth Press.
Briere, J. & Elliott, D.M. (2003). Prevalence and psychological sequelae of self-reported childhood physical and sexual abuse in a general population sample of men and women. *Child Abuse & Neglect, 27(10)*: 1205-1222.
Brilliant Maps (2018). Map of the 53 Countries that ban the corporal punishment of children. https://brilliantmaps.com/corporal-punishment/
British Association for Counselling and Psychotherapy (BACP) (2010). *BACP: Ethical Framework: Providing a Good Standard of Practice and Care*. www.bacp.co.uk/ethical_framework/good_standard.php
Brody, V.A. (1997). *The Dialogue of Touch: Developmental Play Therapy*. Lanham, MD: Jason Aronson.

Brown, C.C. (Ed.) (1984). *The Many Facets of Touch: The Foundation of Experience: Its Importance Through Life, with Initial Emphasis for Infants and Young Children.* Skillman, NJ: Johnson & Johnson Baby Product Company.

Brown, L.S. (1988). Harmful effects of post-termination sexual and romantic relationships with former clients. *Psychotherapy: Theory, Research, Practice, Training, 25(2)*:249–255.

Brown, M. (1973). The new body psychotherapies. *Psychotherapy: Theory, Research and Practice, 10(2)*:98–116.

Brown, M.J., Thacker, L.R., & Cohen, S.A. (2013). Association between adverse childhood experiences and diagnosis of cancer. *PLoS ONE, 8(6)*:e65524.

Buist, A. & Janson, H. (2001). Childhood sexual abuse, parenting and postpartum depression — a 3-year follow-up study. *Child Abuse & Neglect, 25(7)*:909–921.

Burgoon, J.K., Buller, D.B., Hale, J.L. & de Turck, M. (1984). Relational messages associated with nonverbal behavior. *Human Communication Research, 10(3)*:351–378.

Burgoon, J.K., Buller, D.B. & Woodall, W.G. (1996). *Nonverbal Communication: The Unspoken Dialogue* (2nd ed.). New York: McGraw-Hill.

Burns, D. & Nolen-Hoeksema, S. (1992). Therapist empathy and recovery from depression in cognitive-behavioral therapy: a structural equation model. *Journal of Counseling Psychology, 60(3)*:441–449.

Butler, S. & Zelen, S.L. (1977). Sexual intimacies between therapists and patients. *Psychotherapy: Theory, Research and Practice, 14(2)*:139–145.

Butler, S.R. & Schanberg, S.M. (1977). Effect of maternal deprivation on polyamine metabolism in pre-weanling rat brain and heart. *Life Sciences, 21(6)*:877–884.

Butler, S.R., Suskind, M.R. & Schanberg, S.M. (1978). Maternal behavior as a regulator of polyamine biosynthesis in brain and heart of the developing rat pup. *Science, 199(4327)*:445–447.

Byrne D. & Clore, C.L. (1970). A reinforcement model of evaluative responses. *Personality: An International Journal, 1(2)*:103–128.

Cady, S.H. & Jones, G.E. (1997). Massage therapy as a workplace intervention for reduction of stress. *Perceptual & Motor Skills, 84(1)*:157–158.

Caldji, C., Diorio, J., Anisman, H. & Meaney, M.J. (2004). Maternal behavior regulates Benzodiazepine/$GABA_A$ Receptor subunit expression in brain regions associated with fear in BALB/c and C57BL/6 Mice. *Neuropsychopharmacology, 29(7)*:1344–1352.

Caldji, C., Diorio, J. & Meaney, M.J. (2003). Variations in maternal care alter $GABA_A$ Receptor subunit expression in brain regions associated with fear. *Neuropsychopharmacology, 28(11)*:1950–1959.

Caldwell, C. (2002, June). *Using touch in psychotherapy.* Paper presented at the USA Body Psychotherapy Conference, Baltimore. In J.E.

Phelan (Ed.). (2009). Exploring the use of touch in the psychotherapeutic setting: a phenomenological review. *Psychotherapy: Theory, Research, Practice, Training, 46(1)*:98.

Cannon, W.B. (1929). *Bodily Changes in Pain, Hunger, Fear, and Rage.* New York: Appleton-Century-Crofts.

Capitanio, J., Mendoza, S., Lerche, N. & Mason, W. (1998). Social stress results in altered glucocorticoid regulation and shorter survival in simian acquired immune deficiency syndrome. *Proceedings of the National Academy of Sciences of the USA, 95(8)*:4714–4719.

Carlsson, E., Frostell, A., Ludvigsson, J. & Faresjö, M. (2014). Psychological stress in children may alter the immune response. *Journal of Immunology, 192(5)*:2071–2081.

Caroprese, M., Napolitano, F., Albenzio, M., Annicchiarico, G., Musto, M. & Sevi, A. (2006). Influence of gentling on lamb immune response and human-lamb interactions. *Applied Animal Behaviour Science, 99(1–2)*:118–131.

Casement, P. (1985). *On Learning from the Patient.* London: Tavistock Publications.

Cashar, L. & Dixson, B. (1967). The therapeutic use of touch. *Journal of Psychiatric Nursing, 5(5)*:442–451.

Cashmore, J. & Shackel, R. (2013). *The Long-term Effects of Child Sexual Abuse.* Child Family Community Australia (CFCA), Paper No. 11, Australian Institute of Family Studies.

Center for AIDS Information and Advocacy (2012). Sexual abuse in childhood raises risk of HIV and other sexual infections. *The Body Pro.* www.thebodypro.com/content/68532/sexual-abuse-in-childhood-raises-risk-of-hiv-and-o.html

Centers for Disease Control and Prevention (CDC) (2008). *Child Maltreatment Surveillance: Uniform Definition for Public Health and Recommended Data Elements.* Version 1.0. Atlanta, Georgia, USA.

Chambers, R.A., Bremner, J., Moghaddam, B., Southwick, S., Charney, D. & Krystal, J. (1999). Glutamate and PTSD. *Seminars in Clinical Neuropsychiatry, 4(4)*:274–281.

Chapin, H.D. (1915). A plea for accurate statistics in children's institutions. *Transactions of the American Pediatric Society, 27*:180–185.

Chang, M.Y., Wang, S.Y. & Cheng, C.H. (2002). Effects of massage on pain and anxiety during labor: a randomized controlled trial in Taiwan. *Journal of Advanced Nursing, 38(1)*:68–73.

Charpak, N., Ruiz, J.G., Zupan, J., Cattaneo, A; Figueroa, Z; Tessier, R., Cristo, M., Anderson, G., Ludlington, S., Mendoza, S., Mokhachane, M. & Worku, B. (2005). Kangaroo mother care: 25 years after. *Acta Paediatrica, 94(5)*:514–522.

Chartier, M.J., Walker, J.R. & Naimark, B. (2009). Health risk behaviors and mental health problems as mediators of the relationship between childhood abuse and adult health. *American Journal of Public Health, 99(5)*:847–854.

Cheng, H.G., Huang, Y. & Anthony, J.C. (2011). Childhood physical punishment and later alcohol drinking consequences: evidence from a Chinese context. *Journal of Studies on Alcohol and Drugs, 72(1)*:24–33.

Child Family Community Australia (CFCA) (2019). *The Long-Term Effects of Child Sexual Abuse*. Melbourne, Victoria: Australian Institute of Family Studies, Australian Government.

Children Act (1989, 16th November). *Parliamentary Debates (Hansard)*. London: House of Commons.

Cigales, M., Field, T., Lundy, B., Cuadra, A. & Hart, S. (1997). Massage enhances recovery from habituation in normal infants. *Infant Behavior and Development, 20(1)*:29–34.

Clance, P.C. & Petras, V.J. (1998). Therapists' recall of their decision-making processes regarding the use of touch in ongoing psychotherapy: a preliminary study. In E.W.L. Smith, R.C. Clance & S. Imes (Eds). *Touch in Psychotherapy: Theory, Research and Practice*: 92–108. New York: Guilford Press.

Clarkin, J.F. & Levy, K.N. (2004). The influence of client variables on psychotherapy. In M.J. Lambert (Ed.). *Bergin & Garfield's Handbook of Psychotherapy and Behavior Change* (5th ed.): 194–226. New York: Wiley.

Cohen, J. & Crnic, L. (1982). Glucocorticoids, stress and the immune response. In D. Webb (Ed.). *Immunopharmacology and the Regulation of Leucocyte Function*: 61–91. New York: Marcel Dekker.

Cohen, J.A., Deblinger, E., Mannarino, A.P. & Steer, R.A. (2004). A multisite, randomized controlled trial for children with sexual abuse-related PTSD symptoms. *Journal of the American Academy of Child & Adolescent Psychiatry, 43(4)*:393–402.

Cohen, R.A., Grieve, S., Hoth, K.F., Paul, R.H., Sweet, L., Tate, D., Gunstad, J., Stroud, L., McCaffery, J., Hitsman, B., Niaura, R., Clark, C.R., McFarlane, A., Bryant, R., Gordon, E. & Williams, L.M. (2006). Early life stress and morphometry of the adult anterior cingulate cortex and caudate nuclei. *Biological Psychiatry, 59(10)*:975–982.

Cohen, R.T., Canino, G.J., Bird, H.R. & Celedón, J.C. (2008). Violence, abuse, and asthma in Puerto Rican children. *American Journal of Critical Care Medicine, 178(5)*:453–459.

Cohen, S.S. (1987). *The Magic of Touch*. New York: Harper & Row.

Collette, J.C., Millam, J.R., Klasing, K.C. & Wakenell, P.S. (2000). Neonatal handling of Amazon parrots alters the stress response and immune function. *Applied Animal Behaviour Science, 66(4)*:335–349.

Colman, R.A. & Widom, C.S. (2004). Childhood abuse and neglect and adult intimate relationships: a prospective study. *Child Abuse & Neglect, 28(11)*:1133–1151.

Coogan, P.F., Wise, L.A., O'Connor, G.T., Brown, T.A., Palmer, J.R. & Rosenberg, L. (2013). Abuse during childhood and adolescence and risk of adult-onset asthma in African American women. *Journal of Allergy Clinical Immunology, 131(4)*:1058–1063.

Cornell, D., Gregory, A., Huang, F. & Fan, X. (2013). Perceived prevalence of teasing and bullying predicts high school dropout rates. *Journal of Educational Psychology, 105(1)*:138–149.

Cowen, E.L., Weissberg, R.P. & Lotyczeuski, B.S. (1983). Physical contact in interactions between clinicians and young children. *Journal of Consulting and Clinical Psychology, 50(2)*:219–225.

Crusco, A.H. & Wetzel, C.G. (1984). The Midas touch: the effects of interpersonal touch on restaurant tipping. *Personality and Social Psychology Bulletin, 10(4)*:512–517.

Cuddy, E. & Reeves, R.V. (2014). *Hitting Kids: American parenting and physical punishment*. Social Mobility Papers. Washington, DC: The Brookings Institution.

Cullen, C., Field, T., Escalona, A. & Hartshorn, K. (2000). Father-infant interactions are enhanced by massage therapy. *Early Child Development and Care, 164(1)*:41–47.

Cutajar, M.C., Mullen, P.E., Ogloff, J.R.P., Thomas, S.D., Wells, D.L. & Spataro, J. (2010a). Schizophrenia and other psychotic disorders in a cohort of sexually abused children. *Archives of General Psychiatry, 67(11)*:1114–1119.

Cutajar, M.C., Mullen, P.E., Ogloff, J.R.P., Thomas, S.D., Wells, D.L. & Spataro, J. (2010b). Suicide and fatal drug overdose in child sexual abuse victims: a historical cohort study. *Medical Journal of Australia, 192(4)*:184–187.

Dahlberg, C. (1970). Sexual contact between patient and therapist. *Contemporary Psychoanalysis, 6(2)*:107–124.

Danese, A., Moffit, T.E., Harrington, H.L., Milne, B.J., Polanczyk, G., Pariante, C.M., Poulton, R. & Caspi, A. (2009). Adverse childhood experiences and adult risk factors for age-related disease. *Archives of Pediatrics & Adolescent Medicine, 163(12)*:1135–1143.

Dannlowski, U., Stuhrmann, A., Beutelmann, V., Zwanzger, P., Lenzen, T., Grotegerd, D., Domschke, K., Hohoff, C., Ohrmann, P., Bauer, J., Lindner, C., Postert, C., Konrad, C., Arolt, V., Heindel, W., Suslow, T. & Kugel, H. (2011). Limbic scars: long-term consequences of childhood maltreatment revealed by functional and structural magnetic resonance imaging. *Biological Psychiatry, 71(4)*:286–293.

Danto, E.A. (2005). *Freud's Free Clinics: Psychoanalysis and Social Justice, 1918–1938*. New York: Columbia University Press.

Davidson, K., Jacoby, S. & Brown, M.S. (2000). Prenatal perineal massage: preventing lacerations during delivery. *Journal of Obstetric, Gynecologic, & Neonatal Nursing, 29(5)*:474–479.

Davidson, R.J. & McEwen, B.S. (2012). Social influences on neuroplasticity: stress and interventions to promote well-being. *Nature Neuroscience, 15(5)*:689–695.

De Bellis, M.D., Chrousos, G.P., Dorn, L.D., Burke, L., Helmers, K., Kling, M.A., Trickett, P.K. & Putnam, F.W. (1994). Hypothalamic-pituitary-adrenal axis dysregulation in sexually abused girls. *Journal of Clinical Endocrinology & Metabolism, 78(2)*:249–255.

De Bellis, M.D., Keshavan, M.S., Clark, D.B., Casey, B.J., Giedd, J.N., Boring, A.M., Frustaci, K. & Ryan, N.D. (1999). Bennett research award. Developmental traumatology. Part II: brain development. *Biological Psychiatry, 45(10)*:1271–1284.

De Bellis, M.D., Keshavan, M.S., Shifflett, H., Iyengar, S., Beers, S.R., Hall, J. & Moritz, G. (2002). Brain structures in pediatric maltreatment-related posttraumatic stress disorder: a sociodemographically matched study. *Biological Psychiatry, 52(11)*:1066–1078.

De Bellis, M.D. & Kuchibhatla, M. (2006). Cerebellar volumes in pediatric maltreatment-related posttraumatic stress disorder. *Biological Psychiatry, 60(7)*:697–703.

Delaney, J.P., Leung, K.S., Watkins, A. & Brodie, D. (2002). The short-term effects of myofascial trigger point massage therapy on cardiac autonomic tone in healthy subjects. *Journal of Advanced Nursing, 37(4)*:364–371.

Delozier, P.P. (1994). Therapist sexual misconduct. *Women and Therapy, 15(1)*:55–67.

Denenberg, V.H. & Karas, G.G. (1959). Effects of differential infantile handling upon weight gain and mortality in the rat and mouse. *Science, 130(3376)*:629–630.

Denenberg, V.H. & Karas, G.G. (1960). Interactive effects of age and duration of infantile experience on adult learning. *Psychological Preports, 7(2)*:313–322.

Denenberg, V.H. & Whimbey, A.E. (1963). Behavior of adult rats is modified by the experience their mothers had as infants. *Science, 142(3596)*:1192–1193.

Derlega, V.J. & Berg, J.H. (Eds). (1987). *Self-Disclosure; Theory, Research, and Therapy*. New York: Plenum Press.

Desai, S., Arias, I., Thompson, M.P. & Basile, K.C. (2002). Childhood victimization and subsequent adult revictimization assessed in a nationally representative sample of women and men. *Violence and Victims, 17(6)*:639–653.

Descartes, R. (1642). *Meditations*. Amsterdam: Louis Elzevir.

Diego, M.A., Field, T. & Hernandez-Reif, M. (2005). Vagal activity, gastric motility, and weight gain in massaged preterm neonates. *Journal of Pediatrics, 147(1)*:50–55.

Diego, M.A., Field, T. & Hernandez-Reif, M. (2009). Procedural pain heart rate responses in massaged preterm infants. *Infant Behavior and Development, 32(2)*:226–229.

Diego, M.A., Field, T. & Hernandez-Reif, M. (2014). Preterm infant weight gain is increased by massage therapy and exercise via different underlying mechanisms. *Early Human Development, 90(3)*:137–140.

Diego, M.A., Field, T., Hernandez-Reif, M., Deeds, O., Ascencio, A. & Begert, G. (2007). Preterm infant massage elicits consistent increases in vagal activity and gastric motility that are associated with greater weight gain. *Acta Paediatrica, 96(11)*:1588–1591.

Diego, M.A., Field, T., Hernandez-Reif, M., Shaw, J.A., Rothe, E.M., Catellanos, D. & Mesner, L. (2002b). Aggressive adolescents benefit from massage therapy. *Adolescence, 37(147)*:597–607.

Diego, M.A., Hernandez-Reif, M., Field, T., Friedman, L. & Shaw, K. (2001). HIV adolescents show improved immune function following massage therapy. *International Journal of Neuroscience, 106(1–2)*:35–45.

Dieter, J., Field, T., Hernandez-Reif, M., Emory, E.K. & Redzepi, M. (2003). Stable preterm infants gain more weight and sleep less after five days of massage therapy. *Journal of Pediatric Psychology, 28(6)*:403–411.

Diette, T.M., Goldsmith, A.H., Hamilton, D. & Darity, W.A. Jr. (2017). Child abuse, sexual assault, community violence and high school graduation. *Review of Behavioral Economics, 4(3)*:215–240.

Dinwiddie, S., Heath, A.C., Dunne, M.P., Bucholz, K.K., Madden, P.A., Slutske, W.S., et al. (2000). Early sexual abuse and lifetime psychopathology: a co-twin-control study. *Psychological Medicine, 30(1)*:41–52.

Dolinski, D. (2010). Touch, compliance and homophobia. *Journal of Nonverbal Behavior, 34(3)*:179–192.

Dominian, J. (1971). The psychological significance of touch. *Nursing Times, 67(26)*:896–898.

Dong, M., Dube, S.R., Felitti, V.J., Giles, W.H. & Anda, R.F. (2003). Adverse childhood experiences and self-reported liver disease: new insights into the causal pathway. *Archives of Internal Medicine, 163(16)*:1949–1956.

Dong, M., Giles, W.H., Felitti, V.J., Dube, S.R., Williams, J.E., Chapman, D.P. & Anda, R.F. (2004). Insights into causal pathways for ischemic heart disease: adverse childhood experiences study. *Circulation, 110(13)*:1761–1766.

Dorahy, M.J. & Clearwater, K. (2010). Shame and guilt in men exposed to childhood sexual abuse: a qualitative investigation. *Journal of Child Sexual Abuse, 21(2)*:155–175.

Dozier, M., Peloso, E., Lewis, E., Laurenceau, J-P. & Levine, S. (2008). Effects of an attachment-based intervention on the cortisol production of infants and toddlers in foster care. *Development and Psychopathology, 20(3)*:845–859.

Draper, B., Pfaff, J.J., Pirkis, J., Snowdon, J., Lautenschlager, N.T., Wilson, I. & Almeida, O.P. (2008). Long-term effects of childhood abuse on the quality of life and health of older people: results from the depression and early prevention of suicide in general practice project. *Journal of the American Geriatrics Society, 56(2)*:262–271.

Draper, P. (1973). Crowding among hunter-gatherers: The! Kung Bushmen. *Science, New Series, 182(4109)*:301–303.

Donoyama, N., Munakata, T. & Shibasaki, M. (2010). Effects of Anma therapy (traditional Japanese massage) on body and mind. *Journal of Bodywork and Movement, 14*: 55–64.

Dozier, M., Peloso, E., Lewis, E. & Laurenceau, J-P (2008). Effects of an attachment-based intervention on the cortisol production of infants and toddlers in foster care. *Development and Psychopathology, 20(3)*:845–850.

Drossman, D.A. (1995). Sexual and physical abuse and gastrointestinal illness. *Scandinavian Journal of Gastroenterology, 30(Sup.208)*:90–96.

Dube, S.E., Fairweather, D., Pearson, W.S., Felitti, V.J., Anda, R.F. & Croft, J.B. (2009). Cumulative childhood stress and autoimmune diseases in adults. *Psychosomatic Medicine, 71(2)*:243–250.

Dube, S.R., Felitti, V.J., Dong, M., Chapman, D.P., Giles, W.H. & Anda, R.F. (2003). Childhood abuse, neglect, and household dysfunction and the risk of illicit drug use: the adverse childhood experiences study. *Pediatrics, 111(3)*:564–572.Dunbar, R.I.M. (2010). The social role of touch in humans and primates: behavioural function and neurobiological mechanisms. *Neuroscience & Biobehavioral Reviews, 34(2)*:260–268.

Duncan, B.L., Hubble, M.A. & Miller, S.D. (1997). *Psychotherapy with Impossible Cases: Efficient Treatment of Therapy Veterans*. New York: Norton.

Dunne, C., Bruggen, P. & O'Brian, C. (1982). Touch and action in group therapy of younger adolescents. *Journal of Adolescence, 5(1)*:31–38.

Durfee, H. & Wolf, K. (1933). Anstaltspflege und Entwiklung im Ersten Lebensjahr [Institutional Care and Development in the first year – translated in Spitzer, 1940]. *Zeitschrift fur Kinderforschung, 42(3)*:273–320.

Dussich, J.P.J. & Maekoya, C. (2007). Physical child harm and bullying-related behaviors: a comparative study in Japan, South Africa, and the United States. *International Journal of Offender Therapy & Comparative Criminology, 51(5)*:495–509.

Eaton, M., Mitchell-Bonair, I.L., & Friedmann, E. (1986). The effect of touch on nutritional intake of chronic organic brain syndrome patients. *Journal of Gerontology, 41(5)*:611–616.

Ebrecht, M., Hextall, J., Kirtley, L.G., Taylor, A., Dyson, M. & Weinman, J. (2004). Perceived stress and cortisol levels predict speed of wound healing in healthy male adults. *Psychoneuroendocrinology, 29(6)*:798–809.

Edmiston, E.E., Wang, F., Mazure, C.M. Guiney, J., Sinha, R., Mayes, L.C. & Blumberg, H.P. (2011). Corticostriatal gray matter morphology in adolescents with self-reported exposure to childhood maltreatment. *Archives of Pediatrics and Adolescent Medicine, 165(12)*:1069–1077.

Edwards, D.J.A. (1981). The role of touch in interpersonal relations: implications for psychotherapy. *South African Journal of Psychology, 11(1)*:29–37.

Eiden, B. (1998). The use of touch in psychotherapy. *Self & Society, 26(2)*:3–8.

Eiden, B. (2002). *Can the Profession of Psychotherapy Afford to Be Untouched Any Longer?: The Use of Touch in Psychotherapy*. www.chironcentre.freeserve.co.uk/articles/untouched.html

El-Baz, R.H., Abo-El-Ezz, W.F., El-Hadidy, M.A.E. & El-Boraie, H.A. (2016). Child abuse experiences in adolescents with externalizing disorders. *Egyptian Journal of Psychiatry, 37(2)*:46–52.

Eluvathingal, T.J., Chugani, H.T., Behen, M.E., Juhász, C., Muzik, O., Magbool, M., Chugani, D.C. & Makki, M. (2006). Abnormal brain connectivity in children after early severe socioemotional deprivation: a diffusion tensor imaging study. *Pediatrics, 117(6)*:2093–2100.

Epel, E.S. (2009). Review: psychological and metabolic stress: a recipe for accelerated cellular aging? *Hormones, 8(1)*:7–22.

Erfanian, M. (2018). Childhood trauma: a risk for major depression in patients with psoriasis. *Psychiatry and Clinical Psychopharmacology, 28(4)*:378–385.

Everaerd, D., Klumpers, F., Zwiers, M., Guadalupe, T., Franke, B., van Oostrom, I., Schene, A., Fernández, G. & Tendolkar, I. (2015). Childhood abuse and deprivation are associated with distinct sex-dependent differences in brain morphology. *Neuropsychopharmacology, 41(7)*:1716–1723.

Evison, R. & Horobin, R. (1985). *How to Change Yourself & Your World: A Manual of Co-Counselling Theory and Practice*. Pitlochry, Scotland: Co-Counselling Phoenix.

Evison, R. & Horobin, R. (1999). *Co-Counselling as Therapy*. Pitlochrie, Scotland: Co-Counselling Phoenix.

Fabricius, K., Wortwein, G. & Pakkenberg, B. (2008). The impact of maternal separation on adult mouse behaviour and on the total neuron number in the mouse hippocampus. *Brain Structure and Function, 212(5)*:403–416.

Fagan, J. (1998). Thoughts on using touch in psychotherapy. In E.W.L. Smith, R.C. Clance & S. Imes (Eds). *Touch in Psychotherapy: Theory, Research and Practice*: 145–152. New York: Guilford Press.

Fagan, J. & Silverthorn, A.S. (1998). Research on communication by touch. In E.W.L. Smith, R.C. Clance & S. Imes (Eds). *Touch in Psychotherapy: Theory, Research and Practice*: 59–73. New York: Guilford Press.

Falkensteiner, M., Mantovan, F., Muller, I. & Them, C. (2011). The use of massage therapy for reducing pain, anxiety, and depression in oncological palliative care patients: a narrative review of the literature. *International Scholarly Research Network Nursing*. doi: 10.5402/2011/929868.

Faller, K.C. (1993). *Child Sexual Abuse: Intervention and Treatment Issues: Definitions, Scope, and Effects of Child Sexual Abuse*. Washington, DC: Child Welfare Information Gateway.

Fang, X. & Corso, P.S. (2007). Child maltreatment, youth violence, and intimate partner violence: developmental relationships. *American Journal of Preventive Medicine, 33(4)*:281–290.

Farber, B.A. (2006). *Self-disclosure in Psychotherapy*. New York: Guilford Press.

Farber, E.D. & Joseph, J.A. (1985). The maltreated adolescent: patterns of physical abuse. *Child Abuse & Neglect, 9(2)*:201–206.

Farrah, S. (1971). The nurse, the patient and touch. In M. Duffy (Ed.). *Current Concepts in Clinical Nursing*. St. Louis: C. V. Mosby Co.

Fauci, A.S. & Dale, D.C. (1974). The effect of In Vivo hydrocortisone on subpopulations of human lymphocytes. *The Journal of Clinical Investigation, 53(1)*:240–246.

Feijo, L., Hernandez-Reif, M., Field, T., Burns, W., Valley-Gray, S. & Simco, E. (2006). Mothers' depressed mood and anxiety levels are reduced after massaging their preterm infants. *Infant Behavior and Development, 29(3)*:476–480.

Feiring, C. & Cleland, C. (2007). Childhood sexual abuse and abuse-specific attributions of blame over 6 years following discovery. *Child Abuse & Neglect, 31(11–12)*:1169–1186.

Feldman, R. (2011). Maternal touch and the developing infant. In M.J. Hertenstein & S.J. Weiss (Eds). *The Handbook of Touch: Neuroscience, Behavioral, and Health Perspectives*: 373–407. New York: Springer.

Feldman, R., Rosenthal, Z. & Eidelman, A.L. (2014). Maternal-preterm skin-to-skin contact enhances child physiologic organization and cognitive control across the first 10 years of life. *Biological Psychiatry, 75(1)*:56–64.

Feldman, R., Singer, M. & Zagoory, O. (2010). *Touch Attenuates Infants' Physiological Reactivity to Stress*. Wiley Online Library. doi: 10.1111/j.1467-7687.2009.00890.x

Felitti, V.J. (1991). Long-term medical consequences of incest, rape, and molestation. *Southern Medical Journal, 84(3)*:328–331.

Felitti, V.J., Anda, R.F., Nordenberg, D., Williamson, D.F., Spitz, A.M., Edwards, V., Koss, M.P. & Marks, J.S. (1998). Relationship of childhood abuse and household dysfunction to many of the leading causes of death in adults: the adverse childhood experiences (ACE) Study. *American Journal of Preventive Medicine, 14(4)*:245–258.

Felson, R.B. & Lane, K.J. (2009). Social learning, sexual and physical abuse, and adult crime. *Aggressive Behaviour, 35(6)*:489–502.

Ferber, S.G., Kuint, J., Weller, A., Feldman, R., Dollberg, S., Arbel, E. & Kohelet, D. (2002). Massage therapy by mothers and trained professionals enhances weight gain in preterm infants. *Early Human Development, 67(1–2)*:37–45.

Ferenczi, F. (1930). The principle of relaxation and neocatharsis. *International Journal of Psycho-Analysis, 11*:428–443.

Fergusson, D.M., Horwood, L.I. & Lynskey, M.T. (1997). Childhood sexual abuse, adolescent sexual behaviors and sexual revictimization. *Child Abuse & Neglect, 21(8)*:789–803.

Field, T. (1998). Massage therapy effects. *American Psychologist, 53(12)*:1270–1281.

Field, T. (1999a). Preschoolers in America are touched less and are more aggressive than preschoolers in France. *Early Child Development and Care, 151(1)*:11–17.
Field, T. (1999b). American adolescents touch each other less and are more aggressive towards their peers as compared with French adolescents. *Adolescence, 34(136)*:753–758.
Field, T. (2001a). *Touch.* Cambridge, MS: MIT Press.
Field, T. (2001b). Massage therapy facilitates weight gain in preterm infants. *Current Directions in Psychological Science, 10(2)*:51–54.
Field, T. (2002). Violence and touch deprivation in adolescents. *Adolescence, 37(148)*:735–749.
Field, T. (2010). Postpartum depression effects on early interactions, parenting, and safety practices: a review. *Infant Behavior and Development, 33(1)*:1–6.
Field, T. (2014). Massage therapy research review. *Complimentary Therapies in Clinical Practice, 20(4)*:224–229.
Field, T., Cullen, C., Diego, M., Hernandez-Reif, M., Sprinz, P., Beebe, K., Kissel, B. & Bango-Sanchez, V. (2001). Leukemia immune changes following massage therapy. *Journal of Bodywork and Movement Therapies, 5(4)*:271–274.
Field, T. & Diego, M. (2008a). Vagal activity, early growth and emotional development. *Infant Behavior and Development, 31(3)*:361–373.
Field, T. & Diego, M. (2008b). Cortisol: the culprit prenatal stress variable. *International Journal of Neuroscience, 118(8)*:1181–1205.
Field, T., Diego, M., Cullen, C., Hartshorn, K., Gruskin, A., Hernandez-Reif, M. & Sunshine, W. (2004). Carpal tunnel syndrome symptoms are lessened following massage therapy. *Journal of Bodywork and Movement Therapies, 8(1)*:9–14.
Field, T., Diego, M. & Hernandez-Reif, M. (2008a). Prematurity and potential predictors. *International Journal of Neuroscience, 118(2)*:277–289.
Field, T., Diego, M., Hernandez-Reif, M., Dieter, J.N., Kumar, A.M., Schanberg, S. & Kuhn, C. (2008b). Insulin and insulin-like growth factor-1 increased in preterm neonates following massage therapy. *Journal of Developmental and Behavioral Pediatrics, 29(6)*:463–466.
Field, T., Diego, M. & Hernandez-Reif, M. (2010a). Preterm infant massage therapy research: a review. *Infant Behavior and Development, 33(2)*:115–124.
Field, T., Diego, M. & Hernandez-Reif, M. (2010b). Moderate pressure is essential for massage therapy effects. *International Journal of Neuroscience, 120(5)*:381–385.
Field, T., Diego, M., Hernandez-Reif, M., Deeds, O. & Figueiredo, B. (2009). Pregnancy massage reduces prematurity, low birthweight and postpartum depression. *Infant Behavior & Development, 32(4)*:454–460.

Field, T., Grizzle, N., Scafidi, F., Abrams, S. & Richardson, S. (1996a). Massage therapy for infants of depressed mothers. *Infant Behavior and Development, 19(1)*:107–112.

Field, T., Grizzle, N., Scafidi, F. & Schanberg, S. (1996b). Massage and relaxation therapies' effects on depressed adolescent mothers. *Adolescence, 31(124)*:903–911.

Field, T., Henteleff, T., Hernandez-Reif, M., Martinez, E., Mavunda, K., Kuhn, C. & Schanberg, S. (1998a). Children with asthma have improved pulmonary functions after massage therapy. *Journal of Pediatrics, 132(5)*:854–858.

Field, T., Hernandez-Reif, M., Quintino, O., Schanberg, S. & Kuhn, C. (1998b). Elder retired volunteers benefit from giving massage therapy to infants. *Journal of Applied Gerontology, 17(2)*:229–239.

Field, T. & Hernandez-Reif, M. (2001). Sleep problems in infants decrease following massage therapy. *Early Child Development and Care, 168(1)*:95–104.

Field, T., Hernandez-Reif, M., Diego, M., Feijo, L., Vera, Y., Gil, K. & Sanders, C. (2007a). Still-face and separation effects on depressed mother-infant interactions. *Infant Mental Health Journal, 28(3)*:314–323.

Field, T., Hernandez-Reif, M., Diego, M. & Fraser, M. (2007b). Lower back pain and sleep disturbance are reduced following massage therapy. *Journal of Bodywork and Movement Therapy, 11(2)*:141–145.

Field, T., Hernandez-Reif, M., Diego, M., Schanberg, S. & Kuhn, C. (2005). Cortisol decreases and serotonin and dopamine increase following massage therapy. *International Journal of Neuroscience, 115(10)*:1397–1413.

Field, T., Hernandez-Reif, M., Hart, S., Quintino, O., Drose, L.A., Field, T., Kuhn, C. & Schanberg, S. (1997a). Effects of sexual abuse are lessened by massage therapy. *Journal of Bodywork and Movement Therapies, 1(2)*:65–69.

Field, T., Hernandez-Reif, M., LaGreca, A., Shaw, K., Schanberg, S. & Kuhn, C. (1997b). Massage therapy lowers blood glucose levels in children with diabetes mellitus. *Diabetes Spectrum 10*:237–239.

Field, T., Hernandez-Reif, M., Taylor, S., Quintino, O. & Burman, I. (1997c). Labor pain is reduced by massage therapy. *Journal of Psychosomatic Obstetrics and Gynecology, 18(4)*:286–291.

Field, T., Ironson, G., Scafidi, F., Nawrocki, T., Goncalves, A., Burman, L., Pickens, J., Fox, N., Schanberg, S. & Kuhn, C. (1996a). Massage therapy reduces anxiety and enhances EEG pattern of alertness and math computations. *International Journal of Neuroscience, 86(3–4)*:197–205.

Field, T., Kilmer, T., Hernandez-Reif, M. & Burman, I. (1996b). Preschool children's sleep and wake behavior: effects of massage therapy. *Early Child Development and Care, 120(1)*:39–44.

Field, T., Seligman, S., Scafidi, F. & Schanberg, S. (1996c). Alleviating posttraumatic stress in children following Hurricane Andrew. *Journal of Applied Developmental Psychology, 17(1)*:37–50.

Field, T., Morrow, C., Valdeon, C., Larson, S., Kuhn, C. & Schanberg, S. (1992). Massage reduces anxiety in child and adolescent psychiatric patients. *Journal of the American Academy of Child and Adolescent Psychiatry, 31(1)*:125–131.

Field, T., Scafidi, F. & Schanberg, S. (1987). Massage of preterm newborns to improve growth and development. *Pediatric Nursing, 13(6)*:385–387.

Field, T., Schanberg, S., Scafidi, F., Bauer, C., Vega-Lahr, N., Garcia, R., Nystrom, J. & Kuhn, C. (1986). Tactile/kinesthetic stimulation effects on preterm neonates. *Pediatrics, 77(5)*:654–658.

Fisher, J.D., Rytting, M. & Heslin, R. (1976). Hands touching hands: affective and evaluative effects of an interpersonal touch. *Sociometry, 39(4)*:416–421.

Fisher, S. (1986). *Development and Structure of the Body Image* (2 vols). Hillsdale, NJ: Erlbaum.

Fisher, S. (1990). The evolution of psychological concepts about the body. In T.F. Cash & T. Pruzinsky (Eds). *Body Images: Development, Deviance, and Change*: 3–20. New York: Guilford Press.

Fleming, L.C. & Jacobsen, K.H. (2010). Bullying among middle-school students in low and middle income countries. *Health Promotion International, 25(1)*:73–84.

Foda, M.I., Kawashima, T., Nakamura, S., Kobayashi, M. & Oku, T. (2004). Composition of milk obtained from unmassaged versus massaged breasts of lactating mothers. *Journal of Pediatrics and Gastroenterology Nutrition, 38(5)*:484–487.

Forchuk, C., Baruth, P., Prendergast, M., Holliday, R., Bareham, R., Brimner, S., Schulz, V., Chan, Y.C. & Yammine, N. (2004). Postoperative arm massage: a support for women with lymph node dissection. *Cancer Nursing, 27(1)*:25–33.

Ford, C. (1989). *Where Healing Waters Meet: Touching Mind and Emotion through Body*. New York: Station Hill Press.

Forer, B.R. (1969). The Taboo against touching in psychotherapy. *Psychotherapy: Theory, Research and Practice, 6(4)*:229–231.

Fortes Mayer, A. (2010). www.cuddleworkshop.co.uk/about-us

Foshee, V.A., Benefield, T.S., Ennett, S.T., Bauman, K.E. & Suchindran, C. (2004). Longitudinal predictors of serious physical and sexual dating violence victimization during adolescence. *Preventive Medicine, 39(5)*:1007–1016.

Fowler, J.H. & Christakis, N.A. (2008). Dynamic spread of happiness in a large social network: longitudinal analysis over 20 years in the Framington Heart Study. *British Medical Journal, 337*:a2338. doi: 101136/bmj.a2338

Fox, C. & Hawton, K. (2004). *Deliberate Self-Harm in Adolescence.* London, UK: Jessica Kingsley.

Fox, S. & Pritchard, D. (2001). *Anatomy, Physiology and Pathology for the Massage Therapist.* Melbourne, Australia: Corpus.

Francis, D.D., Diorio, J., Liu, D. & Meaney, M.J. (1999). Nongenomic transmission across generations in maternal behavior and stress responses in the rat. *Science, 286(5442)*:1155–1158.

Frank, J.D. (1961). *Persuasion and Healing.* Baltimore: John Hopkins University Press.

Frank, J.D. (1973). *Persuasion and Healing: A Comparative Study of Psychotherapy* (rev. ed.), Baltimore: John Hopkins University Press.

Frank, L. (1957). Tactile communication. *Genetic Psychology Monographs,* 56:209–255.

Frazer, A. & Hensler, J.G. (1999). Serotonin involvement in physiological function and behavior. In G.J. Siegel, E.W. Agranoff, R.W. Albers, S. Fisher & M.D. Uhler (Eds). *Basic Neurochemistry: Molecular, Cellular and Medical Aspects* (6th ed.). Philadelphia: Lippincott-Raven.

Freud, A. (1936). *The Ego and the Mechanisms of Defence.* Translated into English by C. Baines (1937). English revised version (1968), London: Hogarth Press.

Freud, S. (1912–1913/1955). *Totem and Taboo and Other Works.* In The Standard Edition of the Complete Psychological Works of Sigmund Freud, Vol 13 (1912–1913). Translated and edited by J. Strachey (1955). London: Hogarth Press and the Institute of Psycho-analysis.

Freud, S. (1915/1983). Further recommendations in the technique of psychoanalysis: observations on transference-love. In P. Rieff (Ed.). *Freud: Therapy and Technique*: 167–180. New York: Collier.

Freud, S. (1923/1960). *Das Ich Und Das Es.* Internationaler Psycho-Analytischer Verlag, Vienna & Zurich. Translated and edited by J. Strachey as *The Ego and the Id* (1960). In The Standard Edition of the Complete Psychological Works of Sigmund Freud, Vol. X1X (1923–1925). New York: Norton.

Freud, S. (1927/1957). *The Ego and the Id.* English translation by J. Riviere (1927). The International Psycho-Analytical Library, No. 12. London: The Hogarth Press and The Institute of Psycho-Analysis. Edited by E. Jones (1957) (7th ed.).

Fritz, S. (2016). *Fundamentals of Therapeutic Massage (6th ed.).* Maryland Height: Elsevier, Mosby.

Fromme, D.K., Jaynes, W.E., Taylor, D.K., Hanold, E.G., Daniell, J., Rountree, J.R. & Fromme, M.L. (1989). Nonverbal Behavior and Attitudes toward Touch. *Journal of Nonverbal Behavior, 13(1)*:3–14.

Fuller, B., Simmering, M.J., Marling, L.E., Bennett, R.J. & Cheramie, R.A. (2011). Exploring touch as a positive workplace behavior. *Human Relations, 64(2)*:231–256.

Fuller-Thomson, E., Bottoms, J., Brennenstuhl, S. & Hurd, M. (2011a). Is childhood physical abuse associated with peptic ulcer disease? Findings from a population-based study. *Journal of Interpersonal Violence, 26(16)*:3225–3247.

Fuller-Thomson, E., Sulman, J., Brennenstuhl, S. & Merchant, M. (2011b). Functional somatic syndromes and childhood physical abuse in women: data from a representative community-based sample. *Journal of Aggression, Maltreatment & Trauma, 20(4)*:445–469.

Fuller-Thomson, E. & Brennenstuhl, S. (2009). Making a link between childhood physical abuse and cancer: results from a regional representative survey. *Cancer, 115(14)*:3341–3350.

Fuller-Thomson, E., Brennenstuhl, S. & Frank, J. (2010). The association between childhood physical abuse and heart disease in adulthood: findings from a representative community sample. *Child Abuse & Neglect, 34(9)*:689–698.

Fuller-Thomson, E., Mehta, R. & Valeo, A. (2014). Establishing a link between attention deficit disorder/attention deficit hyperactivity disorder and childhood physical abuse. *Journal of Aggression, Maltreatment & Trauma, 23(2)*:188–198.

Fuller-Thomson, E., Stefanyk, M. & Brennenstuhl, S. (2009). The robust association between childhood physical abuse and osteoarthritis in adulthood: findings from a representative community sample. *Arthritis & Rheumatism, 61(11)*:1554–1562.

Gadow, S. (1984). Touch and technology. *Journal of Religion and Health, 23(1)*:63–69.

Gallace, A. & Spence, C. (2010). The science of interpersonal touch: an overview. *Neuroscience and Biobehavioral Reviews, 34(2)*:246–259.

Gardner, L.I. (1972). Deprivation dwarfism. *Scientific American, 227(1)*: 76–82.

Garfield, S.L. (1992). Eclectic psychotherapy: a common factors approach. In J.C. Norcross & M.R. Goldfried (Eds). *Handbook of Psychotherapy Integration*: 169–201. New York: Basic Books.

Garreau, J. (1981). *The Nine Nations of North America*. New York: Avon Books.

Gaskell, C. (2008). Kids company research and evaluation programme. In *Two Islingtons: Understanding the Problem, Paper 3: What Do Other People Think and Do About Equality and Fairness*. The Islington Fairness Commission. www.islington.gov.uk/fairness

Gastil, R.D. (1975). *Cultural Regions of the United States*. Seattle: University of Washington Press.

Gatti, G., Cavallo, R., Sartori, M.L., Del Ponte, D., Masera, R., Salvadori, A., Carignola, R. & Angeli, A. (1987). Inhibition by cortisol of human natural killer (NK) cell activity. *Journal of Steroid Biochemistry, 26(1)*:49–58.

Gawande, A. (2014, 9th December). *The Problem of Hubris*. The second of the three 2014 Reith Lectures entitled *The Future of Medicine*. BBC.
Geber, M. (1958). The psychomotor development of African children in the first year and the influence of maternal behavior. *Journal of Social Psychology, 47(2)*:185–195.
Gee, D.G., Gabard-Durnam, L.J., Flannery, J., Goff, B., Humphreys, K.L., Telzer, E.H., Hare, T.A., Bookheimer, S.Y. & Tottenham, N. (2013). Early developmental emergence of human amygdala-prefrontal connectivity after maternal deprivation. *Proceedings of the National Academy of Sciences of the United Stated of America, 110(39)*:15638–15643.
Geib, P.G. (1982). The experience of nonerotic physical contact in traditional psychotherapy: a critical investigation of the taboo against touch. *Dissertation Abstracts International, 43(1-B)*, 248.
Geib, P.G. (1998). The experience of nonerotic physical contact in traditional psychotherapy. In E.W.L. Smith, R.C. Clance & S. Imes (Eds). *Touch in Psychotherapy: Theory, Research and Practice*: 109–126. New York: Guilford Press.
Geldard, F. (1960). Some neglected possibilities of communication. *Science, 131(3413)*:1583–1588.
Gerhardt, S. (2004). *Why Love Matters: How Affection Shapes a Baby's Brain*. Hove, UK: Brunner-Routledge.
Gershoff, E.T. (2002). Corporal punishment by parents and associated child behaviors and experiences: a meta-analytic and theoretical review. *Psychological Bulletin, 128(4)*:539–579.
Gershoff, E.T. (2008). *Report on Physical Punishment in the United States: What Research Tells us about Its Effects on Children*. Columbus, OH: Center for Effective Discipline.
Gershoff, E.T. (2013). Spanking and child development: we know enough now to stop hitting our children. *Child Development Perspectives, 7(3)*:133–137.
Gershoff, E.T. (2017). School corporal punishment in global perspective: prevalence, outcomes, and efforts at intervention. *Psychology, Health & Medicine, 22(sup.1)*:224–239.
Gershoff, E.T. & Grogan-Kaylor, A. (2016). Spanking and child outcomes: old controversies and new meta-analyses. *Journal of Family Psychology, 30(4)*:453–469.
Gineste, Y. & Marescotti, R. (2008). *Sensory capture and feedback in the management of behavioural disturbances in demented old patients during basic care*. Production Yves Gineste and Rosette Marescotti, CEC.87220 France. www.cec-formation.net
Ginsberg, F. & Famaey, J.P. (1987). A double-blind study of topical massage with Rado-Salil ointment in mechanical low-back pain. *Journal of International Medical Research, 15(3)*:148–153.
Glaser, B.G. (1978). *Theoretical Sensitivity*. Mill Valley, CA: Sociology Press.

Glaser, R. & Kiecolt-Glaser, J. (2005). Stress-induced immune dysfunction: implications for health. *Nature Reviews Immunology, 5(3)*:243–251.

Gleeson, M. & Timmins, F. (2005). A review of the use and clinical effectiveness of touch as a nursing intervention. *Clinical Effectiveness in Nursing, 9*:69–77.

Glickauf-Hughes, C. & Chance, S. (1998). An individualised and interactive object relations perspective on the use of touch in psychotherapy. In E.W.L. Smith, R.C. Clance & S. Imes (Eds). *Touch in Psychotherapy: Theory, Research and Practice*: 153–169. New York: Guilford Press.

Gluck, S. (2016). *Effects of Child Physical Abuse*. HealthyPlace: Trusted mental health information; Abuse Community. www.healthyplace.com/abuse/child-physical-abuse/effects-of-child-physical-abuse

Goldfarb, W. (1943a). Infant rearing and problem behavior. *American Journal of Orthopsychiatry, 13(2)*:249–265.

Goldfarb, W. (1943b). The effects of early institutional care on adolescent personality. *Journal of Experimental Education, 12(2)*:106–129.

Goldfarb, W. (1945). Effects of psychological deprivation in infancy and subsequent stimulation. *The American Journal of Psychiatry, 102(1)*:18–33.

Golding, J.M., Taylor, D., Menard, L. & King, M. (2000). Prevalence of sexual abuse history in a sample of women seeking treatment for premenstrual syndrome. *Journal of Psychosomatic Obstetrics & Gynecology, 21(2)*:69–80.

Goldman, M. & Fordyce, J. (1983). Prosocial behavior as affected by eye contact, touch, and voice expression. *Journal of Social Psychology, 121(1)*:125–129.

Goldstein, K. (1939). *The Organism: A holistic Approach to Biology Derived from Pathological Data in Man*. American Book Company. Original German (1934).

Goldstein Ferber, S.G., Laudon, M., Kuint, J., Weller, A. & Zisapel, N. (2002). Massage therapy by mothers enhances the adjustment of circadian rhythms to the nocturnal period in full-term infants. *Developmental and Behavioral Pediatrics, 23(6)*:410–415.

Gomba, C. (2015). Corporal punishment is a necessary evil: parents' perceptions on the use of corporal punishment in school. *The International Journal of Research in Teacher Education, 6(3)*:59–71.

Goodman, M. & Teicher, A. (1988). To touch or not to touch. *Psychotherapy, 25(4)*:492–500.

Goodwin, R.D., Fergussen, D.M. & Horwood, L.J. (2005). Childhood abuse and familial violence and the risk of panic attacks and panic disorder in young adulthood. *Psychological Medicine, 35(6)*:881–890.

Goodykoontz, L. (1979). Touch: comfort or threat. *Nursing Forum, 18(1)*:4–17.

Gordon, I. & Feldman, R. (2015). A biopsychosocial perspective on synchrony and the development of human parental care. In S.D. Calkins (Ed.). *Handbook of Infant Biopsychosocial Development*: 283–312. New York: Guilford Press.

244 Bibliography

Gorlin, R.A. (Ed.) (1990). *Codes of Professional Responsibility* (2nd ed.). Washington, DC: The Bureau of National Affairs.

Gould, F., Clarke, J., Heim, C., Harvey, P.D., Majer, M. & Nemeroff, C.B. (2012). The effects of child abuse and neglect on cognitive functioning in adulthood. *Journal of Psychiatric Research, 46(4)*:500–506.

Gould, N. & O'Leary, P. (2009). Men who were sexually abused in childhood and subsequent suicidal ideation: community comparison, explanations and practice implications. *British Journal of Social Work, 39(5)*:950–968.

Gourkow, N., Hamon, S.C. & Phillips, C.J.C. (2014). Effect of gentle stroking and vocalization on behaviour, mucosal immunity and upper respiratory disease in anxious shelter cats. *Preventive Veterinary Medicine, 117(1)*:266–275.

Gow, R. (2012). *Kids Company Schools Nutrition Survey*. London: Kids Company.

Graff, H. & Mallin, R. (1967). The syndrome of the wrist cutter. *American Journal of Psychiatry, 124(1)*:36–42.

Grandin, T. (1992). Calming effects of deep touch pressure in patients with autistic disorder, college students, and animals. *Journal of Child and Adolescent Psychopharmacology, 2(1)*:63–72.

Gray, H., Williams, P.L. & Bannister, L.H. (1995) (38th edition). *Gray's Anatomy: The Anatomical Basis of Medicine and Surgery*. New York: Churchill Livingstone.

Grealish, L., Lomasney, A. & Whiteman, B. (2000). Foot massage. A nursing intervention to modify the distressing symptoms of pain and nausea in patients hospitalized with cancer. *Cancer Nursing, 23(3)*:237–243.

Green, J.H. & Messman-Moore, T.I. (2015). Impact of Physical and Sexual Abuse. In R. Witte & G.S. Mosley-Howard (Eds). *Mental Health Practice in Today's Schools: Issues and Interventions*: Chapter 13: 287–311. New York, Springer.

Green, L. (2017). The trouble with touch? New insights and observations on touch for social work and social care. *British Journal of Social Work, 47(3)*:773–792.

Greenfield, E.A. (2010). Child abuse as a life-course social determinant of adult health. *Maturitas, 66(1)*:51–55.

Grogan-Kaylor, A. (2005). Corporal punishment and the growth trajectory of children's antisocial behavior. *Child Maltreatment, 10(3)*:283–292.

Guéguen, N. & Jacob, C. (2005). The effect of touch on tipping: an evaluation in a French bar. *International Journal of Hospitality Management, 24(2)*:295–299.

Gupta, M.A. (2006). Somatization disorders in dermatology. *International Review of Psychiatry, 18(1)*:41–47.

Gupta, M.A. & Schork, N.J. (1995). Touch deprivation has an adverse effect on body image: some preliminary observations. *International Journal of Eating Disorders, 17(2)*:185–189.

Gursimran, T., Deborah, T., Gould, M., McKenna, P. & Greenberg, N. (2015). Impact of a single-session of havening. *Health Science Journal, 9(5)*. https://kclpure.kcl.ac.uk/portal/en/publications/impact-of-a-singlesession-of-...

Gutheil, T.G. & Gabbard, G.O. (1993). The concept of boundaries in clinical practice: theoretical and risk-management dimensions. *American Journal of Psychiatry, 150(2)*:188–196.

Halambi A.M. & Klapper, S.A. (2005). The impact of child maltreatment on child development. In M.R. Ventrell & D.N. Duquette (Eds), for the National Association of Counsel for Children. *Child Welfare Law and Practice: Representing Children, Parents, and State Agencies in Abuse, Neglect, and Dependency Cases*: 53–77. Denver, CO: Bradford.

Hall, H.E. (1959). *The Silent Language*. New York: Doubleday.

Hall, J.E. (1987). Gender-related ethical dilemmas and ethics education. *Professional Psychology: Research and Practice, 18(6)*:573–579.

Hall, K. (2008). Childhood sexual abuse and adult sexual problems: a new view of assessments and treatment. *Feminism & Psychology, 18(4)*:546–556.

Hammett, F.S. (1921). Studies of the Thyroid Apparatus: I. *American Journal of Psychology, 56*:196–204.

Hammett, F.S. (1922). Studies of the Thyroid Apparatus: V. *Endocrinology, 6*:221–229.

Hanson, J.L., Chung, M.K., Avants, B.B., Shirtcliff, A.E., Gee, J.C., Davidson, R.J. & Pollak, S.D. (2010). Early stress is associated with alterations in the orbitofrontal cortex: a tensor-based morphometry investigation of brain structure and behavioral risk. *Journal of Neuroscience, 30(22)*:7466–7472.

Harlow, H.F. (1958). The nature of love. *American Psychologist, 13(12)*: 673–685.

Harlow, H.F. (1974). *Learning to Love*. New York: Jason Aronson.

Harlow, H.F. & Harlow, M.K. (1962). The effects of rearing conditions on behavior. *Bulletin of the Menninger Clinic, 26(5)*:213–224.

Harlow, H.F. & Harlow, M.K. (1969). Effects of various mother-infant relationships on rhesus monkey behaviors. In B. Foss (Ed.). *Determinants of Infant Behaviour*: 15–36. London: Methuen.

Harlow, H.F., Harlow, M.K. & Hansen, E.W. (1963). The maternal affectional system of rhesus monkeys. In H.L. Rheingold (Ed.). *Maternal Behavior in Mammals*: 277–278. New York: Wiley.

Harlow, H.F. & Zimmerman, R.R. (1959). Affectional responses in the infant monkey. *Science, 130(3373)*:421–432.

Harris, M. & Richards, K.C. (2010). The physiological and psychological effects of slow-stroke back massage and hand massage on relaxation in older people. *Journal of Clinical Nursing, 19(7–8)*:917–926.

Hart, S., Field, T., Hernandez-Reif, M. & Lundy, B. (1998). Preschoolers' cognitive performance improves following massage. *Early Child Development & Care, 143(1)*:59–64.

Hatfield, R.W. (1994). Touch and human sexuality. In V. Bullough, B. Bullough & A. Stein (Eds). *Human Sexuality: An Encyclopedia.* New York: Garland.

Häuser, W., Kosseva, M., Üceyler, N., Klose, P. & Sommer, C. (2011). Emotional, physical, and sexual abuse in fybromyalgia syndrome. A systematic review with meta-analysis. *Arthritis Care and Research, 63(6)*:808–820.

Heim, C., Nater, U.M., Maloney, E., Boneva, R., Jones, J.F. & Reeves, W.C. (2009). Childhood trauma and risk for chronic fatigue syndrome; Association with neuroendocrine dysfunction. *Archives of General Psychiatry, 66(1)*:72–80.

Henley, N.M. (1977). *Body Politics: Power, Sex, and Nonverbal Communication.* Englewood Cliffs, NJ: Prentice-Hall.

Henricson, M. (2008). The outcome of tactile touch on stress parameters in intensive care: a randomized controlled trial. *Complementary Therapies in Clinical Practice, 14(4)*:244–254.

Heppner, P.P., Rosenberg, J.I. & Hedgespeth, J. (1992). Three methods in measuring the therapeutic process: clients' and counselors' constructions of the therapeutic process versus actual therapeutic events. *Journal of Counseling Psychology, 39(1)*:20–31.

Herbert, T.B. & Cohen, S. (1993). Stress and immunity in humans: a meta-analytic review. *Psychosomatic Medicine, 55(4)*:364–379.

Herman, J.L. (1992). *Trauma & Recovery.* New York: Basic Books.

Hernandez-Reif, M., Diego, M. & Field, T. (2007). Preterm infants show reduced stress behaviors and activity after 5 days of massage therapy. *Infant Behavior and Development, 30(4)*:557–561.

Hernandez-Reif, M., Dieter, J., Field, T., Swerdlow, B. & Diego, M. (1998a). Migraine headaches are reduced by massage therapy. *International Journal of Neuroscience, 96(1–2)*:1–11.

Hernandez-Reif, M., Field, T. & Theakston, H. (1998b). Multiple sclerosis patients benefit from massage therapy. *Journal of Bodywork and Movement Therapies, 2(3)*:168–174.

Hernandez-Reif, M., Field, T., Ironson, G., Beutler, J., Vera, Y., Hurley, J., Fletcher, M., Schanberg, S., Kuhn, C. & Fraser, M. (2005). Natural killer cells and lymphocytes increase in women with breast cancer following massage therapy. *International Journal of Neuroscience, 115(4)*:495–510.

Hernandez-Reif, M., Field, T., Krasnegor, J., Theakson, H., Hossain, Z. & Burman, I. (2000a). High blood pressure and associated symptoms were reduced by massage therapy. *Journal of Bodywork and Movement Therapies, 4(1)*:31–38.

Hernandez-Reif, M., Martinez, A., Field, T., Quintero, O. & Hart, S. (2000b). Premenstrual syndrome symptoms are relieved by massage therapy. *Journal of Psychosomatic Obstetrics & Gynecology, 21(1)*:9–15.

Hernandez-Reif, M., Ironson, G., Field, T., Hurley, J., Katz, G., Diego, M., Weiss, S., Fletcher, M.A., Schanberg, S., Kuhn, C. & Burman, I. (2004). Breast cancer patients have improved immune functions following massage therapy. *Journal of Psychosomatic Research, 57(1)*:45–52.

Heron, J. (1979). *Co-Counselling. Human Potential Research Unit*. Guildford: University of Surrey.

Herrenkohl, T.I., Hong, S., Klika, J.B., Herrenkohl, R.C. & Russo, M.J. (2013). Developmental impacts of child abuse and neglect related to adult mental health, substance use, and physical health. *Journal of Family Violence, 28(2)*. doi: 10.1007/s10896-012-9474-9

Herrenkohl, T.I., Mason, W.A., Kosterman, R., Lengua, L.J., Hawkins, J.D. & Abbott, R.D. (2004). Pathways from physical childhood abuse to partner violence in young adulthood. *Violence and Victims, 19(2)*:123–136.

Herringa, R.J., Birn, R.M., Ruttle, P.L., Burghy, C.A., Stodola, D.E., Davidson, R.J. & Essex, M.J. (2013). Childhood maltreatment is associated with altered fear circuitry and increased internalizing symptoms by late adolescence. *Proceedings of the National Academy of Sciences of the USA, 110(47)*:19119–19124.

Hertenstein, M.J., Verkamp, J.M., Kerestes, A.M. & Holmes, R.M. (2006). The communicative functions of touch in humans, nonhuman primates, and rats: a review and synthesis of the empirical research. *Genetic, Social and General Psychology Monographs, 132(1)*:5–94.

Heslin, R. (1974). Steps toward a taxonomy of touching. In R. Heslin (Ed.). *Getting Close: Research and Theory on Spatial Distance, Touching and Eye Contact*. Symposium presented at the Midwestern Psychological Association, Chicago.

Heslin, R. & Alper, T. (1983). Touch: a bonding gesture. In J.M. Wiemann & R.P. Harrison (Eds). *Nonverbal Communication* (Vol. 11 of *Sage Annual Reviews of Communication Research*). Beverly Hills, CA: SAGE.

Hilbert, J.E., Sforzo, G.A. & Swensen, T. (2003). The effects of massage on delayed onset muscle sorenes. *British Journal of Sports Medicine, 37(1)*:72–75.

Hillman, S. & Wainwright, L. (2012). *Need Analysis on a Sample of High-Risk Clients (Its OK)*. London: Kids Company.

Hinde R.A. & Spencer-Booth, Y. (1971). Effects of brief separation from mother on rhesus monkeys. *Science, 173(3992)*:111–118.

Hofer, M.A. (1984). Relationships as regulators: a psychobiologic perspective on bereavement. *Psychosomatic Medicine, 46(3)*:183–197.

Hofer, M.A. (1995). Hidden regulators: implications for a new understanding of attachment, separation and loss. In S. Goldberg, R. Muir & J. Kerr (Eds). *Attachment Theory: Social, Developmental and Clinical Perspectives*: 203–230. Hillside, NJ: Analytic Press.

Holden, G.W. (2002). Perspectives on the effects of corporal punishment: comment on Gershoff (2002). *Psychological Bulletin, 128(4)*:590–595.

Hollender, M.H. (1961). Prostitution, the body, and human relations. *International Journal of Psychoanalysis, 42(4–5)*:404–413.
Hollender, M.H. (1970). The need or wish to be held. *Archives of General Psychiatry, 22(5)*:445–453.
Hollender, M.H., Luborsky, L. & Scaramella, T.J. (1969). Body contact and sexual excitement. *Archives of General Psychiatry, 20(2)*:188–191.
Hollender, M.H. & Mercer, A.J. (1976). Wish to be held and wish to hold in men and women. *Archives of General Psychiatry, 33(1)*:49–51.
Hollinger, L. (1986). Communicating with the elderly. *Journal of Gerontological Nursing, 12(3)*:8–13.
Holroyd, J.C. & Brodsky, A.M. (1977). Psychologists' attitudes and practices regarding erotic and nonerotic physical contact with patients. *American Psychologist, 32(10)*:843–849.
Holroyd, J.C. & Brodsky, A. (1980). Does touching patients lead to sexual intercourse? *Professional Psychology, 11(5)*:807–810.
Horner, A. (1968). To touch or not to touch. *Voices, 14(2)*:26–28.
Hornik, J. (1992). Tactile stimulation and consumer response. *Journal of Consumer Research, 19(3)*:449–458.
Horton, I. (1996). Towards the construction of a model of counselling: some issues. In R. Bayne, I. Horton & J. Bimrose (Eds). *New Directions in Counselling*: 281–296. London: Routledge.
Horton, J. (1998). Further research on the patient's experience of touch in psychotherapy. In E.W.L. Smith, R.C. Clance & S. Imes (Eds). *Touch in Psychotherapy: Theory, Research and Practice*: 127–141. New York: Guilford Press.
Horton, J.A., Clance, P.R., Sterk-Elifson, C. & Emshoff, J. (Eds) (1995). Touch in psychotherapy: survey of patients' experiences. *Psychotherapy, 32(3)*:443–457.
Horvath, A.O. & Greenberg, L.S. (1989). Development and validation of the working alliance inventory. *Journal of Counseling Psychology, 36(2)*:223–233.
Hou, W.H., Chiang, P.T., Hsu, T.Y., Chiu, S.Y., Yen, Y.C. (2010). Treatment effects of massage therapy in depressed people: a meta-analysis. *Journal of Clinical Psychiatry, 71(7)*:894–901.
Howard, G.S. (1991). Culture tales: a narrative approach to thinking, cross-cultural psychology, and psychotherapy. *American Psychologist, 46(3)*:187–197.
Howe, D. (1993). *On Being a Client: Understanding the Process of Counselling and Psychotherapy*. London: SAGE.
Hubble, M.A., Duncan, B.L. & Miller, S.D. (1999). *The Heart and Soul of Change*. Washington: American Psychological Association.
Hubble, M.A., Noble, F.C. & Robinson, E.E. (1981). The effect of counselor touch in an initial counseling session. *Journal of Counseling Psychology, 28(6)*:533–535.

Huesmann, L.R., Eron, L.D., Lefkowitz, M.M. & Walder, L.O. (1984). The stability of aggression over time and generations. *Developmental Psychology, 20(6)*:1120–1134.

Humphreys, J., Epel, E.S., Cooper, B.A., Lin, J., Blackburn, E.H. & Lee, K.A. (2012). Telomere shortening in formerly abused and never abused women. *Biological Research for Nursing, 14(2)*:115–123.

Hunter, C., for Child Family Community Australia (CFCA) (2014). *Effects of Child Abuse and Neglect for Adult Survivors*. CFCA Resource Sheet: e1–15. Australian Institute of Family Studies, Australian Government.

Hunter, M. & Struve, J. (1998). *The Ethical Use of Touch in Psychotherapy*. London: SAGE.

Huss, A.J. (1977). 1976 Eleanor Clarke Slagle Lecture: touch with care or a caring touch? *American Journal of Occupational Therapy, 31(1)*:11–18.

Hussain, D. (2010). Stress, immunity, and health: research findings and implications. *International Journal of Psychosocial Rehabilitation, 15(1)*:94–100.

Hyman, I.A. (1996). Using research to change public policy: reflections on 20 years of effort to eliminate corporal punishment in schools. *Pediatrics, 98(4, pt 2)*:818–821.

Imes, S. (1998). Long-term clients' experience of touch in gestalt therapy. In E.W.L. Smith, P.R. Clance & S. Imes (Eds). *Touch in Psychotherapy: Theory, Research and Practice*: 170–200. New York: Guilford Press.

Ingham, A. (1989). A review of the literature relating to touch and its use in intensive care. *Intensive Care Nursing, 5(2)*:65–75.

Inskipp, F. (1966). New directions in supervision. In R. Bayne, I. Horton & J. Bimrose (Eds). *New Directions in Counselling*: 268–280. London: Routledge.

Irigaray, T.Q., Pacheco, J.B., Grassi-Oliveira, R., Fonseca, R.P., de Carvalho Leite, J.C. & Kristensen, C.H. (2013). Child maltreatment and later cognitive functioning: a systematic review. *Psicologia: Reflexão e Crítica, 26(2)*:376–387.

Irish, L., Kobayashi, I. & Delahanty, D.L. (2010). Long-term physical health consequences of childhood sexual abuse: a meta-analytic review. *Journal of Pediatric Psychology, 35(5)*:450–461.

Ironson, G., Field, T., Scafidi, F., Hashimoto, M., Kumar, M., Kumar, A., Price, A., Goncalves, A., Burman, I., Tetenman, C., Patarca, R. & Fletcher, M.A. (1996). Massage therapy is associated with enhancement of the immune system's cytotoxic capacity. *International Journal of Neuroscience, 84(1–4)*:205–217.

Jackins, H. (1962). *Fundamentals of Co-Counseling Manual*, Seattle, Washington: Personal Counselors.

Jackins, H. (1982). *Fundamentals of Co-Counseling* (3rd revised ed.). Seattle, Washington: Rational Island Publishers.

Jacob, B.A. & Ryan, J. (2018). *Child Maltreatment and Academic Performance*. Youth Policy Lab & Child and Adolescent Data Lab, University of Michigan.

Jacobson, N.S., Follette, W.C. & Revenstorf, D. (1984). Psychotherapy outcome research: methods for reporting variability and evaluating clinical significance. *Behavior Therapy, 15(4)*:336–352.

Jacques-Tiura, A.J., Tkatch, R., Abbey, A. & Wegner, R. (2010). Disclosure of sexual assault: characteristics and implications for posttraumatic stress symptoms among African American and caucasian survivors. *Journal of Trauma & Dissociation, 11(2)*:174–192.

Jakubiak, B.K. & Feeney, B.C. (2017). Affectionate touch to promote relational, psychological, and physical well-being in adulthood: a theoretical model and review of the research. *Personality and Social Psychology Review, 21(3)*:228–252.

Jamali, S., Ramezanli, S., Jahromi, M.K., Zare, A. & Poorgholami, F. (2016). Effects of massage therapy on physiologic responses in patients with congestive heart failure. *Biosciences Biotechnology Research Asia, 13(1)*:383–388.

Jamieson, D.J. & Steege, J.F. (1977). The association of sexual abuse with pelvic pain complaints in a primary care population. *American Journal of Obstetrics & Gynecology, 177(6)*:1408–1412.

Jesperson, A.F., Lalumiére, M.L. & Seto, M.C. (2009). Sexual abuse history among adult sex offenders and non-sex offenders: a meta-analysis. *Child Abuse & Neglect, 33(3)*:179–192.

Johansson, C. (2013). Views on and Perceptions of Experiences of Touch Avoidance: An Exploratory Study. *Current Psychology*, 32: 44–59. doi: https://doi.org/10.1007/s12144-012-9162-1

Johnson, B.S. (1965). The meaning of touch in nursing. *Nursing Outlook, 13(2)*:59–60.

Johnson, D.E. & Gunnar, M.R. (2011). Growth failure in institutionalised children. *Monographs of the Society for Research in Child Development, 76(4)*:92–126.

Johnson, J.G., Bromley, E. & McGeoch, P.G. (2009). Childhood experiences and development of maladaptive and adaptive personality traits. In J.M. Oldham, A.E. Skodol & D.S. Bender (Eds). *Essentials of Personality Disorders*:143–157. Virginia, USA: American Psychiatric Publishing.

Jonas, S., Bebbington, S., McManus, S., Meltzer, H., Jenkins, R. & Kuipers, E. et al. (2011). Sexual abuse and psychiatric disorder in England: results from the 2007 adult psychiatric morbidity survey. *Psychological Medicine, 41(4)*:709–719.

Jones, E. (1961). *The Life and Work of Sigmund Freud: Edited and Abridged in One Volume By Lionel Trilling and Steven Marcus*. New York: Basic Books.

Jones, E., Dimmock, P.W. & Spencer, S.A. (2001). A randomized controlled trial to compare methods of milk expression after preterm delivery. *Archives of Disease in Childhood – Fetal and Neonatal Edition, 85(2)*:91–95.

Jones, W.H. & Russell, D. (1982). The social reticence scale: an objective instrument to measure shyness. *Journal of Personality Assessment, 4(6)*:629–631.

Jones, S.E. & Yarbrough, A.E. (1985). A naturalistic study of the meaning of touch. *Communication Monographs, 52(1)*:19–56.
Joshi, P.D., Almeida, M. & Shete, P.D. (2010). Attitudes toward physical contact in a therapeutic setting: role of gender and expertise. *Journal of the Indian Academy of Applied Psychology, 36(1)*:35–43.
Joule, R.V. & Guéguen, N. (2007). Touch, compliance, and awareness of tactile contact. *Perceptual and Motor Skills, 104(2)*:581–588.
Jourard, S.M. (1963). *Personal Adjustment* (2nd ed.). New York: MacMillan.
Jourard, S.M. (1964). *The Transparent Self. Self-disclosure and Well-being*. New York: Van Nostrand Reinhold.
Jourard, S.M. (1966). An exploratory study of body accessibility. *British Journal of Social and Clinical Psychology, 5(3)*:221–231.
Jourard, S.M. (1968). *Disclosing Man to Himself*. New York: Van Nostrand Reinhold Company.
Jourard, S.M. (1974). *Healthy Personality*. New York: MacMillan.
Jourard, S.M. & Friedman, R. (1970). Experimenter-subject difference and self-disclosure. *Journal of Personal and Social Psychology, 14(3)*:278–282.
Jourard, S.M. & Rubin, J.E. (1968). Self-disclosure and touching: a study of two modes of interpersonal encounter and their interrelation. *Journal of Humanistic Psychology, 8(1)*:39–48.
Jovchelovitch, S. & Concha N. (2013). *Kids Company; A Diagnosis of the Organisation and Its Interventions; Final Report*. The London School of Economics and Political Science (LSE).
Jump, V.K., Fargo, J.D. & Akers, J. (2006). Impact of massage therapy on health outcomes among orphaned infants in Ecuador: results of a randomized clinical trial. *Family and Community Health, 29(4)*:314–319.
Jung, M.J. & Fouts, H.N. (2011). Multiple caregivers' touch interactions with young children among the Bofi foragers in Central Africa. *International Journal of Psychology, 46(1)*:24–32.
Kabat-Zinn J., Lipworth, L., Burncy, R. & Sellers, W. (1986). Four-year follow-up of a meditation-based program for the self-regulation of chronic pain. *The Clinical Journal of Pain, 2(3)*. https://journals.lww.com/clinicalpain/Abstract/1986/02030/Four_Year_Follow_Up_of_a_Meditation_Based_Program.4.aspx
Kabat-Zinn, J., Wheeler, E., Light, T., Skillings, A., Scharf, M.J., Cropley, T.G., Hosmer, D. & Bernhard, J.D. (1998). Influence of a mindfulness meditation-based stress reduction intervention on rates of skin clearing in patients with moderate to severe psoriasis undergoing phototherapy (UVB) and photochemotherapy (PUVA). *Psychosomatic Medicine, 60(5)*:625–632.
Kalra, G. & Bhugra, D. (2013). Sexual violence against women: understanding cross-cultural intersections. *Indian Journal of Psychiatry, 55(3)*:244–249.
Kamiya, Y., Timonen, V. & Kenny, R.A. (2016). The impact of childhood sexual abuse on the mental and physical health, and healthcare utilization of older adults. *International Psychogeriatrics, 28(3)*:415–422.

Kanitz, E., Tuchscherer, M., Puppe, B., Tuchscherer, A. & Stabenow, B. (2004). Consequences of repeated early isolation in domestic piglets (Susscrofa) on their behavioural, neuroendocrine, and immunological responses. *Brain Behavior and Immunity, 18(1)*:35–45.

Kardener, S., Fuller, M. & Mensh, I. (1973). A survey of physicians' attitudes and practices regarding erotic and nonerotic contact with patients. *American Journal of Psychiatry, 130(10)*:1077–1081.

Karsh, E.B. (1983). The effects of early handling on the development of social bonds between cats and people. In A.H. Katcher & A.M. Beck (Eds). *New Perspectives on our Lives with Companion Animals*: 22–28. Philadelphia: University of Pennsylvania Press.

Kashani, F. & Kashani, P. (2014). The effect of massage therapy on the quality of sleep in breast cancer patients. *Iranian Journal of Nursing and Midwifery Research, 19(2)*:113–118.

Katz, J., Wowk, A., Culp, D. & Wakeling, H. (1999). Pain and tension are reduced among hospital nurses after on-site massage treatments: a pilot study. *Journal of Perianesthesia Nursing, 14(3)*:128–133.

Kaufman, J. & Zigler, E. (1987). Do abused children become abusive parents? *American Journal of Orthopsychiatry, 57(2)*:186–192.

Keinan-Boker, L., Vin-Raviv, N., Liphshitz, I., Linn, S. & Barchana, M. (2009). Cancer incidence in Israeli Jewish survivors of World War 11. *Journal of the National Cancer Institute (US), 101(21)*:1489–1500.

Keith-Spiegel, P. & Koocher, G.R. (1985). *Ethics in Psychology: Professional Standards and Cases*. New York: Random House.

Keleman, S. (1981). *Your Body Speaks Its Mind*. Berkeley, CA: Center Press.

Kemeny, M.E. & Schedlowski, M. (2007). Understanding the interaction between psychosocial stress and immune-related diseases: a stepwise progression. *Brain, Behavior and Immunity, 21(8)*:1009–1018.

Kendall-Tackett, K.A. (2002). The health effects of childhood abuse: four pathways by which abuse can influence health. *Child Abuse & Neglect, 6/7*:715–730.

Kendall-Tackett, K.A. (2003). *Treating the Lifetime Health Effects of Childhood Victimization*. Kingston, NJ: Civic Research Institute.

Kendall-Tackett, K.A. & Marshall, R. (1999). Victimization and diabetes: an exploratory study. *Child Abuse & Neglect, 23(6)*:593–596.

Kendler, K.S., Bulik, C.M., Silberg, J., Hettema, J.M., Myers, J. & Prescott, C.A. (2000). Childhood sexual abuse and adult psychiatric and substance use disorders in women: an epidemiological and cotwin control analysis. *Archives of General Psychiatry, 57(10)*:953–959.

Kernberg, O.F., Burstein, E., Coyne, L., Applebaum, A., Horowitz, L. & Voth, H. (1972). Psychotherapy and psychoanalysis: final report of the menninger foundation's psychotherapy research project. *Bulletin of the Menninger Clinic, 36(1)*:1–277.

Kertay, L. & Reviere, S.L. (1998). Touch in context. In E.W.L. Smith, P.R. Clance & S. Imes (Eds). *Touch in Psychotherapy: Theory, Research and Practice*: 16–35. New York: Guilford Press.

Khajehei, M. & Behroozpour, E. (2018). Endorphins, oxytocin, sexuality and romantic relationships: an understudied area. *World Journal of Obstetrics and Gynecology, 7(2)*:17–23.

Khilnani, S., Field, T., Hernandez-Reif, M. & Schanberg, S. (2003). Massage therapy improves mood and behavior of students with attention-deficit/hyperactivity disorder, *Adolescence, 38*: 623–638.

Killion, B. & Weyandt, L.L. (2018). Brain structure in childhood maltreatment-related PTSD across the lifespan: a systematic review. *Applied Neuropsychology. Child*: 1–15. doi: 10.1080/21622965.2018.1515076.

Kim, J. (2008). Type-specific intergenerational transmission of neglectful and physically abusive parenting behaviors among young parents. *Children and Youth Services Review, 31(7)*:761–767.

Kim, M.S., Cho, K.S., Woo, H. & Kim, J.H. (2001). Effects of hand massage on anxiety in cataract surgery using local anesthesia. *Journal of Cataract & Refractive Surgery, 27(6)*:884–890.

Kim, J.E. & Park, H.J. (2011). Stress hormone and skin disease. In U. Khopkar (Ed.). *Skin Biopsy – Perspectives*: Chapter 11, 209–222. Croatia, China: InTechOpen: 4.

Kirkengen, A.L. (2010). *The Lived Experience of Violation: How Abused Children Become Unhealthy Adults*. Zeta Books, Bucharest – a slightly revised and corrected version of the second (2009) edition of the original Norwegian publication – *Hvordan Krekende barn blir syke Voksne*, (2005). Oslo, Norway: Universitetsforlaget.

Kleinke, C.L. (1977). Compliance to requests made by gazing and touching experimenters in field settings. *Journal of Experimental Social Psychology, 13(3)*:218–223.

Knable, J. (1981). Handholding: one means of transcending barriers of communication. *Heart and Lung, 10(6)*:1106–1110.

Koci, A. & Strickland, O. (2007). Relationship of adolescent physical and sexual abuse to perimenstrual symptoms (PMS) in adulthood. *Issues in Mental Health Nursing, 28(1)*:75–87.

Kohut, H. (1977). *The Restoration of the Self*. New York: International Universities Press.

Kolko, D.J. & Kolko, R.P. (2010). Psychological impact and treatment of child physical abuse. In C. Jenny (Ed.). *Child Abuse & Neglect: Diagnosis, Treatment, and Evidence*: 476–489. New York: Saunders/Elsevier.

Konner, M.J. (1976). Maternal care, infant behavior, and development among the !Kung. In R.B. Lee & I. Devore (Eds). *Kalahari Hunter Gatherers*: 218–245. Cambridge, MA: Harvard University Press.

Konturek, P.C., Brzozowski, T. & Konturek, S.J. (2011). Stress and the gut: pathophysiology, clinical consequences, diagnostic approach and treatment options. *Journal of Physiology and Pharmacology, 62(6)*:591–599.

Koocher, G.P. & Keith-Spiegel, P. (2016). *Ethics in Psychology and the Mental Health Professions; Standards and Cases* (4th ed.). New York: Oxford University Press.

Koole, S.L., Tjew, M., Sin, A. & Schneider, I.K. (2014). Embodied terror management: interpersonal touch alleviates existential concerns among individuals with low-self-esteem. *Psychological Science, 25(1)*:30–37.

Kovan, N.M., Chung, A.L. & Sroufe, L.A. (2009). The intergenerational continuity of observed early parenting: a prospective, longitudinal study. *Developmental Psychology, 45(5)*:1205–1213.

Krajewski, W., Wojciechowska, J., Krefft, M., Hirnie, L. & Kolodziej, A. (2016). Urogenital tract disorders in children suspected of being sexually abused. *Central European Journal of Urology, 69(1)*:112–117.

Kraus, M.W., Huang, C. & Keltner, D. (2010). Tactile communication, cooperation and performance: an ethological study of the NBA. *Emotion, 10(5)*:745–749.

Krieger, D. (1975). Therapeutic touch: the imprimatur of nursing. *American Journal of Nursing, 75(5)*:784–787.

Krueger, D.W. (1989). *Body Self and Psychological Self.* New York: Brunner/Mazel.

Krueger, D.W. (1990). Developmental and psychodynamic perspectives on body-image change. In T.F. Cash & T. Pruzinsky (Eds). *Body Images: Development, Deviance, and Change.* New York: Guilford Press.

Kruk, J. & Aboul-Enein, H.Y. (2004). Psychological stress and the risk of breast cancer: a case-control study. *Cancer Detection and Prevention, 28(6)*:399–408.

Kübler-Ross, E. (1969). *On Death and Dying.* New York: Collier Books, MacMillan.

Kubsch, S.M., Neveau, T. & Vandertie, K. (2000). Effect of cutaneous stimulation on pain reduction in emergency department patients. *Complementary Therapies in Nursing & Midwifery, 6(1)*:25–32.

Kuhn, C.M., Schanberg, S., Field, T., Symanski, R., Zimmerman, E., Scafidi, F. & Roberts, J. (1991). Tactile-kinesthetic stimulation effects on sympathetic and adrenocortical function in preterm infants. *Journal of Pediatrics, 119(3)*:434–440.

Kuhn, C.M., Evoniuk, G. & Schanberg, S.M. (1979). Loss of tissue sensitivity to growth hormone during maternal deprivation in rats. *Life Sciences, 25(24–25)*:2089–2097.

Kumari, V., Uddin, S., Premkumar, P., Young, S., Gudjonsson, G., Raghuvanshi, S., Barkataki, I., Sumich, A., Taylor, P. & Das, M. (2014). Lower anterior cingulate volume in seriously violent men with antisocial personality disorder or schizophrenia and a history of childhood abuse. *Australian & New Zealand Journal of Psychiatry, 48(2)*:153–161.

Kunz, D. & Peper, E. (1982). Fields and their clinical implications – Part 1. *The American Theosophist, 70(11)*:395–401.

Kupfermann, K. & Smaldino, C. (1987). The vitalising and revitalising experience of reliability: the place of touch in psychotherapy. *Clinical Social Work Journal, 15(3)*:223–235.

Labrecque, M., Eason, E. & Marcoux, S. (2001). Women's views on the practice of prenatal perineal massage. *British Journal of Obstetrics & Gynaecology, 108(5)*:499–504.
Ladd, G.W., Ettekal, I. & Kochenderfer-Ladd, B. (2017). Peer victimization trajectories from kindergarten through high school: differential pathways for children's school engagement and achievement? *Journal of Educational Psychology, 109(6)*:826–841.
Lambert, M.J. & Barley, D.E. (2001). Research summary of the therapeutic relationship and psychotherapy outcome. *Psychotherapy 38(4)*:357–361.
Langland, R. & Panicucci, C. (1982). Effects of touch on communication with elderly confused patients. *Journal of Gerontological Nursing, 8(3)*:152–155.
Lansford, J.E., Miller-Johnson, S., Berlin, L.J., Dodge, K.A., Bates, J.E. & Pettit, G.S. (2007). Early physical abuse and later violent delinquency: a prospective longitudinal study. *Child Maltreatment, 12(3)*:233–245.
Lanzenberger, R., Wadsak, W., Spindelegger, C., Mitterhauser, M., Akimova, E., Mien, L-K., Fink, M., Moser, U., Savli, M., Kranz, G.S., Hahn A., Kletter, K., & Kaspar (2010). Cortisol plasma levels in social anxiety disorder patients correlate with serotonin-1A receptor binding in limbic brain regions. *International Journal of Neuropsychopharmacology, 13(9)*:1129–1143.
Larsen, K.S. & LeRoux, J. (1984). A study of same sex touching attitudes: scale development and personality predictors. *The Journal of Sex Research, 20(3)*:264–278.
Laudenslager, M.L. & Boccia, M.L. (1996). Some observations on psychosocial stressors, immunity, and individual differences in nonhuman primates. *American Journal of Primatology, 39(4)*:205–221.
Laudenslager, M.L., Capitanio, J. & Reite, M. (1985). Possible effects of early separation experiences on subsequent immune function in adult macaque monkeys. *American Journal of Psychiatry, 142(7)*:862–864.
Law, A.J., Pei, Q., Walker, M., Gordon-Andrews, H., Weickert, C.S., Feldon, J., Pryce, C.R. & Harrison, P.J. (2009). Early parental deprivation in the marmoset monkey produces long-term changes in hippocampal expression of genes involved in synaptic plasticity and implicated in mood disorder. *Neuropsychopharmacology, 34(6)*:1381–1394.
Lawler, S. & Cameron, L. (2006). A randomized, controlled trial of massage therapy as a treatment for migraine. *Annual Behavior and Medicine, 32(1)*:50–59.
Lawn, J.E., Mwansa-Kambafwile, J., Horta, B.L., Barros, F.C. & Cousens, S. (2010). 'Kangaroo mother care' to prevent neonatal deaths due to preterm birth complications. *International Journal of Epidemiology, 39(Sup.1)*:i144–i154.
Lawry, S.S. (1998). Touch and clients who have been sexually abused. In E.W.L. Smith, P.R. Clance & S. Imes (Eds). *Touch in Psychotherapy: Theory, Research and Practice*: 201–210. New York: Guilford Press.

Lazarus, A.A. (1994). How certain boundaries and ethics diminish therapeutic effectiveness. *Ethics and Behavior, 4(3)*:255–261.
LeMay, A. (1986). The human connection. *Nursing Times, 82(47)*:28–32.
Lemma, A. (2010). The power of relationship: a study of keyworking as an intervention with traumatized young people. *Journal of Social Work Practice, 24(4)*:409–427.
Leserman, J.L. & Drossman, D.A. (2007). Relationship of abuse history to functional gastrointestinal disorders and symptoms: some possible mediating mechanisms. *Trauma, Violence, and Abuse, 8(3)*:331–343.
Levine, P. (1997). *Waking the Tiger*. Berkeley, CA: North Atlantic Books.
Lev-Wiesel, R., Daphna-Tekoah, S. & Hallak, M. (2009). Childhood sexual abuse as a predictor of birth-related posttraumatic stress and postpartum posttraumatic stress. *Child Abuse & Neglect, 33(12)*:877–887.
Lewis, H.R. & Streitfeld, H.S. (1972). *Growth Games*. New York: Bantam Books.
Liddell, H.S. (1956). Neonate-mother relationship in goat and man. In B. Schaffner (Ed.). *Group Processes*: 94–140. New York: Josiah Macy, Jr., Foundation.
Liedloff, J. (1975). *The Continuum Concept*. London: Gerald Duckworth & Co.
Lincoln, L.W. & Wakerly, J.B. (1974). Electrophysiological evidence for the activation of supraoptic neurones during the release of oxytocin. *Journal of Physiology, 242(2)*:533–554.
Linden, D.J. (1915). *Touch: The Science of Hand, Heart, and Mind*. London, UK: Viking/Penguin.
Linden, J. (1968). On expressing physical affection to a patient. *Voices, 4(2)*:34–38.
Linehan, M. (1988). Perspectives on the interpersonal relationship in behavior therapy. *Journal of Integrative and Eclectic Psychotherapy, 7(3)*:278–290.
Liss, J. (1976). Why touch? In D. Boadella (Ed.). *In the Wake of Reich*: 236–248. London: Coventure Ltd.
Little, M.I. (1981). *Transference Neurosis and Transference Psychosis*. New York: Jason Aronson.
Liu, D., Tannenbaum, B., Caldji, C., Francis, D.D., Freedman, A., Sharma, S. et al. (1997). Maternal care, hippocampal glucocorticoid receptor gene expression and hypothalamic- pituitary-adrenal responses to stress. *Science, 277(5332)*:1659–1662.
Liu, R.T. (2010). Early life stressors and genetic influences on the development of bipolar disorder: the roles of childhood abuse and brain-derived neurotrophic factor. *Child Abuse & Neglect, 34(7)*:516–572.
Liu, R.T., Scopelliti, K.M., Pittman, S.K. & Zamora, A.S. (2018). Childhood maltreatment and non-suicidal self-injury: a systematic review and meta-analysis. *Lancet Psychiatry, 5(1)*:51–64.

Liu, Y., Croft, J.B., Chapman, D.P., Perry, G.S., Greenlund, K.J., Zhao, G. & Edwards, V.J. (2013). Relationship between adverse childhood experiences and unemployment among adults from five US states. *Social Psychiatry and Psychiatric Epidemiology, 48(3)*:357–369.

Lloyd, C., Smith, J. & Weinger, K. (2005). Stress and diabetes: a review of the links. *Diabetes Spectrum, 18(2)*:121–127.

Lomranz, J. & Shapiro, A. (1974). Communicative patterns of self-disclosure and touching behavior. *Journal of Psychology, 88(2)*:223–227.

Lousada, O. (2009). *Hidden Twins; What Adult Opposite Sex Twins Have to Teach Us.* London: Karnac Books.

Ludlington-Hoe, S.M. & Golant, S.K. (1993). *Kangaroo Care: The Best You Can Do To Help Your Preterm Infant.* New York: Bantam Books.

Ludlington-Hoe, S.M., Hadeed, A. & Anderson, G.C. (1991). Physiologic responses to skin-to-skin contact in hospitalised premature infants. *Journal of Perinatology, 11(1)*:19–24.

Lynch, M.A. (1978). The prognosis of child abuse. *Journal of Child Psychology and Psychiatry and Allied Disciplines, 19(2)*:175–180.

MacGill, M. (2017). What is oxytocin? Why is oxytocin called the love hormone? *Medical News Today.* MNT Knowledge Centre. www.medicalnewstoday.com/articles/275795.php

Madden, V., Domoney, J., Aumayer, K., Sethna, V., Iles, J., Hubbard, I. Giannakakis, A., Psychogiou, L. & Ramchandani, P. (2015). Intergenerational transmission of parenting: findings from a UK longitudinal study. *European Journal of Public Health, 25(6)*:1030–1035.

Mahler, M.S. & McDevitt, J.B. (1982). Thoughts on the emergence of the sense of self, with particular emphasis on the body self. *Journal of the American Psychoanalytic Association, 30(4)*, 827–848.

Mahler, M., Pine, F. & Bergman, A. (1975). *The Psychological Birth of the Human Infant.* New York: Basic Books.

Main, M. (1990). Parental aversion to infant-initiated contact is correlated with the parents' own rejection during childhood: the effects of experience on signals of security with respect to attachment. In K.E. Barnard & T.B. Brazelton (Eds). *Clinical Infant Reports. Touch: The Foundation of Experience.* Full revised and expanded proceedings of Johnson & Johnson Pediatric Round Table X: 461–495. Madison, CT: International Universities Press.

Majno, G. (1975). *The Healing Hand: Man and Wound in the Ancient World.* Boston, MA: Harvard University Press.

Major, B. & Heslin, R. (1982). Perception of cross-sex and same-sex non-reciprocal touch: it is better to give than to receive. *Journal of Nonverbal Behavior, 6(3)*:148–162.

Malmquist, C., Kiresuk, T. & Spano, R. (1966). Personality characteristics of women with repeated illegitimate pregnancies: descriptive aspects. *American Journal of Orthopsychiatry, 36(3)*:476–484.

Maniglio, R. (2013). Prevalence of child sexual abuse among adults and youths with bipolar disorder: a systematic review. *Child Psychology Review, 33(4)*:561–573.

Mantis, I., Mercuri, M., Stack, D.M. & Field, T.M. (2019). Depressed and non-depressed mothers' touching during social interactions with their infants. *Developmental Cognitive Neuroscience, 35*:57–65.

Mariotti, A. (2015). The effects of chronic stress on health: new insights into the molecular mechanisms of brain-body communication. *Future Science OA, 1(3)*:FSO23. doi: 10.4155/fso.15.21

Marshall, L. (1976). *The! Kung of Nyae Nyae*: 315–318. Cambridge, MA: Harvard University Press.

Martin, P. (1997). *The Sickening Mind*. London: Harper Collins.

Maslow, A. (1968). *Towards a Psychology of Being*. New York: D. van Nostrand Co.

Masters, W.H. & Johnson, V.E. (1976). Principles of the new sex therapy. *American Journal of Psychiatry, 133(5)*:548–554.

Mathai, S., Fernandez, A., Mondkar, J. & Kanbur, W. (2002). Effects of tactile-kinesthetic stimulation on preterms: a controlled trial. *Indian Pediatrics, 38(10)*:1091–1098.

Mathews, C.A., Kaur, N. & Stein, M.B. (2008). Childhood trauma and obsessive-compulsive symptoms. *Depression and Anxiety, 25(9)*:742–751.

McCorkle, R. (1974). Effects of touch on severely ill patients. *Nursing Research, 23(2)*:126–132.

McCrory, E., De Brito, S.A. & Viding, E. (2010). Research review: the neurobiology and genetics of maltreatment and adversity. *Journal of Child Psychology and Psychiatry, 51(10)*:1079–1095.

McEwen, B.S. (2000). The neurobiology of stress: from serendipity to clinical relevance. *BrainResearch, 886(1–2)*:172–189.

McEwen, B.S. (2008). Central effects of stress hormones in health and disease: understanding the protective and damaging effects of stress and stress mediators. *European Journal of Pharmacology, 583(2–3)*:174–185.

McEwen, B.S. (2017). Neurobiological and systemic effects of chronic stress. *Chronic Stress*. doi: 10.1177/2470547017692328

McEwen, B.S. & Morrison, J.H. (2013). Brain on stress: vulnerability and plasticity of the prefrontal cortex over the life course. *Neuron, 79(1)*:16–29.

McEwen, B.S. & Sapolsky, R.M. (1995). Stress and cognitive function. *Current Opinion in Neurobiology, 5(2)*:205–216.

McNamara, M.E., Burnham, D.C, Smith, C. & Carroll, D.L. (2003). The effects of back massage before diagnostic cardiac catheterization. *Alternative Therapies, 9(1)*:50–57.

McNeely, A.D. (1987). *Touching: Body Therapy and Depth Psychology*. Toronto: Inner City Books.

Mead, M. (1935). *Sex and Temperament in Three Primitive Societies*. New York: William Morrow.
Meek, S.S. (1993). Effects of slow stroke back massage on relaxation in hospice clients. *Journal of Nursing Scholarship, 25(1)*:17–21.
Mehrabian, A. (1971). *Silent Messages*. Belmont, CA: Wadsworth Publishing Company.
Mendes, E.W. & Procianoy, R.S. (2008). Massage therapy reduces hospital stay and occurrence of late-onset sepsis in very preterm neonates. *Journal of Perinatology, 28(12)*:815–820.
Mercer, L.S. (1966). Touch: comfort or threat. *Perspectives in Psychiatric Care, 4(3)*:20–25.
Merleau-Ponty, M. (1962). *Phenomenology of Perception* (trans. C. Smith). London: Routledge and Kegan Paul.
Milakovich, J. (1998). Differences between therapists who touch and those who do not. In E.W.L. Smith, P.R. Clance & S. Imes (Eds). *Touch in Psychotherapy: Theory, Research and Practice*: 72–91. New York: Guilford Press.
Miller, A. (1983). *For Your Own Good; The Roots of Violence in Child-rearing*: 109–129. New York: Ferrar, Straus & Giroux. (Original German version, 1980.)
Miller, S.D., Duncan, B.L. & Hubble, M.A. (1997). *Escape from Babel: Toward a Unifying Language for Psychotherapy Practice*. New York: Norton.
Mimiaga, M.J., Noonan, E., Donnell, D., Safren, S.A., Koenan, K.C., Gortmaker, S., O'Cleirigh, C., Chesney, M.A., Coates, T.J., Koblin, B.A. & Mayer, K.H. (2009). Childhood sexual abuse is highly associated with HIV risk–taking behavior and infection among MSM in the EXPLORE study. *Journal of Acquired Immune Deficiency Syndromes, 51(3)*:340–348.
Mintz, E.E. (1969a). On the rationale of touch in psychotherapy. *Psychotherapy: Theory, Research and Practice, 6(4)*:232–235.
Mintz, E.E. (1969b). Touch and the psychoanalytic tradition. *Psychoanalytic Review, 56(3)*:365–376.
Mintz, E.E. (1973). On the rationale of touch in psychotherapy. In E. Hendrik & M. Ruitenbeck (Eds). *The Analytic Situation. How Patient and Therapist Communicate*: 184–190. Chicago: Aldine Publishing Company.
Mitchell, G.D. (1970). Abnormal behavior in primates. In L.A. Rosenblum (Ed.). *Primate Behavior*: 195–249. New York: Academic Press.
Mitchell, G. (1979). *Behavioral Sex Differences in Nonhuman Primates*. New York: Van Nostrand Reinhold.
Moe, B.K., King, A.R. & Bailly, M.D. (2004). Retrospective accounts of recurrent parental physical abuse as a predictor of adult laboratory-induced aggression. *Aggressive Behavior, 30(3)*:217–228.

Moghaddam, B., Bolinao, M., Stein-Behrens, B. & Sapolsky, R. (1994). Glucocorticoids mediate the stress-induced accumulation of glutamate. *Brain Research, 655*(1–2):251–254.

Money, J. (1992). *The Kaspar Hauser Syndrome of "Psychosocial Dwarfism"*. New York: Prometheus Books.

Money, J., Annecillo, C. & Kelley, J.F. (1983). Growth of intelligence: failure and catch-up associated respectively with abuse and rescue in the syndrome of abuse dwarfism. *Psychoneuroendocrinology, 8(3)*:309–319.

Money, J., Annecillo, C. & Werlwas, J. (1976). Hormonal and behavioral reversals in hyposomatotropic dwarfism. In E. Sacher (Ed.). *Hormones, Behavior, and Psychopathology:* 243–252. New York: Raven.

Montagu, A. (1986). *Touching: The Human Significance of the Skin* (3rd ed.). (Original 1971). New York: Harper & Row.

Montagu, A. & Matson, F. (1979). *The Human Connection*. New York: McGraw-Hill Books.

Moore, S.E., Norman, R.E., Suetani, S., Thomas, H.J., Sly, P.D. & Scott, J.G. (2017). Consequences of bullying victimization in childhood and adolescence: a systematic review and meta-analysis. *World Journal of Psychiatry, 7(1)*:60–76.

Moran, D. (2010). Sartre on embodiment, touch, and the 'double sensation'. *Philosophy Today, 54(Sup.)*:135–141.

Moran, P.B., Vuchinich, S. & Hall, N.K. (2004). Associations between types of maltreatment and substance use during adolescence. *Child Abuse & Neglect, 28(5)*:565–574.

Morey, N.M., Boggero, I.A., Scott, A.B. & Segerstrom, S.C. (2015). Current directions in stress and human immune function. *Current Opinion in Psychology, 5*:13–17. doi: 10.1016/j.copsyc.2015.03.007

Morgan, B. (1995). *To Touch or Not to Touch; A Critical Analysis of the Use of Touch in Gestalt Individual Psychotherapy*. Unpublished dissertation, London Gestalt Centre.

Morgan, B.E., Horn, A.R. & Bergman, N.J. (2011). Should neonates sleep alone? *Biological Psychiatry, 70(9)*:817–825.

Moriam, S. & Sobhani, M.E. (2013). Epigenetic effect of chronic stress on dopamine signaling and depression. *Genetics and Epigenetics, 5*:11–16. doi: 10.4137/GEG.S11016.

Morris, D. (1971). *Intimate Behavior*. New York: Random House.

Morrison, I. (2016). Keep calm and cuddle on: social touch as a stress buffer. *Adaptive Human Behavior and Physiology, 2(4)*:344–362.

Muller, R.T., Hunter, J.E. & Stollak, G. (1995). The intergenerational transmission of corporal punishment: a comparison of social learning and temperament models. *Child Abuse & Neglect, 19(11)*:1323–1335.

Muñoz-Hoyos, A., Molina-Carballo, A., Augustin-Morales, M., Contreras-Chova, F., Naranio-Gómez, A., Justicia-Martinez, F. & Uberos, J. (2011). Psychosocial dwarfism: psychopathological aspects and putative neuroendocrine markers. *Psychiatry Research, 188(1)*:96–101.

Muzik, M. & Borovska, S. (2010). Perinatal depression: implications for child mental health. *Mental Health in Family Medicine, 7(4)*:239–247.

Naisbitt, J. (1982). *Megatrends.* New York: Warner Books.

National Institute of Neurological Disorders and Stroke (2019). *Shaken Baby Syndrome Information Page.* www.ninds.nih.gov/Disorders/All-Disorders/Shaken-Baby-Syndrome-Information-Page

Negele, A., Kaufhold, J., Kellenbach, L. & Leuzinger-Bohleber, M. (2015). Childhood trauma and its relation to chronic depression in adulthood. *Depression Research and Treatment, 2015*:650–804. doi: 10.1155/2015/650804.

Nelson, D. (1994). *Compassionate Touch: Hands-on Caregiving for the Elderly, the Ill and the Dying.* New York: Station Hill Press.

Nelson, D. (2006). *From the Heart through the Hands: The Power of Touch in Caregiving.* Forres, Scotland: Findhorn Press.

Nelson, E.C., Heath, A.C., Madden, P.A., Cooper, M.L., Dinwiddie, S.H. & Bucholz, K.K. et al. (2002). Association between self-reported childhood sexual abuse and adverse psychosocial outcomes: results from a twin study. *Archives of General Psychiatry, 59(2)*:139–145.

Nelson, S., Baldwin, N. & Taylor, J. (2012). Mental health problems and medically unexplained physical symptoms in adult survivors of childhood sexual abuse: an integrative literature review. *Journal of Psychiatric and Mental Health Nursing, 19(3)*:211–220.

Nepomnaschy, P.A., Welch, K.B., McConnell, D.S., Low, B.S., Strassmann, B.I. & England, B.G. (2006). Cortisol levels and very early pregnancy loss in humans. *Proceedings of the National Academy of Science of the United States of America (PNAS), 103(10)*:3938–3942.

Neumann, D.A., Houskamp, B.M., Pollock, V.E. & Briere, J. (1996). The long-term sequelae of childhood sexual abuse in women: a meta-analytic review. *Child Maltreatment, 1(1)*:6–16.

Neumann, I.D. (2007). Oxytocin: the neuropeptide of love reveals some of its secrets. *Cell Metabolism, 5(4)*:231–233.

Nguyen, M.L., Heslin, R. & Nguyen, R. (1975). The meaning of touch: sex differences. *Journal of Communication, 25(3)*:92–103.

Nixon, M., Teschendorff, J., Finney, J. & Karnilowicz, W. (1997). Expanding the nursing repertoire: the effect of massage on post-operative pain. *Australian Journal of Advanced Nursing, 14*: 21–26.

Noll, J.G., Shenk, C.E. & Putnam, K.T. (2009). Childhood sexual abuse and adolescent pregnancy: a meta-analytic update. *Journal of Pediatric Psychology, 34(4)*:366–378.

Norcross, J.C. (2001). Empirically supported therapy relationships: summary report of the Division 29 task force. *Psychotherapy Research, 38(4)*:345–497.

Norcross, J.C. (2002). *Psychotherapy relationships that work: therapist contributions and responsiveness to patients' needs.* New York: Oxford University Press.

Norman, R.E., Byambaa, M., De, R., Butchart, A., Scott, J. & Vos, T. (2012). The long-term health consequences of child physical abuse, emotional abuse, and neglect: a systematic review and meta-analysis. *PLoS Medicine, 9(11)*:e101349. doi: 10:1371/journal.pmed.1001349

Office for National Statistics (ONS) (2016). *International Comparison of Teenage Births.* www.ons.gov.uk/ons/rel/vsob1/births-by-area-of-usual-residence-of-mother

Offit, A. (1977). *The Sexual Self.* New York: J.B. Lippencott. In M. Hunter & J. Struve (Eds). (1998). *The Ethical Use of Touch in Psychotherapy.* London: SAGE.

Ogden, P. & Minton, K. (2000). Sensorimotor therapy: one method for processing traumatic memory. *Traumatology, 6(3)*:149–173.

Ogloff, J.R.P., Cutajar, M.C., Mann, E., Mullen, P., Wei, F.T.Y., Hassan, H.A.B. & Yih, T.H. (2012). Child sexual abuse and subsequent offending and victimisation: a 45 year follow-up study. *Trends & Issues in Crime & Criminal Justice, 440*:1–6.

O'Hearne, J.J. (1972). How can we reach patients most effectively? *International Journal of Group Psychotherapy, 22(4)*:446–454.

Older, J., (1977). Four taboos that may limit the success of psychotherapy. *Psychiatry, 40(3)*:197–204.

Older, J. (1981). A restoring touch for abusing families. *Child Abuse & Neglect, 5(4)*:487–489.

Older, J. (1982). *Touching is Healing.* New York: Stein & Day.

Oliver, J. (1993). Intergenerational transmission of child abuse: rates, research and clinical implications. *American Journal of Psychiatry, 150(9)*:1315–1324.

Onozawa, K., Glover, V., Adams, D., Modi, N. & Kumar, R.C. (2001). Infant massage improves mother-infant interaction for mothers with postnatal depression. *Journal of Affective Disorders, 63(1–3)*:201–207.

Osaka, I., Kurihara, Y., Tanaka, K., Nishizaki, H., Aoki, S. & Adachi, I. (2009). Endocrinological evaluations of brief hand massages in palliative care. *Journal of Alternative and Complementary Medicine, 15(9)*:981–985. doi: 10.1089/acm.2008.0241

Paige, C. & McLain, T. (2019). Corporal punishment. In A.P. Giardino, M.A. Lyn & E.R. Giardino (Eds). *A Practical Guide to the Evaluation of Child Physical Abuse and Neglect* (3rd ed.), Chapter 14. [Non-Print Legal Deposit e-book] www.bl.uk

Panksepp, J. (1998). *Affective Neuroscience: The Foundations of Human and Animal Emotions.* Oxford: Oxford University Press.

Pani, L., Porcella, A. & Gessa, G.L. (2000). The role of stress in the pathophysiology of the dopaminergic system. *Molecular Psychiatry, 5(1)*:14–21.

Paolucci, E., Genuis, M. & Violato, C. (2001). A meta-analysis of the published research on the effects of child sexual abuse. *Journal of Psychology, 135(1)*:17–36.

Parkes, C.M., Stevenson-Hinde, J. & Marris, P. (Eds). (1991). *Attachment across the life cycle.* New York: Tavistock/Routledge.

Parry, R, (2011). *A Critical Examination of Bion's Concept of Containment and Winnicott's Concept of Holding, and their Psychotherapeutic Implications.* MA Research Report, University of Witwatersrand, Johannesburg, South Africa.

Pattison, J.E. (1973). Effects of touch on self-exploration and the therapeutic relationship. *Journal of Consulting and Clinical Psychology, 40(2)*:170–175.

Pauk, J., Kuhn, C., Field, T. & Schanberg, S. (1986). Positive effects of tactile versus kinesthetic or vestibular stimulation on neuroendocrine and ODC activity in maternally deprived rat pups. *Life Sciences, 39(22)*:2081–2087.

Pearlman, L.A. & Saakvitne, K.W. (1995). *Trauma and the Therapist: Countertransference and Vicarious Traumatization in Psychotherapy with Incest Survivors.* New York: Norton.

Pedersen, D. (1973). Self-disclosure, body accessibility, and personal space. *Psychological Reports, 33(3)*:975–980.

Peloquin, S.M. (1989). Helping through touch: the embodiment of caring. *Journal of Religion and Health, 28(4)*:299–322.

Pereda, N. (2015). Childhood victimization and prostitution. A developmental victimology perspective. *Crime Psychology Review, 1(1)*:5–20.

Perry, B.D & Szalavitz, M. (2008). Child maltreatment: a neurodevelopmental perspective on the role of trauma and neglect in psychopathology. In T.P. Beauchaine & S.P. Hinshaw (Eds). *Child and Adolescent Psychopathology*: 93–128. Hoboken: John Wiley & Sons.

Phelan, J.E. (2009). Exploring the use of touch in the psychotherapeutic setting: a phenomenological review. *Psychotherapy: Theory, Research, Practice, Training, 46(1)*:97–111.

Pisano, M.D., Wall, S.M. & Foster, A. (1986). Perceptions of nonreciprocal touch in romantic relationships. *Journal of Nonverbal Behavior, 10(1)*:29–40.

Plato (360? B.C.) *Pheado.* First translated into Latin from the original Greek by H. Aristippus in 1160. First English edition printed in London by T.R. & N.T. for James Magnes & Richard Bentley in 1675.

Poornima, K.N., Karthick, N. & Sitalakshmi, R. (2014). Study of the effect of stress on skeletal muscle function in geriatrics. *Journal of Clinical and Diagnostic Research, 8(1)*:8–9.

Pope, K.S. (1990a). Therapist-patient sex as sex abuse: six scientific, professional, and practical dilemmas in addressing victimization and rehabilitation. *Professional Psychology: Research and Practice, 21(4)*:227–239.

Pope, K.S. (1990b). Therapist-patient sexual involvement: a review of the research. *Clinical Psychology Review, 10(4)*:477–490.

Pope, K.S. (2001). Sex between therapists and clients. In J. Worell (Ed.). *Encyclopedia of Women and Gender: Sex Similarities and Differences and the Impact of Society on Gender, Volume 2*: 955–962. London, UK: Academic Press.

Pope, K.S. & Bouhoutsos, J.C. (1986). *Sexual Intimacy between Therapist and Patients.* New York: Praeger.

Pope, K.S., Keith-Spiegel, P. & Tebachnik, B.G. (1986). Sexual attraction to clients: the human therapist and the (sometimes) inhuman training system. *American Psychologist, 41(2)*:147–158.

Pope, K.S., Sonne, J.L. & Holroyd, J. (1994). *Sexual Feelings in Psychotherapy: Explorations for Therapists and Therapists-in-training.* Washington, DC: American Psychological Association.

Pope, K.S., Tebachnik, B.G. & Keith-Spiegel, P. (1987). The beliefs and behaviors of psychologists as therapists. *American Psychologist, 42(11)*:1003–1006.

Porche, M.V., Fortuna, L.R., Lin, J. & Alegria, M (2011). Childhood trauma and psychiatric disorders as correlates of school dropout in a national sample of young adults. *Child Development, 82(3)*:982–998.

Ports, K.A., Holman, D.M., Guinn, A.S., Pampati, S., Dyer, K.E., Merrick, M.T., Lunsford, N.B. & Metzler, M. (2018). Adverse childhood experiences and the presence of cancer risk factors in adulthood: a scoping review of the literature from 2005 to 2015. *Journal of Pediatric Nursing, 44(2019)*:81–96.

Powell, E. (2008). *Catharsis in Psychology and Beyond: A Historic Overview*: e1–8. https://pdfs.semanticscholar.org/8209/acea45d32a4e84d596701aca9b9adb17feba.pdf.

Powell, G.F., Brasel, J.A. & Blizzard, R.M. (1967a). Emotional deprivation and growth retardation simulating idiopathic hypopituitarism: I. Clinical evaluation of the syndrome. *New England Journal of Medicine, 276(23)*:1271–1278.

Powell, G.F., Brasel, J.A., Raiti, S. & Blizzard, R.M. (1967b). Emotional deprivation and growth retardation simulating idiopathic hypopituitarism: II. Endocrinologic evaluation of the syndrome. *New England Journal of Medicine, 276(23)*:1279–1283.

Prescott, J.H. (1971). Early somatosensory deprivation as an ontogenetic process in the abnormal development of the brain and behavior. In E.I. Goldsmith & J. Moor-Jankowski (Eds). *Medical Primatology*: 1–20. Basel & New York: S. Karger.

Prescott, J.H. (1975). Body pleasure and the origins of violence. *The Bulletin of the Atomic Scientists, 31(9)*:10–20.

Prescott, J.H. & Wallace, D. (1976). *Developmental Sociobiology and the Origins of Aggressive Behavior.* Paper presented at the 21st International Congress of Psychology, July 18th–25th, Paris.

Preyde, M. (2000). Effectiveness of massage therapy for subacute low-back pain: a randomized controlled trial. *Canadian Medical Association Journal, 162(13)*:1815–1820.

Procianoy, R.S., Mendes, E.W. & Silveira, R.C. (2010). Massage therapy improves neurodevelopment outcome at two years corrected age for very low birth weight infants. *Early Human Development, 86(1)*:7–11.

Pudrovska, T., Carr, D., McFarland, M. & Collins, C. (2013). Higher-status occupations and breast cancer: a life-course stress approach. *Social Science and Medicine, 89*:53–61.

Purtilo, R. (1978). *Health Professional/Patient Interaction*. Philadelphia: W.B. Saunders.
Puszko, S. (2009). Geriatric massage: a new face for the future. *Massage Therapy Canada*. www.massagetherapycanada.com/technique/geriatric-massage-1551
Rayworth, B.B., Wise, L.A. & Harlow, B.L. (2004). Childhood abuse and risk of eating disorders in women. *Epidemiology, 15(3)*:271–278.
Read, J., Agar, K., Argyle, N. & Aderhold, V. (2003). Sexual and physical abuse during childhood and adulthood as predictors of hallucination, delusions and thought disorder. *Psychology and Psychotherapy, 76(1)*:1–22.
Rebellon, C.J. & Straus, M. (2017). Corporal punishment and adult antisocial behavior: a comparison of dyadic concordance types and an evaluation of mediating mechanisms in Asia, Europe, and North America. *International Journal of Behavioral Development, 41(4)*:503–513.
Reich, W. (1948). *Character Analysis* (3rd ed.). Vision Press. Original (1933) published in German as *Charakteranalyse*. Sexpol Verlag.
Reinhart, J.B. & Drash, A.L. (1969). Psychosocial Dwarfism: environmentally induced recovery. *Psychosomatic Medicine, 31(2)*:165–172.
Reite, M. & Field, T. (Eds) (1985). *The Psychobiology of Attachment and Separation*. New York: Academic Press.
Relier, J-P. (2001). Influence of maternal stress on fetal behavior and brain development. *Biology of the Neonate, 79(3–4)*:168–171.
Remland, M.S., Jones, T.S. & Brinkman, H. (1995). Interpersonal distance, body orientation, and touch: effects of culture, gender, and age. *Journal of Social Psychology, 135(3)*:281–297.
Rey, E.S. & Martínez, H.G. (1983). Manejo rational de nino prematuro. *Conference Proceedings 1: Curso de Medicina Fetal y Neonatal: 137–151*. Bogota, Colombia. (English translation from the Spanish available from UNICEF, 3 UN Plaza, New York, NY 10017.
Richert, K.A., Carrion, V.G., Karchemskiy, A. & Reiss, A.L. (2006). Regional differences of the prefrontal cortex in pediatric PTSD: an MRI study. *Depression and Anxiety, 23(1)*:17–25.
Rinder, A.N. & Sutherland, C.J. (1995). An investigation of the effects of massage on quadriceps performance after exercise fatigue, *Complement Ther Nurs Midwifery, 1*: 99–102.
Robertiello, R. (1974a). Addendum to object-relations technique. *Psychotherapy: Theory, Research, and Practice, 11(4)*:197–204.
Robertiello, R. (1974b). Physical techniques with schizoid patients. *Journal of the American Academy of Psychoanalysis, 2(4)*:361–367.
Roberts, A.L., Glymour, M.M. & Koenen, K.C. (2013). Does maltreatment in childhood affect sexual orientation in adulthood? *Archives of Sexual Behavior, 42(2)*:161–171.
Roberts, M.E., Fuemmeler, B.F., McClernon, F.J. & Beckham, J.C. (2008). Association between trauma exposure and smoking in a population-based sample of young adults. *Journal of Adolescent Health, 42(3)*:266–274.

Rogers, C.R. (1957). The necessary and sufficient conditions of therapeutic personality change. *Journal of Consulting Psychology, 21(2)*:95–103.

Rogers, C.R. (1961). *On Becoming a Person: A Therapist's View of Psychotherapy*. London: Constable & Company.

Rogers, M. (1970). *An Introduction to the Theoretical Basis of Nursing*. Philadelphia: FA Davis.

Rohde, P., Ichikawa, L., Simon, G.E., Ludman, E.J., Linde, J.A., Jeffery, R.W. & Operskalski, B.H. (2008). Associations of child sexual and physical abuse with obesity and depression in middle-aged women. *Child Abuse & Neglect, 32(9)*:878–887.

Rokade, P.B. (2011). *Release of Endomorphin Hormone and Its Effects on Our Body and Moods: A Review*. International Conference on Chemical, Biological and Environment Sciences, Bangkok.

Romano, E. & De Luca, R. (2001). Male sexual abuse: a review of effects, abuse characteristics, and links with later psychological functioning. *Aggression and Violent Behaviour, 6(1)*:55–78.

Rosenberg, K. & Trevathan, W. (1995). Bipedalism and human birth: the obstetrical dilemma revisited. *Evolutionary Anthropology: Issues, News, and Reviews, 4(5)*:161–168.

Rosenthal, V. (1975). Holding: a way through the looking glass? *Voices, 11(2)*:2–7.

Roth, A. and Fonagy, P. (2005). *What Works for Whom?: A Critical Review of Psychotherapy Research* (2nd ed.). New York: Guilford Press.

Rothschild, B. (2000). *The Body Remembers: The Psychophysiology of Trauma and Trauma Treatment*. Los Angeles: Norton.

Rubin, R. (1963). Maternal touch. *Nursing Outlook, 11(11)*:828–831.

Ruppenthal, G.C., Arling, G.L., Harlow, H.F., Sackett, G.P. & Suomi, S.J. (1976). A 10-year perspective of motherless mother monkey behavior. *Journal of Abnormal Psychology:* 267–279, *85(4)*:341–349.

Russell, J. (1996). Sexual exploitation in Counselling. In R. Bayne, I., Horton & J. Bimrose (Eds). *New Directions in Counselling*: 65–78. London: Routledge.

Rutter, M. (1980). Attachment and the development of social relations. In M. Rutter (Ed.). *Developmental Psychiatry:* 267–279. Washington, DC: American Psychiatric Press.

Sachs, F. (1988). The intimate sense. *The Sciences, 28(1)*:28–34.

Sackett, G.P. (1968). Abnormal behavior in laboratory reared rhesus monkeys. In M. Fox (Ed.). *Abnormal Behavior in Animals:* 293–331. Philadelphia: Saunders.

Safren, S.A., Gershuny, B.S., Marzol, P.B.A., Otto, M.W. & Pollack, M.H. (2002). History of childhood abuse in panic disorder, social phobia, and generalized anxiety disorder. *The Journal of Nervous and Mental Disease, 190(7)*:453–456.

Sajedi, F., Kashaninia, Z., Hoseinzadeh, S. & Abedinipoor, A. (2011). How effective is Swedish massage on blood glucose level in children with diabetes mellitus? *Acta Medica Iranica, 49(9)*:592–597.

Sanderson, B.A. (1995). *It's Never OK: A Handbook for Professionals on Sexual Exploitation by Counselors and Therapists*. Saint Paul: Minnesota Department of Corrections.
Sansone, R.A., Watts, D.A. & Wiederman, M.W. (2013). Childhood trauma and pain and pain catastrophizing in adulthood: a cross-sectional survey study. *Primary Care Companion for CNS Disorders, 15(4)*. doi: 10.4088/PCC.13m01506
Santa Mina, E.E. & Gallop, R.M. (1998). Childhood sexual and physical abuse and adult self-harm and suicidal behaviour: a literature review. *Canadian Journal of Psychiatry, 43(8)*:793–800.
Sapolsky, R.M. (1996). Why stress is bad for your brain. *Science, 273(5276)*:749–750.
Sartre, J.-P. (1943). *L'Etre et le Néant, Essai d'Ontologie Phénoménologique*. Gallimard, Paris. Translated by Hazel Barnes as *Being and Nothingness: An Essay on Phenomenological Ontology* (1995). London: Routledge.
Saunders, K.E. & Smith, K.A. (2016). Interventions to prevent self-harm: what does the evidence say? *Evidence-Based Mental Health, 19(3)*:69–72.
Sayre-Adams, J. & Wright, S. (1995). *The Theory and Practice of Therapeutic Touch*. London: Churchill Livingstone.
Scafidi, F.A, Field, T.M., Schanberg, S.M., Bauer, C.R., Tucci, K., Roberts, J., Morrow, C. & Kuhn, C.M. (1990). Massage stimulates growth in preterm infants: a replication. *Infant Behavior and Development, 13(2)*:167–188.
Scafidi, F.A., Field, T.M., Schanberg, S.M., Bauer, C.R., Vega-Lahr, N. & Garcia, R. (1986). Effects of tactile/kinesthetic stimulation on the clinical course and sleep/wake behavior of preterm neonates. *Infant Behavior and Development, 9(1)*:91–105.
Schanberg, S.M. & Field, T. (1987). Sensory deprivation and supplemental stimulation in the rat pup and preterm human neonate. *Child Development, 58(6)*:1431–1447.
Schanberg, S.M. & Khun, C. (1980). Maternal deprivation: an animal model of psychosocial dwarfism. In E. Usdin, T.L. Sourkes & M.B.H. Youdin (Eds). *Enzymes and Neurotransmitters in Mental Disease*: 374–393. New York: Wiley.
Schechter, M. & Roberge, L. (1976). Child sexual abuse. In R. Helfer & C. Kempe (Eds). *Child Abuse and Neglect: The Family and the Community*: 127–142. Cambridge: Ballinger.
Scheflen, A.E. & Scheflen, A. (1972). *Body Language and the Social Order*. Englewood Cliffs, NJ: Prentice-Hall.
Schiffman, M. (1971). *Gestalt Self Therapy and Further Techniques for Personal Growth*. California: Self Therapy Press.
Schilder, (1935). *The Image and Appearance of the Human Body*. New York: International Universities Press.
Schmahl, J.A. (1964). Ritualism in nursing practice. *Nursing Forum, 3(4)*:74–84.

Schneiderman, I., Zagoory-Sharon, O., Leckman, J.F. & Feldmana, R. (2012). Oxytocin during the initial stages of romantic attachment: relations to couples' interactive reciprocity. *Psychoneuroendocrinology, 37(8)*:1277–1285.

Schore, A.N. (1994). *Affect Regulation and the Origin of the Self.* New Jersey: Lawrence Erlbaum.

Schore, A.N. (2002). Dysregulation of the right brain: a fundamental mechanism of traumatic attachment and the psychopathogenesis of posttraumatic stress disorder. *Australian and New Zealand Journal of Psychiatry, 36(1)*:9–30.

Schore, A.N. (2003). *Affect Regulation and the Repair of the Self.* New York: Norton.

Schultz, L.G. (1975). A survey of social workers' attitudes and use of body and sex psychotherapies. *Clinical Social Work Journal, 3(2)*:90–99.

Schultz, W. (1967). *Joy.* New York: Grove Press.

Scott, K., Smith, D.R. & Ellis, P.M. (2010). Prospectively ascertained child maltreatment and its association with DSM-1V mental disorders in young adults. *Archives of General Psychiatry, 67(7)*:712–719.

Seagull, A. (1968). Doctor don't touch me, I'd love it!. *Voices, 4*:86–90.

Seay, B.M., Alexander, B.K. & Harlow, H.F. (1964). Maternal behavior of socially deprived rhesus monkeys. *Journal of Abnormal and Social Psychology, 69(4)*:345–354.

Seay, B.M., Hansen, E.W. & Harlow, H.F. (1962). Mother-infant separation in monkeys. *Journal of Child Psychology and Psychiatry, 3(3–4)*:123–132.

Seay, B.M. & Harlow, H.F. (1965). Maternal separation in the rhesus monkey. *Journal of Nervous and Mental Diseases, 140(6)*:434–441.

Sedlak, A.J., Mettenberg, J., Basena, M., Petta, I., McPherson, K., Green, A. & Li, S. (2010). *Fourth National Incidence Study of Child Abuse and Neglect (NIS-4): Report to Congress, Executive Summary.* U.S. Department of Health & Human Services, Administration for Children and Families, Washington, DC.

Seib, C., Whiteside, E., Humphreys, J., Lee, K., Thomas, P., Chopin, L., Crisp, G., O'Keefe, A.O., Kimlin, M., Stacey, A. & Anderson, D. (2014). A longitudinal study of the impact of chronic psychological stress on health-related quality of life and clinical biomarkers: protocol for the Australian Healthy Aging of Woman Study. *BMC Public Health, 14(9)*:e1–7.

Seligman, M.E.P. (1972). Learned helplessness. *Annual Review of Medicine, 23(1)*:407–412.

Selye, H. (1936). A syndrome produced by diverse nocuous agents. *Nature, 138(3479)*:32.

Selye, H. (1956). *The Stress of Life.* London, UK: McGraw-Hill Book Company.

Senn, T.E. & Carey, M.P. (2010). Child maltreatment and women's adult sexual risk behavior: childhood sexual abuse as a unique risk factor. *Child Maltreatment, 15(4)*:324–335.

Senn, T.E., Carey, M.P. & Vanable, P.A. (2008). Childhood and adolescent sexual abuse and subsequent sexual risk behaviour: evidence from controlled studies, methodological critique, and suggestions for research. *Clinical Psychology Review, 28(5)*:711–735.

Shapiro, A.K. & Morris, L.A. (1978). Placebo effects in medical and psychological therapies. In S.L. Garfield & A.E. Bergin (Eds). *Hand-Book of Psychotherapy and Behavior Change: An Empirical Analysis* (2nd ed): 369–410. New York: Wiley.

Sheu, Y-S., Polcari, A., Anderson, C.M. & Teicher, M.H. (2010). Harsh corporal punishment is associated with increased T2 relaxation time in dopamine-rich regions. *Neuroimage, 53(2)*:412–419.

Shields, M.E., Hovdestad, W.E., Gilbert, C.P. & Tonmyr, L.E. (2016a). Childhood maltreatment as a risk factor for COPD: findings from a population-based survey of Canadian adults. *International Journal of Chronic Obstructive Pulmonary Disease, 11(1)*:2641–2650.

Shields, M.E., Hovdestad, W.E., Pelletier, C., Dykxhoorn, J.L., O'Donnell, S.C. & Tonmyr, L. (2016b). Childhood maltreatment as a risk factor for diabetes: findings from a population-based survey of Canadian adults. *BioMed Central Public Health, 16(1)*:879. doi: 10.1186/s12889-016-3491-1

Shepherd, I. (1979). Intimacy in psychotherapy, *Voices, 15(1)*:9–15.

Shin, Y.H., Kim, T.I., Shin, M.S. & Juon, H.S. (2004). Effect of acupressure on nausea and vomiting during chemotherapy cycle for Korean postoperative stomach cancer patients. *Cancer Nursing, 27(4)*:267–274.

Shonkoff, J.P. & Garner, A.S. (2012). The lifelong effects of early childhood adversity and toxic stress. *Pediatrics, 129(1)*:232–248.

Shor-Posner, G., Hernandez-Reif, M., Miguez, M., Fletcher, M., Quintero, N., Baez, J., Perez-Then, E., Soto, S., Mendoza, R., Castillo, R. & Zhang, G. (2006). Impact of a massage therapy clinical trial on immune status in young Dominican children infected with HIV-1. *Journal of Alternative and Complementary Medicine, 12(6)*:511–516.

Shostrum, E.L. (1965). (Film). *Three Approaches to Psychotherapy; Gloria*, Part 1. Orange, CA: Psychological Films. www.psicoterapiaintegrativa.com/texts/rogers/transcription%20Gloria.doc

Shulman, K.R. & Jones G.E. (1996). The effectiveness of massage therapy intervention on reducing anxiety in the workplace. *Journal of Applied Behavioral Science, 32(2)*:160–173.

Siegel, B.S. (1989). *Peace, Love & Healing*. New York: Harper & Row.

Siev-Ner, L., Gamus, D., Lerner-Geva, L. & Achiron, A. (2003). Reflexology treatment relieves symptoms of multiple sclerosis: a randomized controlled study. *Multiple Sclerosis, 9(4)*:356–361.

Silverman, A.B., Reinherz, H.Z. & Giaconia, R.M. (1996). The long-term sequelae of child and adolescent abuse: a longitudinal community study. *Child Abuse & Neglect, 20(8)*:709–723.

Silverman, A.F., Pressman, M.E. & Bartel, H.W. (1973). Self-esteem, and tactile communication. *Journal of Humanistic Psychology, 13(2)*:73–77.

Skuse, D., Albanese, A., Stanhope, R., Gilmour, J., Gilmour, L. & Voss, L. (1996). A new stress-related syndrome of growth failure and hyperphagia in children, associated with reversibility of growth hormone insufficiency. *Lancet, 348(9024)*:353–358.

Smith, E.W.L. (1985). *The Body in Psychotherapy*. Jefferson, NC: McFarland.

Smith, E.W.L. (1992). The ego-syntonic imperative. *Voices, 28(2)*:9–10.

Smith, E.W.L. (1998a). Traditions of touch in psychotherapy. In E.W.L. Smith, P.R. Clance & S. Imes (Eds). *Touch in Psychotherapy: Theory, Research and Practice*: 3–15. New York: Guilford Press.

Smith, E.W.L. (1998b). A taxonomy and ethics of touch in psychotherapy. In E.W.L. Smith, P.R. Clance & S. Imes (Eds). *Touch in Psychotherapy: Theory, Research and Practice*: 36–51. New York: Guilford Press.

Smith, E.W.L., Clance, P.R. & Imes, S. (Eds) (1998). *Touch in Psychotherapy: Theory, Research and Practice*. New York: Guilford Press.

Smith, J. (1989). *Senses and Sensibilities*. New York: John Wiley.

Smith, L.L., Keating, M.N., Holbert, D., Spratt, D.J., McCammon, M.R., Smith, S.S. & Israel, R.G. (1994). The effects of athletic massage on delayed onset muscle soreness, creatine kinase, and neutrophil count: a preliminary report. *Journal of Orthopaedic & Sports Physical Therapy, 19(2)*:93–99.

Smith, M.C., Kemp, J., Hemphill, L. & Vojir, C.P. (2002). Outcomes of therapeutic massage for hospitalized cancer patients. *Journal of Nursing Scholarship, 34(3)*:257–262.

Snyder, C.R., Michael, S.T. & Cheavens, J.S. (1999). Hope as a psychotherapeutic foundation of common factors, placebos and expectancies. In M.A. Hubble, B.L. Duncan & S.D. Miller (Eds). *The Heart and Soul of Change: What Works in Therapy*: 179–200. Washington, DC: American Psychological Society.

Sohlberg S., Norring C. (1992). Ego strength, object relations, and life events as outcome predictors in restricting anorexia nervosa and normal-weight bulimia nervosa. In W. Herzog, H.C. Deter & W. Vandereycken (Eds). *The Course of Eating Disorders*: 337–347. Berlin, Heidelberg: Springer.

Sonne, J., Meyer, B., Borys, D. & Marshall, V. (1985). Clients' reactions to sexual intimacy in therapy. *American Journal of Orthopsychiatry, 55(2)*:183–189.

Sonuga-Barke, E.J.S., Kennedy, M., Kumsta, R., Knights, N., Golm, D., Rutter, M., Schlotz, W. & Kreppner, J. (2017). Child-to-adult neurodevelopmental and mental health trajectories after early life deprivation: the young adult follow-up of the longitudinal English and Romanian Adoptees study. *The Lancet, 389(10078)*:1539–1548.

Sorensen, G. & Beatty, M.J. (1988). The interactive effects of touch and touch avoidance on interpersonal evaluations. *Communication Research Reports, 5(1)*:84–90.
Soydas, E.A., Albayrak, Y. & Sahin, B. (2014). Increased childhood abuse in patients with premenstrual dysphoric disorder in a Turkish sample: a cross-sectional study. *The Primary Care Companion for CNS Disorders, 16(4)*. doi: 10.4088/PCC.14m01647
Sperlich, M. & Seng, J.S. (2008). *Survivor Moms: Women's Stories of Birthing, Mothering and Healing after Sexual Abuse.* Eugene, Oregon: Motherbaby Press.
Spitz, R.A. (1945). Hospitalism: an inquiry into the genesis of psychiatric conditions in early childhood. *The Psychoanalytic Study of the Child, 1(1)*:53–74.
Spitz, R.A. (1946a). Hospitalism: a follow-up report on investigation described in Volume 1, 1945. *The Psychoanalytic Study of the Child, 2(1)*:113–117. New York: International Universities Press.
Spitz, R.A. (1946b). Anaclitic depression. *Psychoanalytic Study of the Child, 2(1)*:313–342.
Spokas, M., Wenzel, A., Stirman, S.W., Brown, G.K. & Beck, A.T. (2009). Suicide risk factors and mediators between childhood sexual abuse and suicide ideation among male and female suicide attempters. *Journal of Traumatic Stress, 22(5)*:467–470.
Spotnitz, H. (1972). Touch countertransference in group psychotherapy. *International Journal of Group Psychotherapy, 22(4)*:455–463.
Springer, K.W., Sheridan, J., Kuo, D. & Carnes, M. (2003). the long-term health outcomes of childhood abuse; An overview and a call to action. *Journal of General Internal Medicine, 18(10)*:864–870.
Springer, K.W., Sheridan, J., Kuo D. & Carnes, M. (2007). Long-term physical and mental health consequences of childhood physical abuse: results from a large population-based sample of men and women. *Child Abuse & Neglect, 31(5)*:517–530.
Srabstein, J.C., (2009). Be aware of bullying: a critical public health responsibility. *AMA (American Medical Association) Journal of Ethics, 11(2)*:173–177.
Sroufe, L.A., Coffino, B. & Carlson, E.A. (2010). Conceptualizing the role of early experience: lessons from the Minnesota longitudinal study. *Developmental Review, 30*: 36–51.
Stack, D.M. & Jean, A.D.L. (2011). Communicating through touch: touching during parent-infant interactions. In M.J. Hertenstein & S.J. Weiss (Eds). *The Handbook of Touch: Neuroscience, Behavioral, and Health Perspectives*: 273–298. New York: Springer.
Steckley, L. (2013). *Therapeutic Containment and Holding Environments: Understanding and Reducing Physical Restraint in Residential Child Care.* Child & Youth Care World Conference, June 25–28, CELCIS Centre for Excellence, University of Strathclyde, Glasgow, UK.

Steele, K. & Colrain, J. (1990). Abreactive work with sexual abuse survivors. In M. Hunter (Ed.). *The Sexually Abused Male, Vol. 2. Application of Treatment Strategies*: 1–55. Lexington, MA: Lexington Books/D. C. Heath and Com.

Stein, M.B., Koverola, C., Hanna, C., Torchia, M.G. & McClarty, B. (1997). Hippocampal volume in women victimized by childhood sexual abuse. *Psychological Medicine, 27(4)*:951–959.

Stein, N. & Sanfilipo, M. (1985). Depression and the wish to be held. *Journal of Clinical Psychology, 41(1)*:3–9.

Sternberg, E. (2001). Neuroendocrine regulation of autoimmune/inflammatory disease. *Journal of Endocrinology, 169(3)*:429–435.

Stiles, W.B. (2012). The client-therapist relationship. In C. Feltham & I. Horton (Eds). *Sage Handbook of Counselling and Psychotherapy* (3rd ed.): 67–77. London: SAGE.

Stipanicic, A., Nolin, P., Fortin, G. & Gobeil, M-E. (2008). Comparative study of the cognitive sequelae of school-aged victims of shaken baby syndrome. *Child Abuse & Neglect, 32(3)*:415–428.

Stock, J.L., Bell, M.A., Boyer, D.K. & Connell, F.A. (1997). Adolescent pregnancy and sexual risk-taking among sexually abused girls. *Family Planning Perspectives, 29(5)*:200–203 & 227.

Stockwell, S.R. & Dye, A. (1980). Effects of counselor touch on counseling outcome. *Journal of Counseling Psychology, 27(5)*:443–446.

Stojanovich, L. & Marisavljevich, D. (2008). Stress as a trigger of autoimmune disease. *Autoimmunity Reviews, 7(3)*:209–213.

Straus, M.A. (1991a). Discipline and deviance: physical punishment of children and violence and other crime in adulthood. *Social Problems, 38(2)*:133–154.

Straus, M.A. (1991b). New theory and old canards about family violence research. *Social Problems, 38(2)*:180–197.

Straus, M.A. & Kantor, G.K. (1994). Corporal punishment of adolescents by parents: a risk factor in the epidemiology of depression, suicide, alcohol abuse, child abuse, and wife beating. *Adolescence, 29(115)*:543–561.

Straus, M.A., Sugarman, D.B. & Giles-Sims, J. (1997). Spanking by parents and subsequent antisocial behavior of children. *Archives of Pediatrics and Adolescent Medicine, 151(8)*:761–767.

Straus, M.A. & Corbin, J. (1990). *Basics of Qualitative Research: Grounded Theory Procedures and Techniques*. London: SAGE.

Strong, S.R. (1978). Social psychological approach to psychotherapy research. In S.L. Garfield & A.E. Bergin (Eds). *Handbook of Psychotherapy and Behavior Change: An Empirical Analysis* (2nd ed.). New York: Wiley.

Strupp, H.H., Fox, R.E. & Lessler, K. (1969). *Patients View Their Psychotherapy*. Baltimore: John Hopkins.

Sue, D.W. & Sue, D. (1990). *Counseling the Culturally Different, Theory & Practice*. Hoboken, USA: Wiley-Interscience Publication, John Wiley & Sons.

Suiter, R. & Goodyear, R. (1985). Male and female counselor and client perceptions of four levels of counselor touch. *Journal of Counseling Psychology, 32(4)*:645–648.
Summitt, R.C. (1983). The child abuse accommodation syndrome. *Child Abuse & Neglect, 7(2)*:177–193.
Sunderland, M. (2016). *What Every Parent Needs to Know*. Dorling Kindersley.
Suomi, S.J. (1984). The role of touch in rhesus monkey social development. In C.C. Brown (Ed.). *The Many Facets of Touch*: 41–50. (Johnson & Johnson Baby Products Company pediatric round table 10). Johnson & Johnson Baby Products Company.
Suomi, S.J. (1990). The role of tactile contact in rhesus monkey social development. In K.E. Barnard & T.B. Brazelton (Eds). *Clinical Infant Reports. Touch: The Foundation of Experience:* Full revised and expanded proceedings of Johnson & Johnson Pediatric Round Table X: 129–164. Madison, CT: International Universities Press.
Suomi, S.J., Collins, H.L. & Harlow, H.F. & Ruppenthal, G.C. (1976). Effects of maternal and peer separations on young monkeys. *Journal of Child Psychology and Psychiatry, 17(2)*:101–112.
Suomi, S.J. & Harlow, H.F. (1972). Social rehabilitation of isolate-reared monkeys. *Developmental Psychology, 6(3)*:487–496.
Swinford, S.P., DeMaris, A., Cernkovich, S.A. & Giordano, P.C. (2004). Harsh physical discipline in childhood and violence in later romantic involvements: the mediating role of problem behaviors. *Journal of Marriage and Family, 62(2)*:508–519.
Tafet, G.E., Idoyaga-Vargas, V.P., Abulafia, D.P., Calandria, J.M., Roffman, S.S., Chiovetta, A. & Shinitzky, M. (2001). Correlation between cortisol level and serotonin uptake in patients with chronic stress and depression. *Cognitive, Affective and Behavioral Neuroscience, 1(4)*:388–393.
Takeuchi, M.S., Miyaoka, H., Tomoda, A., Suzuki, M., Liu, Q. & Kitamura, T. (2010). The effect of interpersonal touch during childhood on adult attachment and depression: a neglected area of family and developmental psychology? *Journal of Child and Family Studies, 19(1)*:109–117.
Tallman, K. & Bohart, A.C. (1999). The client as a common factor: clients as self-healers. In M.A. Hubble, B.L. Duncan & S.D. Miller (Eds). *The Heart and Soul of Change: What Works in Therapy*: 91–131. Washington, DC: American Psychological Society.
Taylor, S.E. (2006). Tend and befriend; Biobehavioral bases of affiliation under stress. *Association for Psychological Science, 15(6)*:273–277.
Taylor, S.E. (2010). Mechanisms linking early life stress to adult health outcomes. *Proceedings of the National Academy of Sciences of the U.S.A., 107(19)*:8507–8512.
Taylor, B. & Wagner, N. (1976). Sex between therapist and clients: a review and analysis. *Professional Psychology: Research and Practice, 7(4)*:593–601.

Teicher, M.H. (2002). Scars that won't heal: the neurobiology of child abuse. *Scientific American, 286(3)*:68–75.

Teicher, M.H., Anderson, C.M. & Polcari, A. (2012). Childhood maltreatment is associated with reduced volume in the hippocampal subfields CA3, dentate gyrus, and subiculum. *Proceedings of the National Academy of Sciences of the U.S.A., 109(9)*:e563–572.

Teicher, M.H., Andersen, S.L., Polcari, A., Anderson, C.M., Navalta, C.P. & Kim, D.M. (2003). The neurobiological consequences of early stress and childhood maltreatment. *Neuroscience and Biobehavioral Reviews, 27(1–2)*:33–44.

Teicher, M.H., Dumont, N.L., Ito, Y., Vaituzis, C., Giedd, J.N. & Andersen, S.L. (2004). Childhood neglect is associated with reduced corpus callosum area. *Biological Psychiatry, 56(2)*:80–85.

Thayer, S. (1982). Social touching. In W. Schiff & E. Foulke (Eds). *Tactual Perception: A Source Book*: 263–304. New York: Cambridge University Press.

Thayer, S. (1986a). History and strategies of research on social touch. *Journal of Nonverbal Behavior, 10(1)*:12–28.

Thayer, S. (1986b). Touch: frontier of intimacy. *Journal of Nonverbal Behavior, 10(1)*:7–11.

Thomas, Z. (1994). *Healing Touch: The Church's Forgotten Language*. Louisville, KY: Westminster /John Knox Press.

Thompson, M.P., Arias, I., Basile, K. & Desai, S. (2002). The association between childhood physical and sexual victimization and health problems in adulthood in a nationally representative sample of women. *Journal of Interpersonal Violence, 17(10)*:1115–1129.

Thompson, R., Kaczor, K., Lorenz, D.J., Bennett, B.L., Meyers, G. & Pierce, M.C. (2017). Is the use of physical discipline associated with aggressive behaviors in young children? *Academic Pediatrics, 17(1)*:34–44.

Thornton, C.P. & Veenema, T.G. (2015). Children seeking refuge: a review of the escalating humanitarian crisis of child sexual abuse and HIV/AIDS in Latin America. *Journal of the Association of Nurses in AIDS Care, 26(4)*:432–442.

Tietjen, G.E. & Peterlin, B.L. (2011). Childhood abuse and migraine: epidemiology, sex differences, and potential mechanisms. *Headache, 51(6)*:869–879.

Timms, R.J. & Connors, P. (1992). *Embodying Healing: Integrating Bodywork and Psychotherapy in Recovery from Childhood Sexual Abuse*. Orwell, OH: Safer Society Press.

Tirnauer, L., Smith, E. & Foster, P. (1996). The American academy of Psychotherapists research committee survey of members. *Voices, 32(2)*:87–94.

Tobiason, S. (1981). Touching is for everyone. *American Journal of Nursing, 81(4)*:729.

Tomasdottir, M.O., Sigurdsson, J.A., Petursson, H., Kirkengen, A.L., Nilson, T.I.L., Hetlevik, I. & Getz, L. (2016). Does 'existential unease' predict adult multimorbidity? Analytical cohort study on embodiment based on the Norwegian HUNT population. *British Medical Journal. BMJ Open, 6*:e012602. doi: 10.1136/bmjopen-2016-012602

Tomoda, A., Suzuki, H., Rabi, K., Sheu, Y-S., Polcari, A. & Teicher, M.H. (2009). Reduced prefrontal cortical grey matter volume in young adults exposed to harsh corporal punishment. *Neuroimage, 47(2)*:T66–71.

Toronto, E.L.K. (2001). The human touch: an exploration of the role and meaning of physical touch in psychoanalysis. *Psychoanalytic Psychology, 18(1)*:37–54.

Torraco, P. (1998). Jean's legacy: on the use of physical touch in long-term psychotherapy. In E.W.L. Smith, P.R. Clance & S. Imes (Eds). *Touch in Psychotherapy: Theory, Research and Practice*: 220–237. New York: Guilford Press.

Tóth, B.E., Vecsernyés, M., Zelles, T., Kádár, K., & Nagy, G.M. (2012). Role of peripheral and brain-derived Dopamine (DA) in immune regulation. *Advances in Neuroimmune Biology, 3(2)*:111–155.

Trask, E.V., Walsh, K. & DiLillo, D. (2011). Treatment effects for common outcomes of child sexual abuse: a current meta-analysis. *Aggression and Violent Behavior, 16(1)*:6–19.

Triandis, H.C. (1972). *The Analysis of Subjective Culture*. New York: Wiley.

Trickett, P.K., Noll, J.G. & Putnam, F.W. (2011). The impact of sexual abuse on female development: lessons from a multigenerational, longitudinal research study. *Development and Psychopathology, 23(2)*:453–476.

Tronick, E.Z. (1995). Touch in mother-infant interaction. In T.M. Field (Ed.). *Touch in Early Development*: 53–65. Mahwah, NJ: Erlbaum:

Tronick, E.Z. (2007). *The Neurobehavioral and Social-Emotional Development of Infants and Children*. New York: Norton.

Truax, C.B. & Carkhuff, R.R. (1965). Client and therapist transparency in the psychotherapeutic encounter. *Journal of Counseling Psychology, 12(1)*:3–9.

Tucker, D. (2007). *Mind from Body: Experience from Neural Structure*. New York: Oxford University Press.

Tune, D. (2001). Is touch a valid therapeutic intervention? Early returns from a qualitative study of therapists' views. *Counselling and Psychotherapy Research, 1(3)*:167–171.

United Nations (2007). *World Fertility Report*. United Nations Publications. www.un.org/en/development/desa/population/publications/pdf/fertility/worldFertilityReport2007.pdf

Uvnäs-Moberg, K., Handlin, L. & Petersson, M. (2014). Self-soothing behaviors with particular reference to oxytocin release induced by non-noxious sensory stimulation. *Frontiers in Psychology, 5*:1529. doi:10.3389/fpsyg.2014.01529 van den Dolder, P.A. & Roberts, D.L. (2003). A trial into the effectiveness of soft tissue massage in the treatment of shoulder pain. *Australian Journal of Physiotherapy, 49(3)*:183–188.

Veenema, A.H. (2009). Early life stress, the development of aggression and neuroendocrine and neurobiological correlates: what can we learn from animal models? *Frontiers in Neuroendocrinology, 30(4)*:497–518.

Venkateshwar, V. & Raman, T.S.R. (2000). Failure to thrive. *Medical Journal Armed Forces India, 56(3)*:219–224.

Verrill, A. (2018). The relationship between childhood abuse and aggressive behavior in adulthood. *Journal of Interdisciplinary Undergraduate Research, 10, Article 2.*

Vogelzangs, N., Beekman, A.T., Milaneschi, Y., Bandinelli, S., Ferrucci, L. & Penninx, B.W. (2010). Urinary cortisol and six-year risk of all-cause and cardiovascular mortality, *Journal of Clinical Endocrinology and Metabolism, 95(11)*:4959–4964.

Voos, A.C., Pelphrey, K.A. & Kaiser, M.D. (2013). Autistic traits are associated with diminished neural response to affective touch. *Social Cognitive and Affective Neuroscience, 8(4)*:378–386.

Vythilingam, M., Heim, C., Newport, J., Miller, A.H., Anderson, E., Bronen, R., Brummer, M., Staib, L., Vermetten, E., Charney, D.S., Nemeroff, C.B. & Bremner, J.D. (2002). Childhood trauma associated with smaller hippocampal volume in women with major depression. *American Journal of Psychiatry, 159(12)*:2072–2080.

Wainright, N.W.J., Surtees, P.G., Wareham, N.J. & Harrison, B.D.W. (2007). Psychosocial factors and incident asthma hospital admissions in the EPIC-Norfolk cohort study. *Allergy, 62(5)*:554–560.

Wainstock, T., Lerner-Geva, L., Glasser, S., Shoham-Vardi, I. & Anteby, E.Y. (2013). Prenatal stress and risk of spontaneous abortion. *Psychosomatic Medicine, 75(3)*:228–235.

Walsh, J. (2000, 25th May). Who wants to be a professional pedant today? London, UK: *The Independent.*

Weber, R. (1990). A philosophical perspective on touch. In K.E. Barnard & T.B. Brazelton (Eds). *Clinical Infant Reports. Touch: The Foundation of Experience.* Full revised and expanded proceedings of Johnson & Johnson Pediatric Round Table X:1–43. Madison, CT: International Universities Press.

Wei, L., David, A., Duman, R.S., Anisman, H. & Kaffman, A. (2010). Early life stress increases anxiety-like behavior in Balb c mice despite a compensatory increase in levels of postnatal maternal care. *Hormones & Behavior, 57(4–5)*:396–404.

Wei, L., Simen, A., Mane, S. & Kaffman, A. (2012). Early life stress inhibits expression of a novel innate immune pathway in the developing hippocampus. *Neuropsychopharmacology, 37(2)*:567–580.

Weiler, B.L. & Widom, C.S. (1996). Psychopathy and violent behaviour in abused and neglected young adults. *Criminal Behaviour and Mental Health, 6(3)*:253–271.

Weininger, O. (1954). Physiological damage under emotional stress as a function of early experience. *Science, 119(3087)*:285–286.
Weiss, S. (1966). The language of touch. *Nursing Research, 28(2)*:76–79.
Weiss, S. (1984). Parental touch and the child's body image. In C.C. Brown (Ed.). *The Many Facets of Touch: The Foundation of Experience: Its Importance Through Life, with Initial Emphasis for Infants and Young Children*: 130–138. Skillman, NJ: Johnson & Johnson Baby Product Company.
Weiss, S. (1986). Psychophysiologic effects of caregiver touch on incidents of cardiac dysrhythmia. *Heart & Lung, 15(5)*:495–505.
Wentworth, L.J., Briese, L.J., Timimi, F.K., Sanvick, C.L., Bartel, D.C., Cutshall, S.M., Tilbury, R.T., Lennon, R. & Bauer, B.A. (2009). Massage therapy reduces tension, anxiety, and pain in patients awaiting invasive cardiovascular procedures. *Progress in Cardiovascular Nursing, 24(4)*:155–161.
Werboff, J., Anderson, A. & Haggett, B.N. (1968). Handling of pregnant mice: gestational and postnatal behavioral effects. *Physiology and Behavior, 3(1)*:35–39.
Werner, E.E. & Smith, R.S. (1992). *Overcoming the Odds: High Risk Children from Birth to Adulthood*. Ithaca, NY: Cornell University Press.
Wheaton, J. & Borgen, F. (1981). Effects of interpersonal touch on clients' perceptions of the counseling relationship. Unpublished manuscript. Iowa State University, Ames.
Wheeden, A., Scafidi, F.A., Field, T., Ironson, G., Valdeon, C. & Bandstra, E. (1993). Massage effects on cocaine-exposed preterm neonates. *Journal of Developmental & Behavioral Pediatrics, 14(5)*:318–322.
White, H.R. & Widom, C.S. (2003). Intimate partner violence among abused and neglected children in young adulthood: the mediating effects of early aggression, antisocial personality, hostility and alcohol problems. *Aggressive Behavior, 29(4)*:332–345.
Widdowson, E.M. (1951). Mental contentment and physical growth. *The Lancet, 1(6668)*:1316–1318.
Widom, C.S. (1989). Child abuse, neglect, and violent criminal behavior. *Criminology, 27(2)*:251–271.
Widom, C.S. (1995, March). *Victims of Childhood Sexual Abuse: Later Criminal Consequences*: 1–8. U.S. Department of Justice, National Institute of Justice.
Widom, C.S. (1999). Posttraumatic stress disorder in abused and neglected children grown up. *American Journal of Psychiatry, 156(8)*:1223–1229.
Widom, C.S. (2000). Childhood victimization: early adversity and subsequent psychopathology. *National Institute of Justice Journal, 242*:3–9.
Widom, C.S., Czaja, S.J. & Dutton, M.A. (2008). Childhood victimization and lifetime revictimization. *Child Abuse & Neglect, 32(8)*:785–796.
Widom, C.S., Czaja, S.J. & Paris, J. (2009). A prospective investigation of borderline personality disorder in abused and neglected children followed up into adulthood. *Journal of Personality Disorders, 23(5)*:433–446.

Widom, C.S. & Kuhns, J.B. (1996). Childhood victimization and subsequent risk for promiscuity, prostitution, and teenage pregnancy: a prospective study. *American Journal of Public Health, 86(11)*:1607–1612.

Widom, C.S., Marmorstein, N.R. & White, H.R. (2006). Childhood victimization and illicit drug use in middle adulthood. *Psychology of Addictive Behaviors, 20(4)*:394–403.

Widom, C.S. & Maxfield, G. (2001). *An Update on the "Cycle of Violence"*. U.S. Department of Justice, National Institute of Justice.

Wilkie, D.J., Kampbell, J., Cutshall, S., Halabisky, H., Harmon, H., Johnson, L.P., Weinacht, L. & Rake-Marona, M. (2000). Effects of massage on pain intensity, analgesics and quality of life in patients with cancer pain: a pilot study of a randomized clinical trial conducted within hospice care delivery. *Hospice Journal, 15(3)*:31–53.

Williams, L.E. & Bargh, J.A. (2008). Experiencing physical warmth promotes interpersonal warmth. *Science, 322(5901)*:606–607.

Willis, F.N. Jr. & Hamm, H.K. (1980). The use of interpersonal touch in securing compliance. *Journal of Nonverbal Behavior, 5(1)*:49–55.

Willison, B.G. & Masson, R.L. (1986). The role of touch in therapy: an adjunct to communication. *Journal of Counseling and Development, 64(8)*:497–500.

Wilson, C.N. & Sathiyasusuman, A. (2015). Associated risk factors of STIs and multiple sexual relationships among youths in Malawi. *PloS One, 10(8)*:e0134286.

Wilson, H.W. & Widom, C.S. (2009). Sexually transmitted diseases among adults who had been abused and neglected as children: a 30-year prospective study. *American Journal of Public Health, 99(Sup.1)*:S197–S203.

Wilson, H.W. & Widom, C.S. (2008). An examination of risky sexual behavior and HIV in victims of child abuse and neglect: a 30-year follow-up. *Health Psychology, 27(2)*:149–158.

Wilson, H.W. & Widom, C.S. (2010). Does physical abuse, sexual abuse, or neglect in childhood increase the likelihood of same-sex sexual relationships and cohabitation? A prospective 30-year follow-up. *Archives of Sexual Behavior, 39(1)*:63–74.

Wilson, J.M. (1982). The value of touch in psychotherapy. *American Journal of Orthopsychiatry, 52(1)*:65–72.

Winnicott, D.W. (1961). Varieties of psychotherapy. In *Home Is Where We Start From*: 101–111. New York: Norton.

Winnicott, D.W. (1965). *The Maturational Process and the Facilitating Environment*. New York: International Universities Press.

Wittman, A.B. & Wall, L.L. (2007). The evolutionary origins of obstructed labor: Bipedalism, encephalization, and the human obstetric dilemma. *Obstetrical & Gynecological Survey, 62(11)*:739–748.

Wolke, D. & Lereya, S.T. (2014). Bullying and parasomnias: a longitudinal cohort study. *Pediatrics, 134(4)*:1040–1048.

Wolke, D. & Lereya, S.T. (2015). Long-term effects of bullying. *Archives of Disease and Childhood, 100(9)*:879–885.

Woodmansey, A.C. (1988). Are psychotherapists out of touch? *British Journal of Psychotherapy, 5(1)*:57–65.

Woon, E.L. & Hedges, D.W. (2008). Hippocampal and amygdala volumes in children and adults with childhood maltreatment-related posttraumatic stress disorder: a meta-analysis. *Hippocampus, 18(8)*:729–736.

World Health Organisation (WHO) (2003a). *Kangaroo Mother Care: A Practical Guide*. Department of Reproductive Health and Research. Geneva: World Health Organization.

World Health Organisation (WHO) (2003b). *Guidelines for Medico-Legal Care for Victims of Sexual Violence*. Geneva: World Health Organisation.

World Health Organisation (WHO) (2019). *Alcohol & Violence; Child Maltreatment and Alcohol*. www.who.int/violence_injury_prevention/violence/world_report/factsheets/fs_d

Wrenn, C. (1985). The culturally encapsulated counselor revisited. In P. Pedersen (Ed.). *Handbook of Cross-Cultural Counseling and Therapy*: 323–329. Westport, CT: Greenwood.

Wyschogrod, E. (1981). Empathy and sympathy as tactile encounter. *Journal of Medicine and Philosophy, 6(1)*:25–43.

Yakeley, J. (2012). Psychoanalytic Therapy (Sigmund Freud, 1856–1939). In C. Feltham & I. Horton (Eds). *The Sage Handbook of Counselling and Psychotherapy*: 268–272 London: SAGE.

Yang, M-Y., Font, S.A., Ketchum, M. & Kim, Y.K. (2018). Intergenerational transmission of child abuse and neglect: effects of maltreatment type and depressive symptoms. *Children and Youth Services Review, 91*:364–371.

Yaribeygi, H., Panahi, Y., Sahraei, H., Johnston, T.P. & Sahebkar, A. (2017). The impact of stress on body function: a review. *Experimental and Clinical Sciences (EXCLI) Journal, 16*:1057–1072. doi: 10.17179/excli2017-480

Zainuddin, Z., Newton, M., Sacco, P. & Nosaka, K. (2005). Effects of massage on delayed-onset muscle soreness, swelling, and recovery of muscle function. *Journal of Athletic Training, 40(3)*:174–180.

Zajonc, R.B. (1968). Attitudinal effects of mere exposure. *Journal of Personality and Social Psychology, 9(2, Pt 2)*:1–27.

Zhang, T.Y., Chrétien, P., Meaney, M.J. & Gratton, A. (2005). Influence of naturally occurring variations in maternal care on prepulse inhibition of acoustic startle and the medial prefrontal cortical dopamine response to stress in adult rats. *The Journal of Neuroscience, 25(6)*:1493–1502.

Zolotor, A.J., Theodore, A.D., Chang, J.J., Berkoff, M.C. & Runyan, D.K. (2008). Speak softly – and forget the stick: corporal punishment and child physical abuse. *American Journal of Preventive Medicine, 35(4)*:364–369.

Zur, O. (2007a). Touch in therapy and the standard of care in psychotherapy and counseling. Bringing clarity to illusive relationships. *U.S. Association of Body Psychotherapy Journal, 6(2)*:61–93.

Zur, O. (2007b). *Boundaries in Psychotherapy: Ethical and Clinical Explorations.* Washington, DC: APA Books.

Zur, O. & Nordmarken, N. (2016). *To Touch or Not to Touch: Exploring the Myth of Prohibition on Touch in Psychotherapy and Counseling.* www.zurinstitute.com/touchintherapy.html

Index

Note: Page numbers followed by "n" denote endnotes.

Abs, P. 170
acceptance: in everyday life 105, 108, 111, 113; in therapy 121, 124, 127, 129, 133, 136, 152; see also self-acceptance
ACE (adverse childhood experience) 24–25, 61
Ader, R. 12
adrenalin 24, 49, 50
Ainsworth, M.D.S. 29
anger: in everyday life 29, 30, 32, 54, 56, 64, 93, 113; in therapy 158, 185, 186
Anglo and non-Anglo tactility see tactility
anxiety: in animals 13; in humans, in everyday life 27, 31, 33, 35, 39, 40, 41, 48, 49, 50, 51, 54, 55, 61, 63, 64, 66, 109, 112; in humans, in therapy 125, 149, 153, 155, 156
attachment 35, 171

Bar-Levav, R. 171, 220n2
Barron, D.H. 8–9
Batmanghelidjh, C. 36–37
Berkeley-Hill, B. 43–47
Bernstein, L. 12–13
bicultural upbringing 98, 100–101, 164
Biddulph, S. 38
Biggar, M.L. 30, 32
body psychotherapy 207–208

Bohart, A.C. 134
Bordin, E.S. 120
Bouhoutsos, J.C. 157
Brodsky, A.M. 180n1
Brody, V.A. 30–31, 204
bullying 60–61, 62
Byrne, D. 34

caring: in everyday life 30, 31, 34, 37, 42, 43, 47, 51, 110; in therapy 123, 129, 135, 152, 179, 197
child abuse (sexual and/or physical), effects on: behaviour 56–57; brain structure and function 54–55; cognitive ability 57; interpersonal relationships 56; mental health and personality 55–57, 94; physical health 57–58; sexual interaction/relationships 56, 57; society 58–59; tactility 56, 71–72, 93, 94, 103, 112, 147
child abuse: in everyday life 53, 54–59, 71–72, 93, 94, 112; intergenerational transmission of/ the 'sorry-go-round' 58–59, 61; social effects of 58; survivors of abuse in therapy 130, 147, 149, 155–156, 158, 177, 182, 184, 187, 190, 192, 219–220
child physical abuse, effects on: behaviour 60, 61, 62; brain structure and function 59–60, 62;

cognitive ability 59–60, 62; mental health and personality 60, 61, 62–63; physical health/well-being 59–60, 61; interpersonal relationships 60; society 60, 61
child physical abuse in everyday life: 53, 59–63; and academic failure 59, 62; in corporal punishment 61–63; intergenerational transmission of 60
Children Act 41
child sexual abuse, effects on: behaviour 63, 64; mental health and personality 63, 64, 65–66, 93; parenting 64; physical health/wellbeing 63, 64; sexual interaction/relationships 63–64
child sexual abuse: in everyday life 53–54, 63–66; disclosure of 65; sexual abuse survivors in therapy 121, 122, 133–134, 136, 137, 139, 141–142, 183, 196; and sexual orientation 64–65; twin studies 65–66
Christianity 100, 161–162, 167
Clark, P. 197n2
Clore, C.L. 34
comfort 43, 105, 123, 142–143, 152
Conklin, P.M. 12
containment 129–130, 136, 143, 154
corporal punishment 61–63
cortisol 24, 25–27, 38, 39, 48, 49, 50

Denenberg, V.H. 12, 13
depression: in everyday life 27, 29, 31, 32, 38, 39, 40, 48, 49, 50, 51, 55, 61, 62, 66, 109; in therapy 125, 130, 153, 220n2; see also postnatal depression
Descartes, R. 161
Diego, M.A. 33
dissociation 64, 138, 155, 184, 192
dopamine: in animals 14, 19n2; in humans 24, 27, 37, 49
Down syndrome 18
drug use 32–33, 51, 56–57, 58, 61

Edwards, D.J.A. 189–190
Eiden, B. 170, 177, 178
embodiment 107, 122, 128, 152
empathy: in everyday life 39, 43, 108; in therapy 133, 140, 152, 167, 168n2, 179, 191, 195
endorphins 24, 27, 32, 37, 51
environmental change-agents 80

Fagan, J. 157
failure to thrive (FTT) 20–21
fear: in animals 7, 11, 13–14, 16; in humans generally 29, 31, 35, 40, 54, 63, 90, 93, 109, 112, 114, 188; in clients 125, 137, 147, 156, 158, 184, 190, 192; in therapists 176, 177, 178, 179, 196; of therapist-client sexual interaction 170, 171, 175
Field, T. 9, 10, 22–23, 27, 33, 38, 47–50
Fisher, J.D. 33–34
Forer, B.R. 32, 34, 156
Fortes Mayer, A. 182, 206, 208
Francis, D.D. 14
Freud, S. 15, 157, 160–161, 162, 163, 166

GABA (gamma-aminobutyric acid) 14, 19n2
Gabbard, G.O. 180n1
Geib, P.G. 186
gentling of animal mammals: effects of 7, 8, 9, 11–13, 15
Gerhardt, S. 26, 35
Gineste, Y. 39
Green, L. 40
Guéguen, N. 34
guilt: in everyday life 54, 63, 64, 112, 113; in therapy 124, 157, 162, 186
Gutheil, T.G. 180n1

Hammett, F.S. 7
happiness 27, 34, 51, 106, 108, 111, 124–125, 193
'happiness hormones' 23–24, 27, 37
Harlow, H.F. 15–17
Hatfield, R.W. 27

Hippocampus: in animals 13, 19n1; in humans 26
Holroyd, J.C. 180n1
Howard, G.S. 102
Hunter, M. 154, 157, 158, 162, 172, 173–174, 175, 176, 177, 181, 182, 185, 187, 195–196, 197n1

Inskipp, F. 176
integration 127–128, 139, 143–144, 153, 219
intergenerational transmission 58–59, 60

Jacob, C. 34
Johansson, C. 156
Johnson, V.E. 157
Jourard, S.M. 153

Kabat-Zinn, J. 208
Kangaroo care 21–22
Karas, G.G. 13
Karsh, E.B. 12
Kertay, L. 155, 158, 182, 184
Kohut, H. 1
Krueger, D.W. 31
Kübler-Ross, E. 39

lack of touch in therapy 141, 158
Larsen, K.S. 156–157
Lazarus, A.A. 179
Leavitt-Teare, M. 18
LeRoux, J. 156–157
limbic system 18
loneliness 31–32, 38–39, 40, 61, 89, 109, 153
love: in everyday life 15, 20, 26, 29, 31, 34, 35, 37, 38, 39, 43, 44, 71, 105, 108, 110; in therapy 123–124, 125, 126, 128, 129–130, 131, 133, 142, 152, 153, 168n2, 171, 172–173, 195, 196–197, 214, 219–220; loving touch 20, 31, 34, 35, 36, 38, 39, 51, 66, 142, 219

marasmus 20, 52n1
Marescotti, R. 39
Martínez, H.G. 21–22

massage therapy 22–23, 27, 33, 37, 38, 39, 40, 44, 47–50, 80, 161, 195, 207; and purely 'human' touch 50–51
massage therapy, effects on: cognitive ability 27; the dying 40; the elderly 39, 50; emotional state 33–34, 39, 40, 48–49; healthy participants 23, 27, 49–50; illness symptoms 23, 44, 47–49; immunity 48; premature infants 22–23, 27
Masson, R.L. 178, 197n1
Masters, W.H. 157
mere exposure 163
Milakovich, J. 165
Mintz, E.E. 160
monkey experiments 9, 10, 15–17, 19n2
Montagu, A. 7, 11, 13, 28, 35, 90, 217
motives for touching 195–197

needs: importance of meeting them 23, 24, 51, 174; for touch in everyday life 24–25, 34–39, 40, 47, 51, 92–93, 105, 217; for touch in therapy 121–129, 133, 139, 140, 142, 152–153, 172, 173, 174, 194; satisfied by touch in everyday life 105–110; satisfied by touch in therapy 121–129, 134, 149–150, 152–153
Nelson, D. 39
neurotransmitters: in animals 14, 19n2; in humans 54
nonverbal communication/body language 67–68, 124, 140, 191–192
noradrenalin 24, 49, 50

Older, J. 18, 152, 163, 218
oxytocin 37, 51

pain: emotional 56, 89, 135, 138, 143, 145, 146, 149, 154, 184, 194; physical 37, 39, 40, 47, 48, 49, 50, 57, 63, 137, 138, 196
Panksepp, J. 18
Peloquin, S.M. 151

Plato 161
postnatal/postpartum depression 23, 37–38, 50, 64
posttraumatic stress disorder (PTSD) 49, 55, 61, 64, 155,
Prescott, J.H. 32–33
psychoanalysis 135, 156, 160–161, 162–163, 165–166, 167, 168, 177–178

Reite, M. 10
relaxation: in everyday life 37, 39, 51, 105–107, 110, 113; in therapy 121, 134–135, 136, 152, 173
reparenting/filling developmental gaps 36–37, 140, 142–143, 155, 174
revictimisation 59, 66
Riviere, S.L. 155, 158, 182, 184
Rey, E.S. 21
risks and contraindications of touch-use: 184–186
rodent (rat and mouse) experiments 13; mouse experiments 11, 14–15; rat experiments 7, 8, 9–10, 11, 12, 13–14;
Rogers, C.R. 168–169n2
rule of abstinence 163

safety: in everyday life 84, 105, 109; in therapy 122, 124, 127, 129, 132–133, 134, 135, 136, 143, 153, 154, 171, 192–193
Saunders, C. 40
Sayre-Adams, J. 43
Schanberg, S.M. 9–10
Schmahl, J.A. 194
self-acceptance 31, 110, 124, 132, 153, 193
self-disclosure in therapy, effects of touch on: 132–135, 154; to elicit occluded/dormant client experience 135–138, e.g. feelings 136, 137, 138, 154 and memories 137, 141, 154
self-esteem in everyday life 31; improved 47, 109, 111; low 35, 55, 90
self-esteem in therapy: improved 126–127, 141, 146–147, 153, 193; low 141, 156, 158

self-love 123, 142
serotonin: in animals 14, 19n2; in humans 24, 27, 32, 37, 47, 49, 51
sexual feelings in therapy 175, 180n1, 183, 185, 206
sexual interaction: fear of, in therapists 170, 171, 175; in monkeys 16; risky 57, 64; in teenagers 36, 57; between therapist and client 157, 159n2, 174, 175, 179, 180n1; in troubled humans 29
sexual orientation 64–65, 196, 197n1
sexual relationships 29, 36, 56, 64, 90, 144–145, 195
shame: in everyday life 41, 54, 64, 112–113; in therapy 124, 146–147, 153
Silverthorn, A.S. 157
Smith, E.W.L. 183
Smith, J. 22
Spitz, R.A. 29
Spotnitz, H. 172, 176–177
stress: alleviation of through touch 40, 43, 50, 105, 153; in animals 8, 13, 19n2; in humans in everyday life 24–27, 40, 54, 107; in therapy 149, 153
stress, effects on: brain structure/cognitive function 26–27; emotional state 27; immunity/physical health 25–26
stress hormones: in animals 8, 13, 19n2; in humans 23, 24, 25, 37, 40, 49, 50, 51
stress response 24, 112
Struve, J. 154, 157, 158, 162, 172, 173–174, 175, 176, 177, 181, 182, 185, 187, 195–196, 197n1
Suomi, S.J. 16, 17
supervision 175, 176, 185, 194–195, 215
support: in everyday life 37, 65, 109; in therapy 123, 133, 139, 152, 154, 169n2, 195
Swade, D. 161
Swanson, D. 38–39

Index 285

tactility: in Anglo cultures 92, 162, 167–168; in Anglo compared with non-Anglo cultures 35, 78–79, 89, 95–102, 114, 164; culture, effects on 94–100, 102; and environmental change-agents 80; family, effects on 92–93; family and cultural 94–95; individual *versus* family 93; and religion 100–101; subcultures, influence on 102, 103, 165–166, 167–168

tactility scale 68–69; considerably tactile 76–77; decreasingly tactile 88–89; fully tactile 78–79; highly tactile 77–78; increasingly tactile 80–88; moderately tactile 74–76; non-tactile 69; reluctantly tactile 70–72; selectively tactile 72–73; slightly tactile 73–74; varyingly tactile 80

tension: in animals 7; in humans, in everyday life 24, 35, 67, 97, 107, 112, 113; in therapy 121, 134, 137, 138, 144, 184, 192

therapeutic relationship 129–132; 133, 140, 153–154; 170; 177, 178; 183; 192–193

therapists who use touch: competencies required 181–184, 191–197

touch in animal mammals, effects on: immunity 10–11, 15; mental ability 12–13, 14–15; physical growth 9–10; physical health 7, 8, 10–11; psyche/personality 11–12, 13–14, 16–17; survival 7–8, 11

touch deprivation in humans, effects on: behaviour 28–30, 36; body image 31; brain structure 27; emotional state 29–30, 35, 38–39; mental health and personality 25, 28–30, 32, 35; newborns 25; physical growth 27–28; self-esteem 31, 35; survival 20–21

touch in everyday life: 'human' compared with structured 50–51; mixed responses to 113–114; negative experience of 70–72, 112–113; in the nursing profession 42–47; personality repair 30–31; social behaviour/ society, effects on 32–34; in the teaching profession 40–42

touch in everyday life, effects on: body image 31, 47, 109; brain structure and function 27; emotional state 31–32, 33–34, 37–38. 40, 49–50, 107–109; hospitalised adults 23 (*see also* massage therapy); mental health and personality 30–34, 37–38, 40; personality repair 30–31; physical growth 27–28; relationships 35, 110–111; society 32–34; survival 20–21, 29

touch in everyday life, functions of 104; communication 105, 111 (*see also* non-verbal communication/body language); fundamental human needs, satisfaction of 105–110; interpersonal relationships, enhancement of 110–111; negative feelings, alleviation of 109; positive change in people's lives, promotion of 111

touch throughout life 34–40; in adolescence 33, 35–37; with the dying 39–40; with the elderly 38–39; in infancy and childhood 34–35 (*see also* touch, effects of, on premature infants, and chapters 1, 2, 3 and 4, etc.); in middle age 38; postpartum 37–38; during pregnancy 37, 38; in single parenthood 38

touch, properties of 186–191; agency 189; duration 186–187; energy 189; location 187; meanings of 189–190; mobile 187–189; modes of 189; personal variables 190; pressure 187; relationship to verbal statements 190; sociocultural factors 190; stillness or mobility 187

touch taboo, dismantling it: create tactile environment 205–215; discuss touch experiences 204–205; explore tactile history 201–202 and response patterns

202–204; hugging circles, hug trails 205; raise awareness of tactile beliefs and habits 198–205; touch diary 198–201; touch exercises 209–215

touch in therapy: at different stages of the therapeutic relationship 192–193; lack of 141, 158; national culture, influence on 161, 162, 163, 164; negative experience of 147–149, 156–157, 186; subculture, influence on 165–166; and talk, the relationship between them 124, 139–140, 190; timing of 184, 192–194

touch in therapy, effects on: body image 153; happiness levels 124–125, 127, 193; interpersonal relationships 127, 144, 145, 154; psychological health/wellbeing/ personality e.g. 141–147, 156; self-esteem 126–127, 141, 146–147, 153, 193

touch in therapy, functions of 120; communication 154, 157, 169n2, 179, 183, 190, 193; developmental gaps, filling of/reparenting 36–37, 136, 140, 142–143, 155, 173–174; fundamental human needs, meeting of 121–129; negative feelings, alleviation of 125; negative relationship patterns, modification of 127, 144–147; therapeutic goals/positive personality change, attainment of, e.g. 141–147; therapeutic relationships, enhancement of 129–132, 133, 140, 153–154

Toro, R. 87, 156
Triandis, H.C. 102
trust: in everyday life 30–31, 37; in therapy 122, 124, 129, 132, 133, 153, 154, 173, 192, 193
Tucker, D. 161

unconditionality 108, 123, 142, 153

violence: in everyday life 32, 56, 58, 60, 61, 62–63; in therapy 181, 184

warmth: in everyday life 50, 96, 105, 107, 115n1; in therapy 125, 126, 129, 133, 139, 140, 144, 152, 167, 172, 178
Weininger, O. 8, 9, 11–12
Whimbey, A.E. 12
Widdowson, E.M. 27–28
Widom, C.S. 56–57
Willison, B.G. 178, 197n1
Wilson, J.M. 31
Woodmansey, A.C. 171, 193, 217
Wright, S. 43
Wyschogrod, E. 153